D1614177

GARDENS AND THE PICTURESQUE

GARDENS AND THE PICTURESQUE

Studies in the History of Landscape Architecture

John Dixon Hunt

The MIT Press
Cambridge, Massachusetts
London, England

This book was set in Bembo by DEKR Corporation and was printed and bound in the United States of America

Library of Congress Cataloging-in-Publication Data

Hunt, John Dixon.
Gardens and the picturesque : studies in the history of landscape architecture / John Dixon Hunt.
p. cm.
Includes bibliographical references and index.
ISBN 0-262-08211-X
1. Gardens, English—History. 2. Gardens—Design—History. 3. Gardens—History. 4. Landscape architecture—History. I. Title.
SB457.6.H865 1992
712′.2—dc20 91-36906
CIP

For Michel and Giselle Baridon

CONTENTS

LIST OF ILLUSTRATIONS

PREFACE

This volume gathers together six essays published between 1971 and 1985, one published in an Italian translation in 1990, and four hitherto unpublished lectures of recent years, revised for this collection. Together they offer analyses of various moments in garden history, and specifically of the relationship of gardens, garden design, and garden theory to various cultural phenomena—in particular the cult of the picturesque, but also traditions of verbal-visual parallels, allegorical imagery and other languages of description, landscape painting, and paintings of gardens.

The rationale for their sequence here is largely historical. To have ordered them in the chronology of their composition would have been of merely biographical interest; to have tried to discover in them some deep and subtle pattern would have been merely ingenious. Instead, it seemed best to let them unfold in roughly chronological sequence of their topics, though with some grouping by theme.

Thus, after an introduction which addresses some of the issues involved in *writing* about what one *sees* in various types of landscape, the first part gathers together five essays on English gardens in the eighteenth and early nineteenth centuries. The second part extends the consideration of picturesque strategies into general landscape studies, though with specific focus upon both John Ruskin's and J. M. W. Turner's affinities with landscape gardening and landscape architecture. A third part, comprising two recent and unpublished pieces, explores both new forms of picturesque in French impressionist pictures of gardens and the way its old forms haunt modernist thinking about garden design. An essay on the utopian dimension of gardens, though without direct links with the preceding themes, seemed to furnish a postscript on the poetic idea of the garden that is indirectly addressed throughout the volume.

One reason for bringing together these various writings was that, like the utopian garden piece, many have appeared in places where those primarily concerned with the study of landscape architecture would not necessarily look. Though my interests in gardens began within literary studies, which therefore explains some of their emphases and perspectives as well as their original places of publication, my work has gradually discovered its own directions and has come to be concerned, for better or for worse, with garden and landscape history and analysis for their own sakes. This volume, through the enterprising auspices of Roger Conover and the MIT Press, therefore offers itself in the first instance—as its subtitle proclaims—to students of landscape architecture.

"Theatre, Gardens and Garden-Theatres" originally appeared in *Essays and Studies*, published by the English Association, 1980; "Emblem and Expression[ism] in the Eighteenth-Century Landscape Garden" came out in *Eighteenth-Century Studies* (1971); "*Ut Pictura Poesis, Ut Pictura Hortus*, and the Picturesque" appeared in the inaugural issue of *Word & Image* (1985); the essay on Humphry Repton was published in the journal then called *Studies in Burke and His Times* (1978); "Picturesque Mirrors and the Ruins of the Past" in *Art History* (1981); the Ruskin essay in *Modern Language Notes* (1978); an Italian version of the Turner essay in *Eidos* (1990); "Gardens in *Utopia*: Utopia in the Garden" appeared in *Between Dream and Nature: Essays on Utopia and Dystopia*, edited by Dominic Baker-Smith and C. C. Barfoot (Amsterdam: Ridolfi, 1987). The text of "Castle Howard Revisited" has grown directly out of the Leventritt Lecture in Art History given at Harvard University in 1989, while the essay on impressionist gardens first came into existence as the 1990 Bakwin Lecture in the History of Art at Wellesley College; to both those institutions I am grateful for the opportunity to develop ideas and to reprint versions of those lectures here. For their careful scrutiny of the essays on Castle Howard and Turner, I am much indebted to Christopher Ridgway and Andrew Wilton respectively.

GARDENS AND THE PICTURESQUE

INTRODUCTION
READING AND WRITING THE SITE

By way of orientation to this collection of essays, it is worth announcing, somewhat schematically, four themes that they have in common. The first, and the lengthiest, concerns how we process the so-called natural or physical world for our consumption. The second briefly addresses gardens as an art of milieu—how gardens, where humans exercise control over space and nature, become the most eloquent expressions of complex cultural ideas. The third invokes the notion of cultural translation—whereby one particular period receives and shapes for its own specific purposes ideas and forms inherited from predecessors elsewhere. The fourth derives from and builds upon the previous three: it explains the claim, implied frequently in the following essays, that gardens and landscapes are "readable."

I

The Roman writer Cicero termed what we would call the cultural landscape a second nature (*alteram naturam*).[1] This was a landscape of bridges, roads, harbors, fields—in short, all of the elements which men and women introduce into the physical world to make it more habitable, to make it serve their purposes. Cicero's phrase "a second nature" of course implies a first; though he does not specify this, we may take it that he implies a primal nature, an unmediated world before humans invaded, altered, and augmented it, a world without any roads, ports, paths, terraced vineyards, etc. Today we might call it the wilderness.

In sixteenth-century Italy, when gardens began to flourish and be elaborated as never before, this art was likened to a third nature by various commentators; one of them, Jacopo Bonfadio, wrote of gardens as being "nature incorporated with art . . . [and made] the creator and conatural of art, and from both is made a third nature [*una terza na-*

tura]."[2] The implication of this third nature, as indeed of Cicero's second, was its augmentation of an existing state of affairs. Gardens went beyond the cultural landscape, and therefore those humanists, drawing upon Cicero, invented new terminology. Gardens were worlds where the pursuit of pleasure probably outweighed the need for utility and accordingly where the utmost resources of human intelligence and technological skill were invoked to fabricate an environment where nature and art collaborated.

The point to emphasize here is the fashion in which first nature has constantly been processed for human consumption, either into second or into second and then third natures, or sometimes directly into third nature. Consumption may involve a search for habitation, agricultural needs, transportation, religious beliefs (whereby sacred places are marked by temples and shrines), and eventually leisure and aesthetic pleasure. To whatever end, though, human reworking of the first nature renders the physical world more amenable, useful, tolerable, pleasant, beautiful (the specific emphasis will clearly depend upon the historical moment, and many—not just ecological enthusiasts—would today of course add ravaged or ruined).

But consumption has also taken less obvious or less palpable forms. One of these, the picturesque, is central to the essays collected in this volume. Much has been written about picturesque taste, both at the time of its greatest popularity and subsequently by modern commentators,[3] but what is never explicitly emphasized is that it was and continues to be a mode of processing the physical world for our consumption or for our greater comfort. The primal world of physical nature—Cicero's implied first nature—can be raw, hostile, discomforting, dangerous: just because few readers of this book may have themselves experienced this first nature in that form does not deny its existence. Whenever humans have encountered it, they tend to tame it, utilize it, and otherwise process it.

This processing can be intellectual as well as physical. A frequent response to the terrifying and threatening spaces of mountains, sea, or desert has been to annex them mentally to what is termed the "sublime," at which point we start talking of the grandeur of the mountains, and so on; while still allowed its primal forcefulness, first nature has now been subsumed and managed culturally (and arguably has ceased to be a pure form of first nature, slipping into a version of the second).

Yet another intellectual intervention into first nature which makes sense and proportion out of empty waste is narrated in Wallace Stevens's poem "Anecdote of the Jar," a parable somewhat in vogue with landscape architects at present. The poet tells how he

placed a jar in Tennessee
And round it was, upon a hill.
It made the slovenly wilderness
Surround that hill.

The wilderness rose up to it,
And sprawled around, no longer wild . . .[4]

The art work—vase or jar—transforms how we regard the first nature in which it is positioned, though without physically altering the hillside (the jar is ecologically sound, so to speak). Gardens, too, may be thought of as jars, set down in otherwise artless landscapes; part of their appeal is that they reorganize our thinking, especially about the natural materials from which they are crafted. Unlike Stevens's jar, though, a garden is itself a consequence of fresh perceptions of second and first nature.

By the end of the eighteenth century the picturesque had become another example of how humans came to accommodate potentially unprepossessing scenery. The physical world could be seen more pleasantly, occupied and visited more safely, if it were thought of as a painting. So it was filtered through sensibilities honed on a study of graphic representations of the world (not necessarily the natural world—that declension, as will be seen in subsequent essays, comes later). William Gilpin, the great popularizer of this picturesque mode, helped his readers to travel and look at the various parts of Great Britain as if its various topographies were safely pictorialized; the world "out there" in Wales, Scotland, the Lake District, even in the Home Counties and the south coast, was turned into "landscapes" or "scenery." Both of which terms, by alluding respectively to paintings and theatrical sets, announced the safe and sanitized nature of the picturesque vision.

An extreme example of Gilpin's helping picturesque travelers come to terms with the larger and difficult world outside their own familiar territory is his proposal for viewing the smelly, muddy world of cattle (which have also been known to get somewhat hostile). Several pages are devoted to a favorable contrast between the "picturesque lines" of the cow and the "nobler" but less satisfactorily picturesque horse; the former, especially "in the months of April, and May, when the old hair is coming off", offers a "contrast between the rougher, and smoother parts of the coat; and often also a pleasing variety of greyish tints, blended with others of a richer hue." The cow is also "better adapted . . . to receive the beauties of light," and its color "often more picturesque." Finally, Gilpin considers how they may be considered as an *ensemble* (fig. 0.1):

> Cattle are so large, that when they ornament a foreground, a few are sufficient. Two cows will hardly combine. Three make a good group—either united—or when one is a little removed from the other two. If you increase the group beyond three; one, or more, in proportion, must necessarily be a *little detached.* This detachment prevents heaviness, and adds variety.

This whole section on accommodating the world of cattle to human sensibility is authorized by appeals to Dutch painters like Nicolaes Berghem and Aelbert Cuyp and even to the august example of Virgil's Aeneas![5]

This may be considered too extreme a manifestation of the picturesque determination to process the messy world of (in this case) second nature for civilized consumption; or it will simply be dismissed as a joke, which is exactly what happened in Gilpin's day: to the lady who thought their modest domestic economy suggested only a couple of cows, Uvedale Price reported her husband's rejoinder—"Lord, my dear, *two* cows you know can never group."[6]

Another humorous but arguably more penetrating view of what is at issue here is Gary Larson's modern cartoon (fig. 0.2). As tourists in the countryside, comfortably ensconced in our automobiles, we expect cows to be lying or standing; that they oblige us by conforming to our preconceptions is, implies Larson, just one way in which we have manipulated the physical world to our own devices and desires.[7] Yet these preconceptions are nothing else but a fossil of Gilpin's picturesque reworking of the agricultural world in his prescriptions for ways of looking at cattle. And the reassurance we have come to expect from a comforting mediation of the physical world through picturesque visions goes a long way to explain the continuing obsession with the picturesque, which is tracked later in this volume through both French impressionist paintings of gardens and the ambivalent attitude toward its picturesque legacy of modernist landscape architecture.[8]

0.1. William Gilpin, plate depicting cattle, from his picturesque Observations *on the Lake District, 1792 edition. Dumbarton Oaks, Trustees for Harvard University.*

0.2. Gary Larson, cartoon. Courtesy of the artist.

That garden art had become intimately allied with the picturesque vogue by the end of the eighteenth century should recall us to the essential fact that gardens, too, have always been ways of mediating the physical world. The motives for such mediation, such processing, may be more varied and complex than are involved with Gilpin's cows; but gardens are, if not ways of actually coming to terms with the first and second natures, at least retrospective ways of registering how we have come to terms with them. By being sophisticated products of our relationship with the world beyond their walls, gardens represent, as do landscape paintings, an art of milieu.[9]

II

Our second point may now be made more quickly. Human beings have processed nature in different ways and for different motives. One such mode is the garden. Each phase of garden art is culturally specific, determined by a whole congeries of ideas and events few of which are explicitly horticultural or architectural: they may be political, social, economic, religious. But because, as the Renaissance humanists implied by their invention of a third nature, gardens go one stage further than the cultural landscape of second nature in representing the extent and significance of control over their environment, gardens may arguably offer a more refined, more acute, and more intricate expression of human experience. This expression will be both conscious and unconscious, just as the subsequent analysis of it will confront both the obvious and the unexpected (there is, however, no automatic correlation between what was taken for granted then and what is seen as obvious about it now).

This is not the place to enquire into exactly what range of human experience gardens have at various times managed to express.[10] But what is today termed landscape architecture has always realized a particular society's, even a particular person's, attitudes toward space and nature. This deliberately constructed milieu invokes selected forms and materials to express, often in a concentrated fashion and certainly in a special way, some human response to and recognition of an environment; this environment will be physical, topographical, but it will also include less tangible, spiritual values. Landscape paintings have also attempted the same expression of experience, though in their case the space is necessarily two-dimensional and therefore illusionary; it is also "easier," in that it requires no physical intervention on the ground as gardens do. To bestow such and such a shape upon a parcel of land is to declare explicitly or implicitly some of the landowner's and designer's more fundamental ideas about their environment.

III

The cultural declarations of landscape architecture may be seen in practice in some of the essays that follow. They are perhaps most visible, in fact, whenever a society attempts to borrow and shape to its own purposes ideas from or about previous cultures. This will be explored most fully in the English eighteenth century; but other versions are canvassed in French impressionism's reformulations of garden imagery or twentieth-century landscape architecture's dialogue with its past. In this process of cultural translation it is the translator's own preoccupations that come to the fore and determine the outcome, which can be better appreciated by comparing it with its original.

In England during the eighteenth century, as is well known, there was much backward contemplation of ancient Rome: classical writers were invoked as contemporary models, and where (as with architecture and certainly landscape architecture) perhaps insufficient antique examples existed, the classical legacy could always be accessed via, say, the works and writings of Italian Renaissance practitioners. But the cult of Palladio in England, for example, makes a further point: his Renaissance buildings were extrapolated for his contemporaries from a careful study of classical remains which were then made anew by him in a fresh context. The English emulation of Palladio in its turn added a further translation: from classical remains into Renaissance buildings, then from those directly or via Palladio's writing in *I Quattro Libri* (1570) into northern ones of the seventeenth and eighteenth centuries.

But a country like England had its own indigenous architectural forms, let alone its own distinct landscapes where (it could be argued) neoclassical buildings did not necessarily sit too happily. Coexisting with the neoclassical taste had always been a fascination with the native Gothic traditions (in literature as well as in architecture) and gradually during the eighteenth century this taste increased. So when writers or architects translated the classical languages of their models, they were obliged at least to address the question of how Vitruvius, Palladio, Horace, or Pliny would function in England and in English. Alexander Pope was actually urged by a friend in the 1720s to "make Homer speak good English," and when he turned his attention to Horace in the 1730s he was even more concerned to register what was capable of translation and what, for various cultural reasons, resisted it.[11]

Exactly the same attitudes to translation seem to have been applied in garden design during the first half of the eighteenth century. The absence of classical precedents forced Englishmen back upon yet further strategies of translation: if they sought to relocate themselves in the villa and garden traditions of Pliny, Horace, and Martial, then they had to translate old verbal accounts into new visual forms.

All this cultural processing of the past for the present and of ancient Rome for modern England could be and was explained by a scheme known as the progress of the arts.[12] What had been the glory of Greece and Rome had (so the narrative went) been lost sight of during the "dark" ages, been recovered and reconstituted by the Italian Renaissance, and from that point of time and place had progressed northward to its final flowering in—according to your nationality—France, the Low Countries, or Great Britain. But at least in the last of these territories the progress of the art of landscaping began to be celebrated as an accommodation of those classical traditions to a new and different culture. Hence, just as Homer and Horace were required to speak modern English in Pope's translations, so landscapes like Castle Howard, discussed in the next essay, felt obliged to honor their indigenous languages of architecture and topography.

One extra example will be useful. When William Kent was called in to redesign Rousham, General Dormer's garden in Oxfordshire, in the late 1730s, he drew attention by various visual hints to that beautiful garden's place in the progress of its art from Rome to England. Allusions to the new garden's Italian models—to the ruined Temple of Fortune at ancient Praeneste or to a sculptural group in the grounds of the Renaissance Villa d'Este—were offered along with indications of the cultural changes that the act of translation had wrought upon the classical originals. Further, throughout the relatively small garden Kent emphasized both the old and the new, classical and Gothick,[13] often side by side (fig. 0.3); by these juxtapositions our attention is drawn to the new English location of classical ideas and forms.

All this was apt for a family with a strong English pedigree: a Dormer had married the aunt of Sir Philip Sidney; the family had been royalist in the Civil Wars, held court appointments in the seventeenth and eighteenth centuries; and yet in the eighteenth century they were

0.3. The classical gateway and Gothic seat (the latter also known as "Cow Castle," since it shelters cattle on the far side), Rousham, Oxfordshire (photograph: author).

attentive to classical culture, especially through architecture and sculpture.[14] Perhaps the most economical and witty fashion in which this cultural translation is underlined occurs on top of the screens with which Kent linked the seventeenth-century house, remodeled to look Tudor-Gothick, to its new wings (fig. 0.4). Giving the "old" central block wings was in the classical-Palladian mode; yet gothicizing them with ogive niches and "battlements" was British, "medieval." So the linking walls have crested parapets or castellations in the shape of the stone balls which decorate similar screen links on the front of Palladio's San Giorgio Maggiore in Venice (fig. 0.5).[15] Thus we are advised that what we see is a translation from an old into a "new" language with a consequent elision of the two.

IV

We have just surveyed what might be called the writing of a site, the inscription of meaning—sometimes with actual words, but just as often by a dumb visual language—onto some segment of terrain. If such a description of the cultural making of gardens is allowed, then it follows that what has been written may also be read, at least if we take the trouble to learn the language. The visual forms that we see at Rousham have a meaning, a content, that is also available to us. In the terms that most of Kent's contemporaries would have understood, his architecture and landscape architecture were "speaking pictures."[16]

It may be objected that a garden like Rousham, or its not too distant neighbor Stowe in Buckinghamshire, is exceptional in the conscious deliberation with which its owners and designers encoded meanings in it. It is indeed true that it was all meant to be readable. Rousham and Stowe have in this respect at least to be situated towards the end of a tradition that found architecture as meaningful, for example, as heraldry.[17]

But it is an underlying argument of these essays that as historians and theorists of landscape architecture we are also able to "read" garden "texts" which did not lay claim to that specific kind of readability. All human creations, especially—it is here argued—gardens, declare their creators; it is the business of cultural historians to extrapolate ideas, beliefs, and other modes of *mentalité* from them. Reading gardens, in other words, does not consist wholly in taking notice of their inscriptions. Many do not have any such verbal devices, and they present themselves substantially if not totally through formal, visual means.

0.4. The garden front of Rousham House, Oxfordshire (photograph: Marina Adams). This side of Kent's link screen is now backed and overshadowed by a higher nineteenth-century wall.

0.5. The facade of San Giorgio Maggiore, Venice (photograph: author).

Yet forms have significance and content, even if that content itself signals a refusal of meaning. No gesture is unreadable. If this volume neglects formal analysis in favor of what forms may contain, that is because the importance of the latter approach needs to be reasserted.

In the first half of the eighteenth century we may detect a growing preference for form at the expense of the ideas that might be expressed through it. A point of equilibrium may be detected in the partnership that Alexander Pope and William Kent somehow established between approximately 1720 and the mid-1740s;[18] an intellectual and social critic like Pope could feed his designer friend with ideas, and Kent, because he was adept at formal invention, could offer the cultural commentary of the satirist significant means of expression. In the end neither had priority in their collaboration. But it would soon be Kent's formal skills that were admired, and the ideas which could be read in and through them became less appreciated and less available as the century advanced. The results of that preference, in both theory and practice, are unfortunately still with us today.

Neither landscape, whether in gardens or on the painted canvas, nor architecture has ever been discursive or didactic as are poetry, rhetoric, and other verbal forms. But there were many during the eighteenth and nineteenth centuries who strived to make them more so. Pope was a landscape gardener who clearly had that ambition; Humphry Repton, after an interlude in landscaping that seemed to downplay meaning in favor of form, also renewed his attention to content; though with many changes in the world where he worked, the agenda of those concerns had clearly altered since Pope's time. The painter J. M. W. Turner was another who valued the meanings that were encoded in and therefore decodable from landscape, and his earliest and most astute critic, John Ruskin, appreciated and tried to explain how Turner grasped the workings of a place with its meanings and implications, and found suitable ways of communicating them.

It is to the modes and possibilities of readability in gardens, landscapes, and landscape gardens, then, that the following essays are addressed rather than to any formal analyses of design and composition. Not that these latter are trivial or to be ignored; it is just that other aspects of the arts of landscape need to be emphasized once again.

PART ONE

Gardens, Words, Pictures

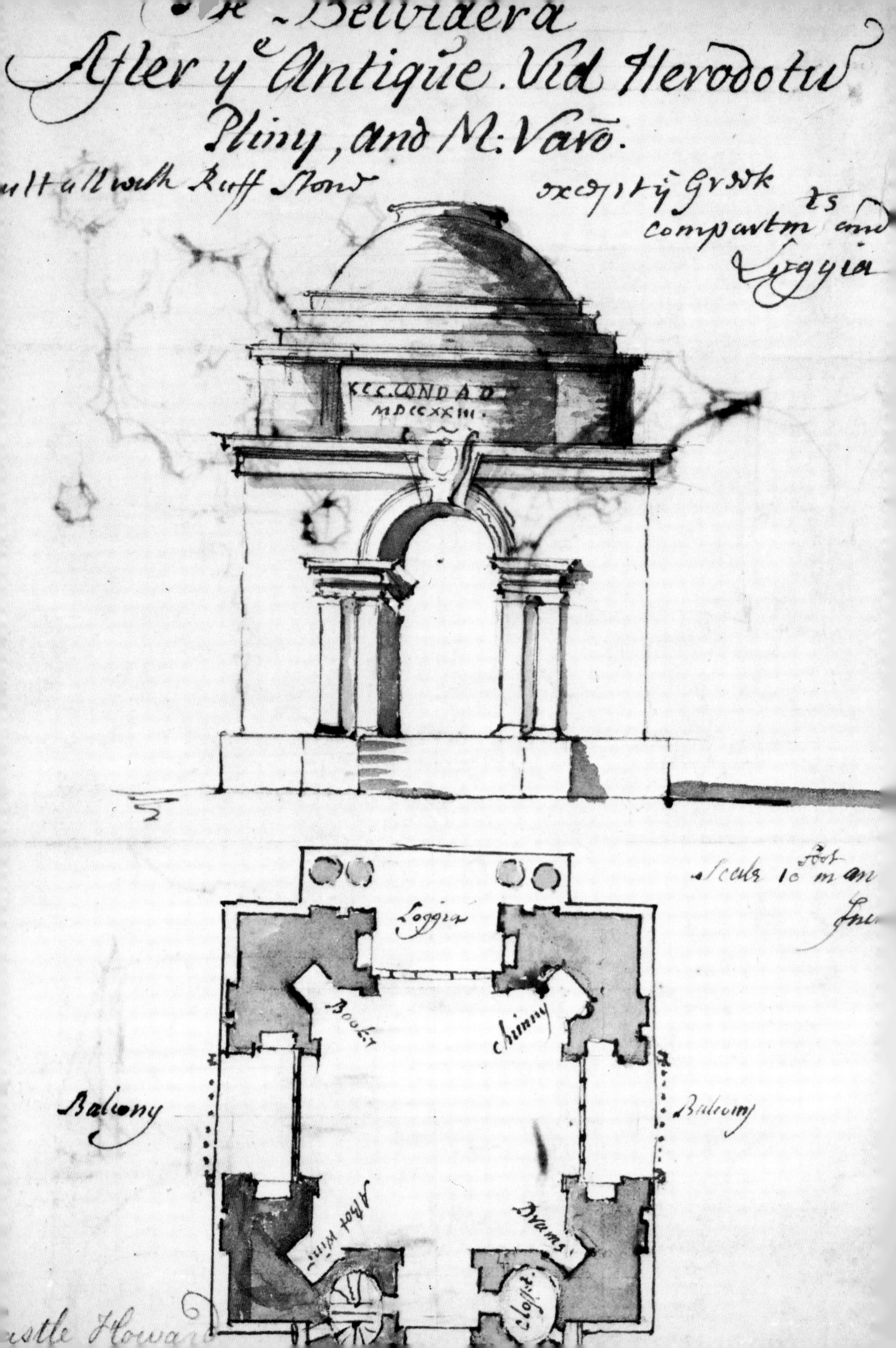

The Belvidera
After ye Antique. Vid Herodotus
Pliny, and M: Varo.

uilt all with Ruff Stone except ye Greek compartments and Loggia

KEC. COND A.D.
MDCCXXIII

Scale 10 foot in an Inch

Loggia

Books

chimny

Balcony

Balcony

A bot Wine

Drams

Closet

stle Howard

1 CASTLE HOWARD REVISITED

This collection of essays reexplores territory which Christopher Hussey opened up for modern scholarship with *The Picturesque: Studies in a Point of View* (1927) and *English Gardens and Landscapes, 1700–1750* (1967). The forty years which elapsed between these two benchmarks in the history and analysis of landscape taste, and the developments over that time in the thinking about their subjects, may perhaps explain why the second seems to be the more durable and continuingly useful.

Not only was *English Gardens and Landscapes* itself a pioneering book, a gathering of some of Hussey's contributions over many years to the weekly *Country Life,* but several of its chapters, for example those on Melbourne Hall, Castle Howard, and Rousham, were the first and are still the last statements worth considering on what are important moments in English landscape garden history. In particular, it seems astonishing that until very recently no further work was undertaken on Castle Howard, since the ideas of landscape that were implemented on that Yorkshire estate from about 1700 onward mark it as one of the earliest, let alone one of the most striking, examples of the English landscape garden.[1] It is for that reason, above all, that I wish to revisit the site in this essay. In addition, I shall be concerned to study Castle Howard in the light of some of the ideas, especially those of cultural representation, that were set out more theoretically in the Introduction and, secondly, as a design which exemplifies many of the themes discussed in subsequent essays.[2]

On the great obelisk raised in 1714 by Charles Howard, third Earl of Carlisle, to Sir John Vanbrugh's design, is an inscription, part of which reads as follows:

If to perfection these plantations rise
If they agreeably my heirs surprise
This faithful pillar will their age declare
As long as time these characters shall spare
Here then with kind remembrance read his name
Who for posterity perform'd the same.

It may be the closest the third Earl ever came to stating his conscious intentions in building Castle Howard and creating its landscape.[3] Yet what strikes the reader of the inscription at once is its allusion simply to the "plantations." Granted it is the woods of this estate that are a great treasure (in every sense of that word), it is still perhaps odd for the inscription not to discuss what we would call the landscaping. Yet the verses point us to where the Earl's most subtle intentions may be discovered: by looking at his Yorkshire plantations in which, at various points, objects like the eloquent obelisk have been inserted, rather than just focusing upon those objects themselves, we will be able to apprehend the larger meaning of the Earl's "performance." There is also perhaps an intention in the use of the word "plantations" of signaling Carlisle's colonization of this landscape.[4]

The obelisk functions like the other objects erected in the landscape that the visitor encounters later: to insert into natural scenery some artificial item like an obelisk gives new meaning to its surroundings even if they remain otherwise unaltered. Like Wallace Stevens's jar, obelisks take dominion everywhere and make wildernesses no longer wild. Especially when obelisks, as does this one, speak to us, we may expect to understand not only their inscriptions but the very face and texture of the landscape in which they are placed and which they thereby subtly alter. What it is that the obelisk alerts visitors to remark, is that it and the surrounding plantations are representations of the third Earl's sense of his place in the political, cultural, and physical world. Some of these representations are explicitly contrived—by inscriptions, by architectural forms and functions, by statuary; some, however, are only implied—the landscape by juxtaposition to the other artifacts assuming its role in this mimetic ensemble.

We reach the obelisk at Castle Howard along the Great Avenue, approximately five miles in length, laid out on a north-south axis in 1709 (see fig. 1.1). The gentle alterations of summit and trough, punctuated by architectural events like the obelisk or gateways, also ensure glimpses through the lines of trees on either side toward distant objects

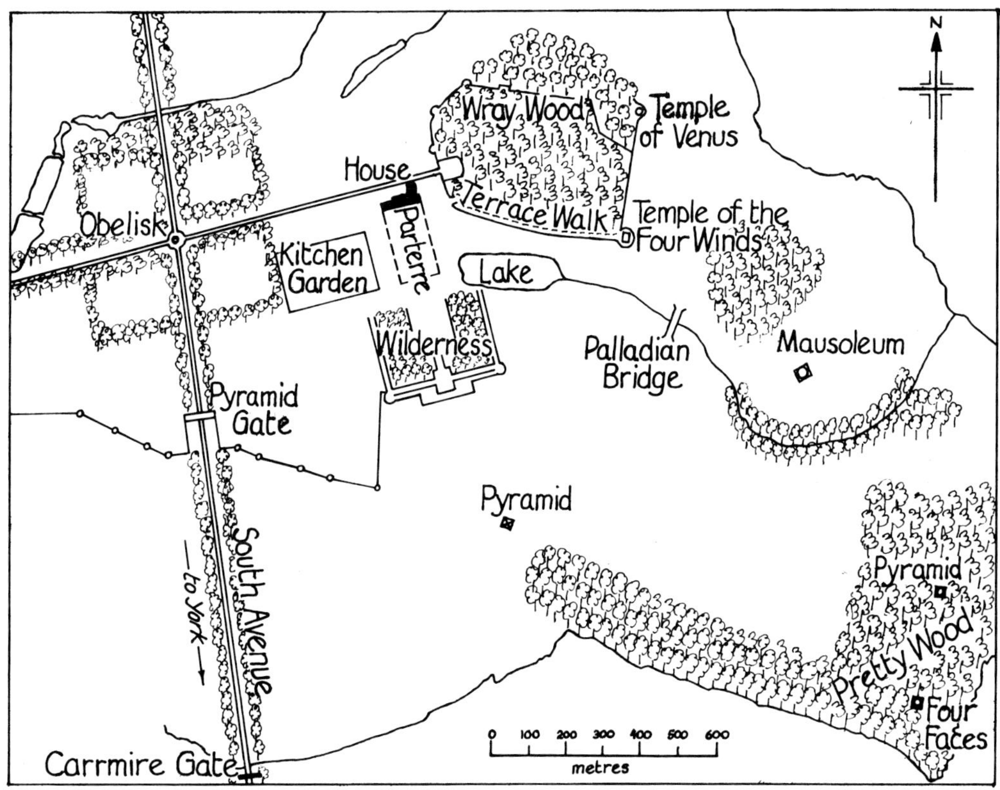

1.1. Plan of Castle Howard, based on early eighteenth-century estate plans, by Robert Williams.

like the Pyramid or Mausoleum. The first idea had been an east-west approach along the top of the ridge where the old Castle had been; this would have ended in the courtyard of the house that then faced its arriving visitors directly. But the decision was taken to orientate the avenue as we have it now, with a road leading off sideways and at right angles from the obelisk toward the house and entering laterally into the courtyard in front of the house, which was also repositioned by Vanbrugh to face north-south (see figs. 1.11–12). This turning of the house also made it part of the alternating experience of revelation and concealment for the approaching visitor who glimpses it from afar.

This experience depends ultimately on the geological structure, the advantages of which would have been lost if the avenue had been laid out from east to west. As Jay Appleton has shown,[5] the Jurassic rocks dip gently toward the north, consisting of shales and sands that include thin bands of grit or limestone which outcrop in a series of tiny escarpments, quite close together, and over which the avenue switchbacks. So the Great Avenue not only incorporates the message of the geological past into this landscape but, as the route all visitors must take in approaching Castle Howard, it inaugurates their response to what the place represents.

From the very beginning, the name Castle Howard signals something medieval, something from English history, what Horace Walpole at Hagley called "the true rust of the barons' wars."[6] And Vanbrugh and Hawksmoor made the approach from the York road a truly castle-like experience—from the York road the visitor passes through two sets of battlemented walls, the first being the Carrmire Gate with towers on either side, then the pyramided gatehouse.

But these strong representations of castle-ness are not unproblematical. To start with, the Carrmire Gate (fig. 1.2) is really very theatrical—pure stage set and, since its extent is so short, clearly incapable of doing any defending at all. Furthermore, while the atmospheric round towers with their arrow slits may look authentic enough, the gateway itself is grandly Italianate after the manner of Giulio Romano; the pyramids that flank the rusticated and pedimented entry, and which are repeated more massively at the next gateway, had Roman associations. The Pyramid Gateway itself (fig. 1.3) is castellar in that it is "protected" by projecting bastions at which the traveler with necessary caution slackens his pace (the Road Works Section of the North Yorkshire County Council is clearly alert to these exigencies of medieval

1.2. The Carrmire Gate, Castle Howard (photograph: author).

1.3. The Pyramid Gate, Castle Howard (photograph: author).

approach and has painted SLOW upon the tarmac). But the central section of this gateway has the force of a Roman triumphal arch and tomb combined, while the rhythms of the architectural bays and classical window types added fifty years later are even more insistently Italian.

This mixture of Gothic and classical which is so clearly announced as we approach turns out to be a dominant theme of the whole estate. It is made explicit once we have arrived at the house itself: from a distance it may seem a jumble of towers and plausible castellations, but close up its baroque dome floats in the air and contrives the effect of a classical temple. All this is clearly intended.

Castle Howard is ultimately a Palladian house,[7] on which a classical dome has been placed. It is true that Palladio also did this, but only to one realized building (and to another that was projected); the novelty, not to say oddity, of a domestic dome is still striking.[8] Yet it is also (in more than just its name) a castle, built after the partial destruction by fire in 1693 of Henderskelfe Castle. At first the remains of that former castle were left on the site, since an estate map of 1694 shows them to the west of the present west wing—in other words, on the same ridge as the obelisk and new house itself. That Vanbrugh may well have wished to retain the older architectural elements of Henderskelfe is supported by his famous advice to the Duchess of Marlborough to retain the ruin of old Woodstock Manor at Blenheim (fig. 1.4). Usually interpreted, because Vanbrugh invoked "the best of Landskip Painters," as a plea for the picturesque *avant la lettre,* it was in fact a strong plea for the representation of earlier history alongside the modern commemoration of Marlborough. Even the Duchess, who turned the idea down as preposterous, noted that the idea contained "something material . . . concerning the occasion of building Blenheim."[9] So, too, at Castle Howard the retention of the old English building as the new Italianate one was going up was significant. By 1724 Vanbrugh is arguing that the "disagreeable Confusion and litter" of the old ruin should be eliminated; yet he also argues that stones from the old building should be put into the foundations of the new wing, thus implying that the eastern block—a quadrant with towers—could be a new "castle" taking the place of the old.[10]

The Palladian layout of the new building is itself a strong mode of representation (we know that Palladio's *I Quattro Libri* was one of the few architecture books used by Vanbrugh);[11] crowning it with a dome is another; siting such an architectural creation not in a landscape of

1.4. Anonymous, the ruined Woodstock Manor at Blenheim, drawing of 1714. Department of Prints and Drawings, British Museum, London.

contemporary mannerist geometry but in a carefully organized representation of different kinds of naturalness is another. All are interconnected, and, basically, their joint theme is one of representing cultural history through the competing styles of Gothick and classical.

The approach to Castle Howard up the Great Avenue is not then simply an introduction to a battle of visual styles. The instructions to the visitor at the obelisk, the mixture of classical and Gothick styles, the concatenation of ancient and modern Italian as well as native or British architecture, the sense of old castle and new Palladian mansion—these work to present the visitor with a play, a picture or representational image of this particular estate's new place in cultural history. It is clear from correspondence and archives that survive at Castle Howard that the exact adjudications of this cultural inheritance were a matter of some concern and debate.

Vanbrugh was clearly an enthusiast for Gothick: he urged its preservation at Woodstock, achieved it in the Holbein Gate at Whitehall, and built himself a castle at Greenwich. He was also associated with several gardens where, as at Castle Howard, bastions or military-style bulwarks set off the gardens from the landscape.[12] Perhaps, since he always like to present himself as the old soldier, Vanbrugh simply associated Gothick with past military glories. And perhaps for a while at Castle Howard he might have been able to bring off a more Gothick structure, apt to set besides the ruins of old Henderskelfe Castle. But there were proponents of classical styles at Castle Howard who enforced different emphases. Indeed, Vanbrugh himself responded to classical forms in ways that showed he too was well aware of their representational power; of his proposals for Kimbolton Castle, Vanbrugh argued that "As to the Outside, I thought, 'twas absolutely best, to give it Something of the Castle air, tho' at the Same time to make it regular" (regular meaning, of course, classical).[13]

It is a precisely similar balance or mixture that he, his coadjutator Hawksmoor,[14] and their patron, Carlisle, contrived at Castle Howard, but clearly after debate about various proposals for a temple in the grounds of Castle Howard—what was presumably to become the Temple of Four Winds.[15] Vanbrugh lined up against Hawksmoor, who was urging something he called a "Turret";[16] Vanbrugh instead proposed that smooth freestone and porticoes facing in each direction were "as cheap as any Gothick Tower."[17] This plea for classical landscape buildings was echoed by Carlisle's son, who was "utterly against anything but an Italian Building in the Place, and entirely approved the first Design."[18] Among those first, Italianate designs may have been a drawing of a temple or belvedere (fig. 1.5) which carries an intriguing annotation in which Hawksmoor (who, generally speaking, acted as organizer, draftsman, and designer for Vanbrugh) justifies a temple or belvedere overlooking the Yorkshire countryside by a caption which reads "After ye Antique. Vide Herodotus, Pliny and M. Varro." Now it really looks nothing like a classical or even a modern Italian temple; but clearly those classical writers on the country life authorized Hawksmoor's design as well as its proposed situation on English land.

The subtext to this drawing and Hawksmoor's annotations concern ideas which much preoccupied late seventeenth- and eighteenth-century English artistic commentators: on the one hand, the rival virtues of ancient and modern culture,[19] and, on the other, the so-called progress of the arts whereby the fortunes of, say, poetry, architecture, or music were traced from classical times through hibernation during the Dark Ages to their revitalization in Renaissance Italy and thence their movement northward across Europe.[20] England could see itself therefore as both the ultimate inheritor of classical traditions (in the sense of the latest and the best) and as the final arbitrator of the old battle of Ancients versus Moderns. Yet it was not an easy role to adopt. For to see England as the ultimate location of classical culture was neither to come down very obviously on the side of the Moderns nor yet to be very attentive to such records of your own native culture as Woodstock Manor or Henderskelfe Castle.

Castle Howard manages the balancing act very cleverly. Hawksmoor's annotation of his drawing of the temple gives it full classical authority, while the design itself attempts more modernist forms; to have set it down in contemporary English scenery would have given it an instant contemporary and local color. Perhaps the problem with it was how to make visible what the verbal annotation could do *only on the drawing*. The solution was to erect the Temple of the Four Winds (fig. 1.6).[21]

This, as various commentators have shown, clearly echoes a whole cluster of Renaissance Italian buildings, including both the Aurora casino in the gardens of the Villa Ludovisi—especially as viewed in the Falda print, where it is interestingly juxtaposed to ruined and castellated Roman walls (fig. 1.7)—and Palladio's Villa Rotunda; further back still, the Temple at Castle Howard alludes by almost direct quotation to

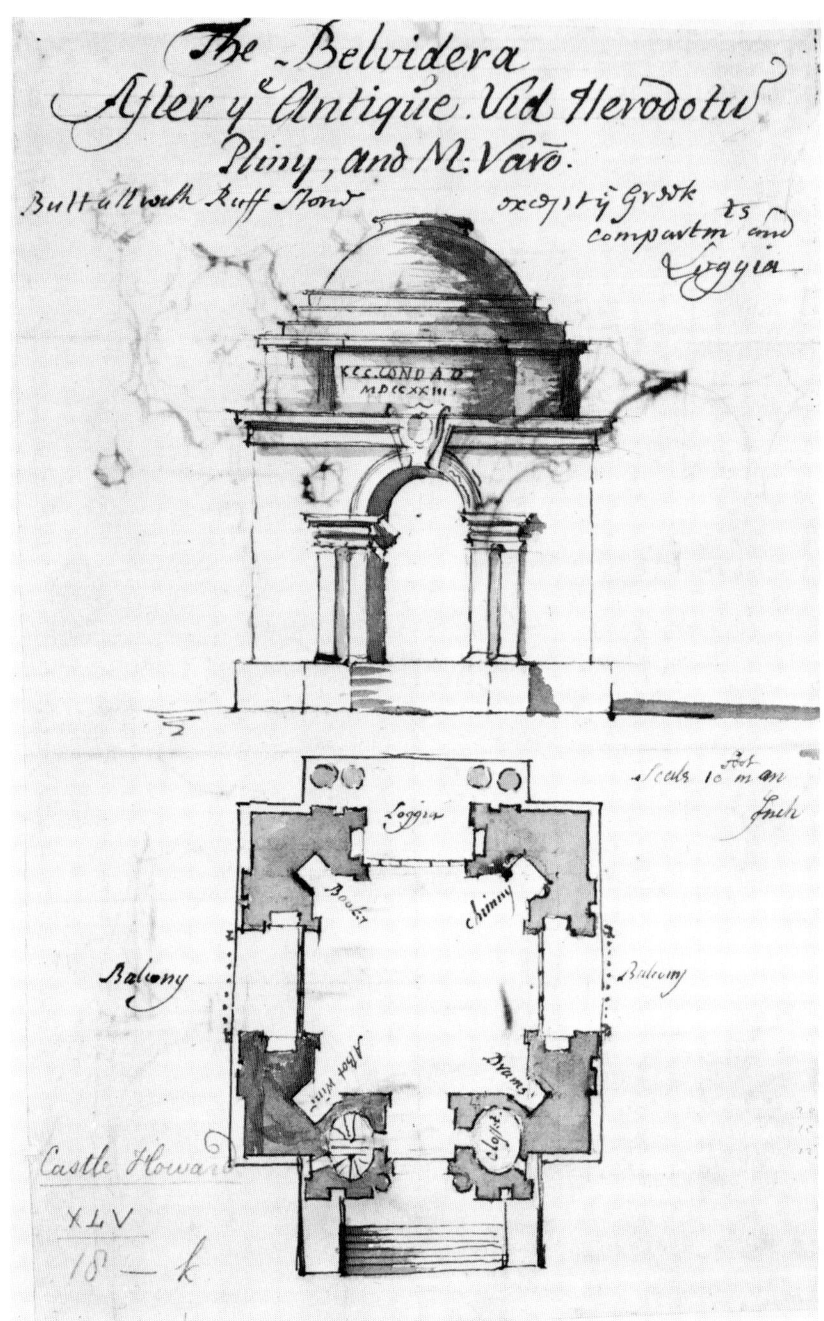

1.5. Nicholas Hawksmoor, design of a temple for Castle Howard, dated 1723 on the proposed building. Map Room, British Library, London.

1.6. The Temple of the Four Winds, Castle Howard (photograph: author).

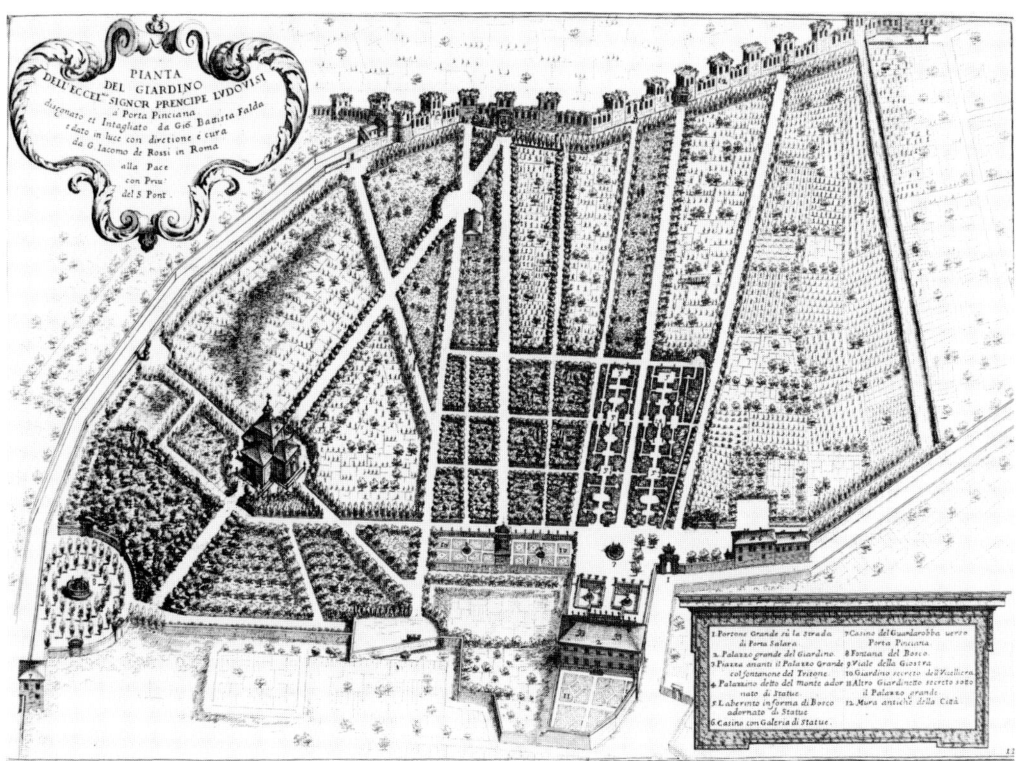

1.7. The Villa Ludovisi, from Falda, Li Giardini di Roma *(Rome, 1683). Dumbarton Oaks, Trustees for Harvard University.*

Palladio's reconstruction of the Temple of Fortune at Praeneste (fig. 1.8).[22] Thus the Temple of the Four Winds represents various stages of cultural history, besides being itself sited upon bulwarks which echo the "castle" walls that the visitor had encountered on his approach from York and which have fine views of *English* countryside.

Exactly the same solution seems to have been followed with the main house itself. Called "Hinderskelfe Castle" (the new house, that is) on an early plan,[23] it used a Palladian villa layout of central block and wings held out to embrace the immediate surroundings, like the Villa Trissino at Meledo. The force of these Palladian representations here at the villa-castle and at the Temple of the Four Winds is, of course, as any owner of *I Quattro Libri* would appreciate, that they represent not only modern Renaissance architecture but a modern style based upon elaborate studies of antique Roman remains. Palladio's is a wholly mediated architecture; it incorporates its own debts to and rehandling of classical sources as part of its meaning. Palladio undergoes a further declension by Vanbrugh in the dramatic play of component parts of the house and in the (late) decision to crown it all with a dome. This last, the first such stone form to be completed in Britain, is a deliberate modern touch, a calculated statement of the progress of arts—not just to Albion's Isle but specifically to Yorkshire. Not for nothing was Charles Howard a member of the patriotic Whig Kit-Cat Club, dedicated to the prosperity and progress of a modern Britain.[24] Nor is it surprising that Colen Campbell included an engraving of Castle Howard in the third installment of the significantly named *Vitruvius Britannicus* (fig. 1.9).

The setting constitutes a crucial part of the ensemble of Castle Howard, as somebody (maybe Vanbrugh) knew when the house was turned from an east-west to a north-south axis and given more extensive views (though this, in its turn, meant that the road from the obelisk had to approach the house sideways, though significantly—as we shall see—terminating in Wray Wood itself). Even the southern garden, which is what the engraving in *Vitruvius Britannicus* displays, played its part in the overall cultural drama.[25] Laid out on another huge fortress-like bastion[26] with views of the Yorkshire countryside beyond and a rectangular pool directly south, it is shown as filled with cabinets and winding walks in dense hedges called the "wood within the walls"; they are decorated with Roman obelisks and terminated with temples. This *bosquet* or *boschetto* on the southern parterre may not seem very

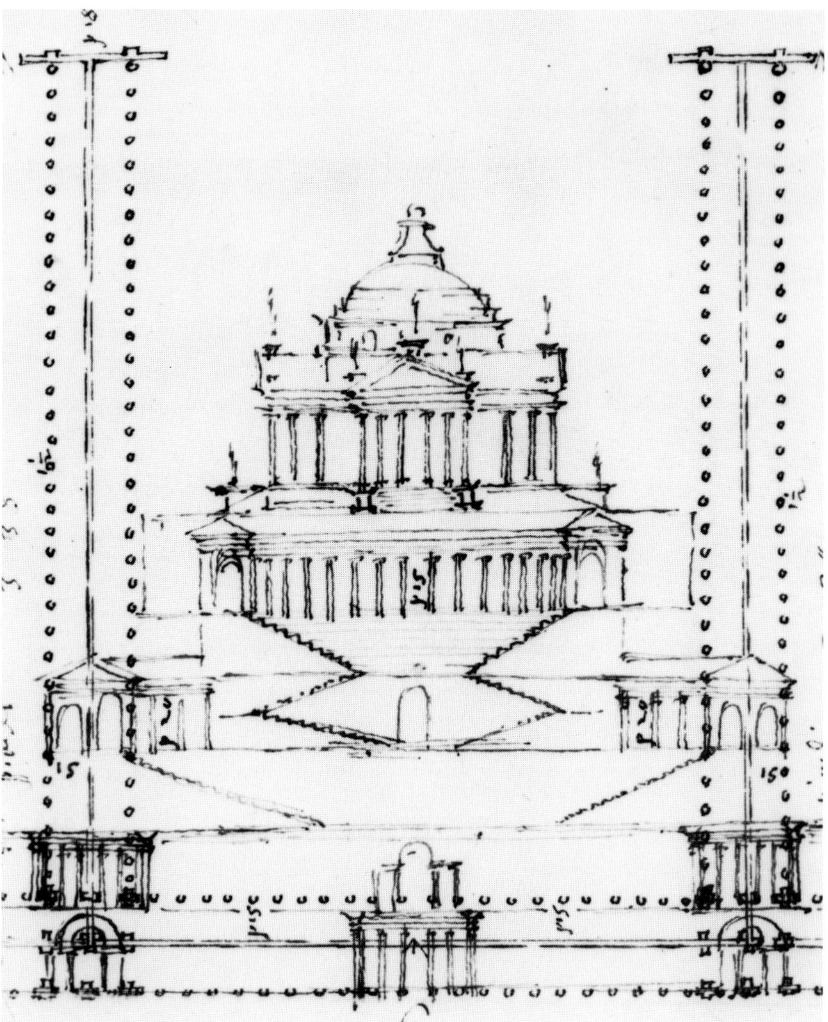

1.8. Andrea Palladio, detail of his reconstruction of the Temple of Fortune, Praeneste (Palestrina). RIBA Drawings Collection, London.

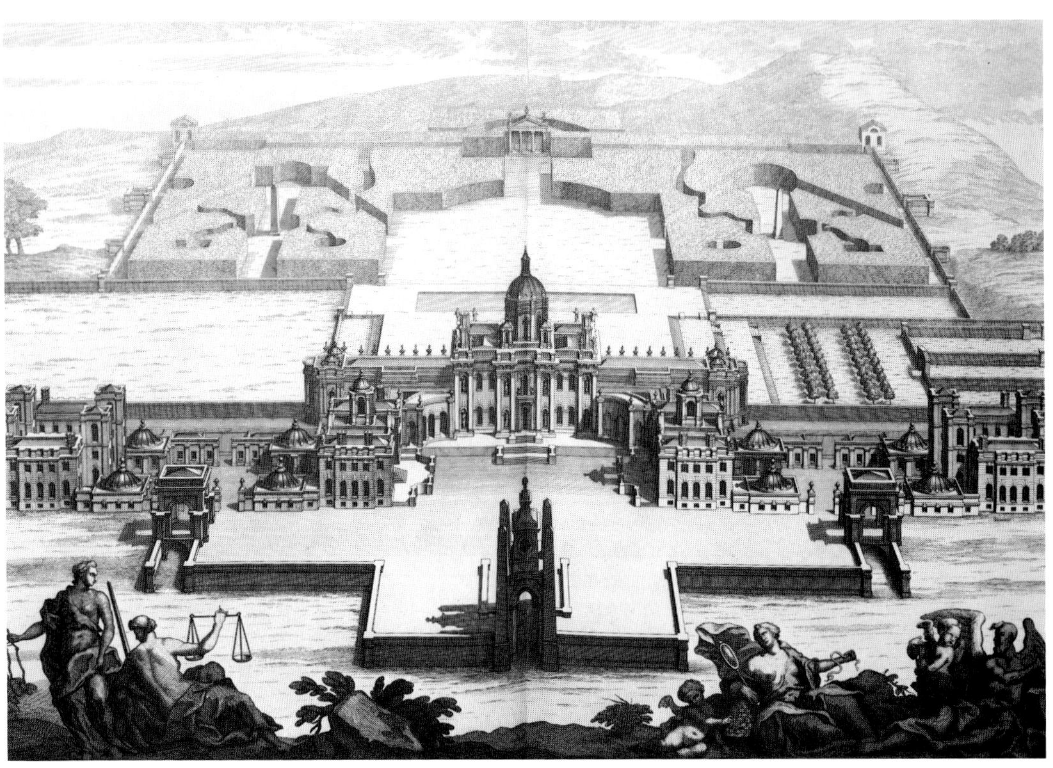

1.9. Castle Howard, engraving from Colen Campbell, Vitruvius Britannicus, *vol. 3, 1725. Dumbarton Oaks, Trustees for Harvard University.*

radical; but in their refusal of current French parterre style and above all in their incorporation near the house of a grove in the antique fashion (compare fig. 1.10), these gardens announced continuities of Italianate gardening.[27]

Similar discriminations affected other parts of the nearby gardenscape. The vegetable garden to the southwest of the house, established early on between 1703 and 1705, was given huge gateways and walls, doubtless to promote warm microclimates within, but with yet another mixture of intimated castleness and European baroque.

More important and difficult of solution seems to have been the area to the northeast of the house, the famous Wray Wood. Praised by Leland,[28] the Tudor chronicler of British culture in the sixteenth century, the 66-acre Wray Wood became the battleground of representation at Castle Howard in the eighteenth. The first of two unexecuted proposals for Wray Wood (fig. 1.11) gave it a brave baroque geometry of avenues and *rond-points,* a form that is used even for the relocated village, pools, and canals.[29] At least the design (if not the drawing) is probably by William Talman.

The second design (fig. 1.12) may have come from George London, who visited Castle Howard once or twice to advise before he was, at least as garden designer, supplanted.[30] This second, also unexecuted, design retains the crossed canals and water theaters to the north of the house, which has now been turned around to face the far better views on either side of the ridge (as opposed to along it). But the proposal which gave offense and probably lost George London the job was to drive avenues through Wray Wood in a star-shaped pattern.

Yet another scheme left the much esteemed and historical wood to speak more in its own voice; this too survives in a drawing (fig. 1.13) which we presume was executed. This was devised by Carlisle himself with some assistance, I suspect, from Stephen Switzer, who praised the final design in his *Ichnographia Rustica* of 1715. But he praised it—this has never been remarked before—in terms of its happy representation or imitation of nature:

> 'Tis there [i.e., Wray Wood] that Nature is truly imitated, if not excell'd, and from which the Ingenious may draw the best of their Schemes in Natural and Rural Gardening: 'Tis there that she is by a kind of fortuitous Conduct pursued through all her most intricate Mazes, and taught ever to exceed her own self in the *Natura-Linear,* and much more Natural and Promiscuous Disposition of all her Beauties.[31]

1.10. William Stukeley, drawing of "The ancient manner of Temples in Groves." Bodleian Library, Gough Maps 229, item 322.

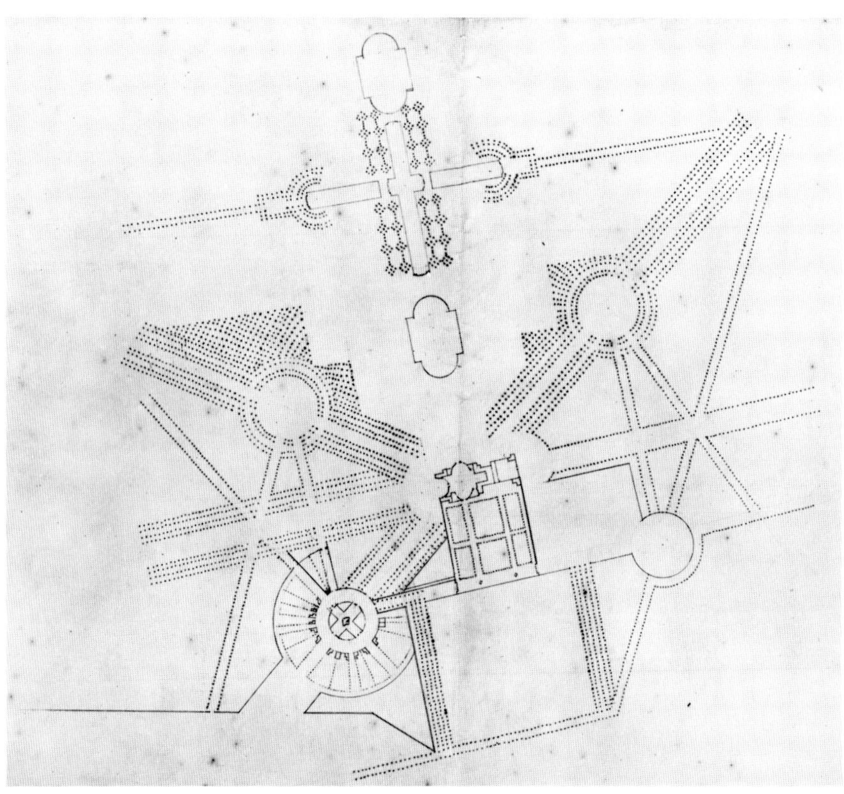

1.11. Proposal for Wray Wood, Castle Howard, pencil, pen, and ink. Victoria and Albert Museum (E 434-1951).

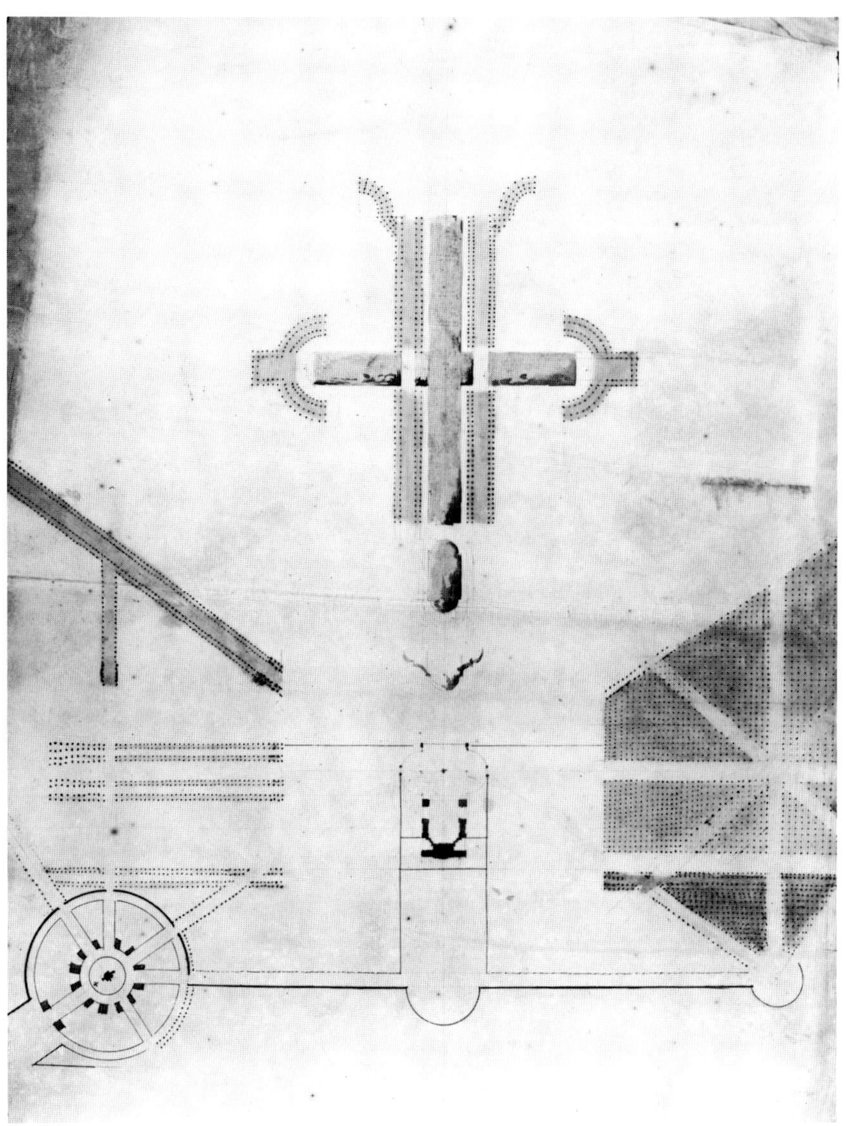

1.12. Second proposal for Wray Wood, Castle Howard, pencil, pen, ink, and watercolor. Victoria and Albert Museum (E 433-1951).

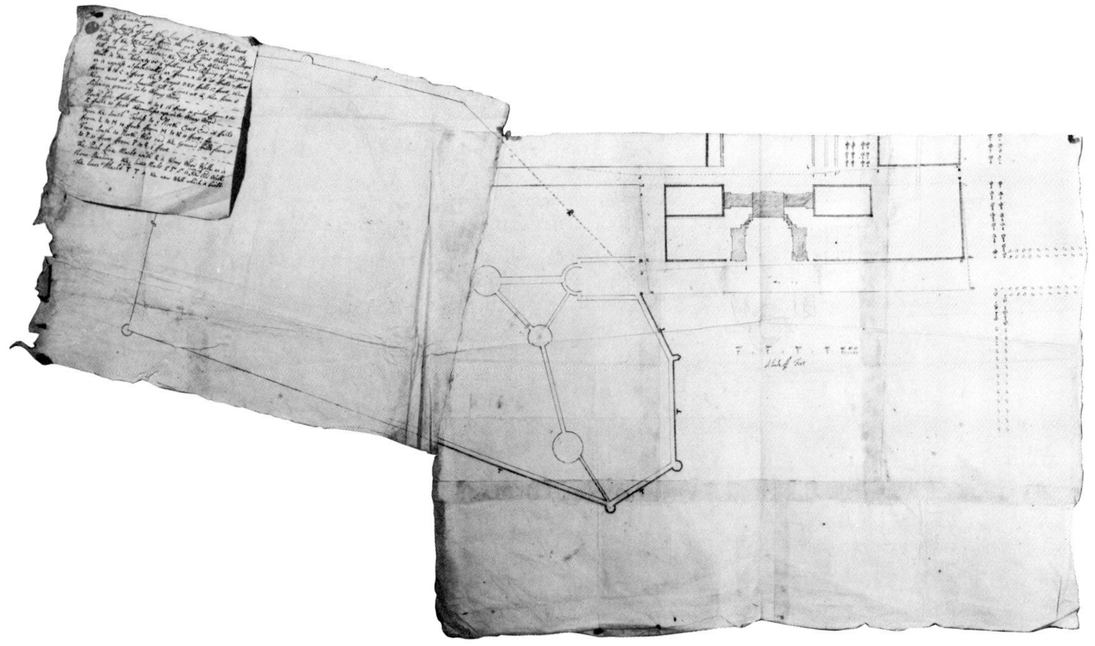

1.13. Third proposal for Wray Wood, Castle Howard, pencil, pen, and ink. Victoria and Albert Museum (E 432-1951).

In another version of this passage Switzer praises "his Lordship's superlative Genius" in giving Wray Wood "that Labyrinth diverting Model we now see" and he concludes by recording (with a pun on George London whose design would "have spoil'd the Wood") Yorkshire's supremacy over London![32]

But the layout of Wray Wood, so praised for its imitation of nature, seems to have been nothing particularly new, let alone naturalistic. From other sources it is clear that it was much like classical Roman descriptions of country seats;[33] much like too the groves of Italian Renaissance villas—those at Villa Lante, at the Medici Villa of Pratolino (fig. 1.14), or at many Frascati villas. Scattered along the walks in the wood were fountains, pools, urns, statues of Diana, Apollo, sybils, and Neptune, and a summerhouse with marine and landscape frescoes. In short, what Carlisle and Switzer between them did was to represent nature by combining in an idealized "natural" form the old woodland which was such a prized feature of the estate, the fortification-like walls shown on the plan and which continue the castle theme of the estate,[34] and, after the manner of Ovid's *Metamorphoses,* a whole range of mythological and narrative emblems, the common theme of which was nature's penetration by god and human alike. It was indeed an imitation or representation of nature, but with the full vocabulary and syntax of Renaissance forms mingling with the native, indigenous trees. These were, as one visitor put it, "the noblest *Beach trees,* which I believe are to be met with in England."[35]

Wray Wood features prominently in any exploration of the grounds. From the house, then as now, one walks eastward along the terrace of the south front and either directs one's steps upwards into the Wray Wood and explores its mixture of endemic Englishness, classical imagery, and Italianate forms, or bending to the right finds oneself walking below the woodland along the old village street, which in its turn had been decorated with classical statues and urns. This invocation of the existing and seemingly random curve of an earlier English settlement for a garden walk mingles (as would Wray Wood, if the visitor went that way) old and new, Italian and English, contrived scenery and actual, for the old village street begins to give visitors fine views over a quintessentially English landscape, the Howardian Hills.

Whichever route visitors take from the house eastward, they reach the *pièce de résistance* of Castle Howard's representations, the point in space and time where the English garden's art of imitation may be seen

1.14. Gustav Utens, lunette depicting the Villa of Pratolino, 1599. Museo Topografico, Florence.

to have reached a crucial stage in its endeavors. The visitor who went either through Wray Wood or along the old village street at its edge would have emerged upon the military-like fortification that surrounds it and at one of two temples placed there (fig. 1.15). Both were at one point termed "turrets" by Hawksmoor,[36] as if continuing to stress the castleness. In fact, both were classical: the Temple of the Four Winds we have already encountered and discussed, and a Temple of Venus, down the northeast side of the wood, only the platform of which now survives. The classical architecture or association of both and the dedication of the latter to a Roman deity of gardens added their distinctive note to the castlelike bastions. From either temple one viewed indigenous scenery and, from the Temple of the Four Winds uniquely, an English landscape transformed—as Wallace Stevens's jar did the Tennessee hillside—by the siting of a massive bridge and a circular temple, like some reconstructed Roman remains (fig. 1.16). The bridge is in fact derived from a design in Palladio's Book III (itself based on the Bridge of Augustus at Rimini); the Mausoleum, for which Hawksmoor refused to use Greek forms,[37] is based instead on a combination of Roman tombs and temples and Bramante's Christian Tempietto in Rome.

Two final insertions of classical monuments into the Yorkshire countryside are encountered if visitors set out to explore that view of woods and fields. Wandering inside Pretty Wood, which lies to the southeast beyond the Mausoleum, and having apparently left behind the classically transformed countryside, they encounter a pyramid (fig. 1.17) and a structure known as the Four Faces (fig. 1.18). Hawksmoor's modern commentator, Kerry Downes, betrays an uncharacteristic lapse when he writes of these two items that they are "utterly pointless"—"you come upon them when you have lost your way, and like Melisande it has no reason for being there and leaves all your questions unanswered."[38] But maybe not. These versions of Roman pyramid and column recall us to cultural origins in ancient Rome and Renaissance Italy, yet they do so on as English a site as could be imagined—the famed woodland of this estate, an English scene which is the final destination and culmination of the progress of the arts. Here in Pretty Wood these objects make the same point as did engraving Castle Howard for a book entitled *Vitruvius Britannicus* or annotating an English belvedere design with references to Pliny and Varro.

These structures and what they represent of cultural history all bring into prominence the Yorkshire scenery in which they have been intro-

1.15. Distant view of the Temple of the Four Winds from the site of the vanished Temple of Venus, Castle Howard (photograph: author).

1.16. Bridge and distant Mausoleum from the Temple of the Four Winds, Castle Howard (photograph: author).

1.17. Pyramid in Pretty Wood, Castle Howard (photograph: Chris Ridgway).

1.18. Four Faces in Pretty Wood, Castle Howard (photograph: Chris Ridgway).

duced. Yet they make the northern wilderness no longer wild; they ensure that it takes its privileged place in the whole represented scene. The view from the Temple of the Four Winds of square temple, bridge, and round Mausoleum may, as has been suggested,[39] look like a Claude Lorrain painting in its choice of Roman forms; but their context is English, indeed Yorkshire, and the whole is orchestrated into some large theatrical representation. Indeed, the vista was actually described by a visitor as providing an amphitheater—"from hence [in Wray Wood] you are carry'd through a winding walk which brings you to a piece of ground laid out in the form of an amphitheatre."[40] This clearly recalls the younger Pliny's famous account of his Tuscan villa where the landscape was shaped into some "vast amphitheatre such as could only be the work of nature."[41]

The sense of amphitheater would remind any early eighteenth-century spectator that he would be expected to attend to some representation. William Kent in the 1730s showed that these were his expectations when, in a pair of drawings related by this subject, contemporary spectators watch in one the transformation of the Chatsworth hillside (see fig. 8.5) and in the other the meeting of the Rivers Thames and Mole in a landscape that features both Tudor-Gothick and Palladian buildings (fig. 1.19). In both drawings the humans are actors and spectators of the representation, and they seem to show they are clearly aware of that dual role in these theaters of landscape. Today we have wholly lost this response; what we see are people simply looking at scenery, without even registering that the word "scenery" has a theatrical connotation.

It is here that we encounter the watershed of garden representation. To those educated and attuned to thinking of art as representation, such a spot as the Temple of the Four Winds at Castle Howard would have declared its cultural history. But to increasing numbers it became just an apparently effortlessly beautiful landscape; for them there was no difference worth observing or bothering about between the landscape and what it represented, between the medium and the message. Instead of temples and bridges, like obelisks or jars, transforming their context and themselves, they were registered simply as items dumped in the landscape.

Subsequent designers like William Kent and Capability Brown continued to bring neoclassical aesthetics to bear upon their designs. Brown especially perfected nature by judicious manipulation of its components, adding a tree here or a concealed head of water there. His art attended

1.19. William Kent, landscape capriccio *with Hampton Court, Esher, and the River Thames (illustration of Michael Drayton's* Polyolbion*). Department of Prints and Drawings, British Museum, London.*

to the formal potential of ground, water, trees, and so gave to English landscape its ideal forms, *la belle nature anglaise*. The difficulty was that less capable imitators and less sophisticated spectators did not see nature perfected, nature represented at her best; they saw simply what they took to be nature— William Chambers thought Brown's landscapes "differ very little from common fields, so closely is common nature copied in most of them."[42]

So we must remind ourselves how to look at the Castle Howard landscape as it was intended before Brown embrowned England and our taste. We must understand just how complex this act of garden landscape representation was. What Carlisle and his architects achieved by mid-century by a gradual process of trial, error, and a growing sense of purpose was the creation of a landscape in which explicit architectural features call into being a wholly calculated representation of an English scene both in the sense of scenery and as a theater of cultural history.

The scenario was complex enough. As Carlisle's son and the family's architects made clear, the Temple of the Four Winds on the bastion at the edge of Wray Wood from which the visitor views this scene had to be Italian. And as if to emphasize this consensus, Carlisle's daughter, Lady Irwin, the author of a poem on Castle Howard of about 1733, wrote "This Wood with Justice Belvedere we name"; to make assurance double-sure she added a footnote to explain that "belvedere" was "Italian for the Fine View."[43] The word and some prominent components of the scene are Italian; the ensemble, the "Fine View" itself, is ineluctably English, like the fortifications from which it is viewed.

These final views at Castle Howard—the last ones a visitor encounters in a walk from the house as well as the last ones to be created—announce both an awareness of history and a sense of the future. The past is there in the castlelike bastions, the Roman as well as Palladian architecture, the Pyramid built to celebrate the third Earl's ancester, Lord William Howard, as well as the Mausoleum. The future is also there in the Mausoleum, since Vanbrugh claimed it as "a Show, and a Noble one, to many future Ages."[44] The future was addressed directly, too, in the Earl's claim upon the obelisk that "for posterity [he] performed the same." The future is there, too, in the confident appeal to a rich agrarian and wooded landscape which would, as it still does in the profitable modern estate, yield future riches to the owners.

The Pyramid itself is eloquent of much of this (fig. 1.20). A strikingly Roman form, it was designed to celebrate the third Earl's English

1.20. The Pyramid, Castle Howard (photograph: author).

ancestry:[45] it thereby dignifies the Howards with Roman attributes and at the same time gives a traditional antique structure a local habitation and a name. Furthermore, locally hewn stone gives this antique form, as indeed it gives to each and every architectural object in the Castle Howard landscape, whether, Gothick, classical, Palladian, or modern, a thoroughly local accent.[46] Yet to celebrate here and in this fashion Lord William Howard, whose gardens at Naworth Castle in Cumberland, filled with Roman antiquities, the third Earl had allowed to fall into decay, was to advance Castle Howard at the expense of Naworth Castle. Much concerned with heraldry and family trees, the third Earl was, as Charles Saumarez-Smith makes very clear in his book on *The Building of Castle Howard,* very conscious of both the great and powerful dynasty to which he belonged and the junior and relatively undistinguished branch from which he himself came. To locate this memorial to his ancestry out in the fields of his enlarged and recreated estate, a pyramid clearly seen from the house, from the old village street turned garden walk, as well as once or twice during the approach along the great avenue, was to promise something too about the future. For the rich agricultural land and valuable woods, about which Carlisle and his landscape architects were always concerned, was an investment for the future just as it was an acknowledgment of traditions of Roman husbandry in which Castle Howard was taking its place. Stephen Switzer, again perhaps influenced by his contacts with Castle Howard, voices it all clearly: for him modern British estates of patriotic (i.e., Whig) landed gentry enshrined the progress of agrarian arts by practicing what he called "Rural and Extensive Gardening"—prospects of "good Woods, fine Pasture, Land, &c . . . open to all View, to the unbounded Felicities of distant prospect, and to the expansive volumes of Nature herself."[47]

Switzer's metaphors are not idly chosen. The prospects were views, but they were also future prospects of agricultural prosperity. And to the careful mixture of old and new, Roman, Italian, and British, we can add that other ancient alliance of beauty and utility, a classical alliance given, once again, fresh formulation on this Yorkshire estate. The volumes of Nature were indeed open for all who chose to read. One who did was Horace Walpole; he recognized something of what was being represented and expressed it in his own way by hailing "woods [as] worthy of being each a metropolis of the Druids." What he does is to invoke an ancient British tribe, which by his time had become a crucial way of registering Britian's historic, indigenous culture.[48]

Castle Howard shows how one particular estate adjudicated between ancient and modern; how the progress of the classical arts of architecture, gardening, and indeed of living and dying (given the Mausoleum) reached not just the northern island of England but invaded even Yorkshire and there melded with the native traditions of Gothick and castle—and all this in a landscape the very extent of which precludes its being artificially reorganized like a garden parterre. In short, we have at Castle Howard a representation of a particular, historical conception of England and Englishness. Yet the whole mode of articulating that idea was quickly to lose its impact and appeal as the eighteenth century advanced into more and more naturalistic landscaping taste.

2 THEATERS, GARDENS, AND GARDEN THEATERS

A subtitle for this essay might be "About Vauxhall and Ranelagh." These London pleasure gardens will serve as text, pretext, and context; to write "about" them is to explore a whole congeries of forms, themes, and ideas of both garden and theater. Variously and collaboratively these two artistic forms shaped each other's development during and after the Renaissance: many writers, for example, have noticed "the close relationship which existed in seventeenth-century Italy between theatrical and garden architecture."[1] This relationship was carried, like much else, into England, and like much else too, adapted to English art and society during the seventeenth and eighteenth centuries. Yet architectural form by itself is not my concern here; it is rather how the physical conditions of garden and/or theater declare contemporary ideas of human nature and existence. Gardens and theaters (including stage scenery) search for their forms in a constantly changing attempt to articulate other, larger and less accessible aspects of life. By close attention to specific examples of garden and theater such as Vauxhall and Ranelagh it is possible to give a sharper focus to those shadows thrown upon the walls of the cave (or, in theatrical terms, even *cavea*) of history.

Vauxhall and Ranelagh were the two most famous, because the most successful and long-lived, of London's pleasure gardens.[2] But for two hundred years or more after the Restoration these two were simply the most prominent among many others, smaller, less ambitious (and so less able to survive by adapting to changing tastes and social customs), yet sharing with their major rivals features of garden and theater which will occasionally be useful in illuminating Vauxhall and Ranelagh. Vauxhall was opened in 1661 as the New Spring Gardens; it comprised fountains, one large room, grass walks dividing the land into plots filled with fruit bushes, roses, shrubs as well as vegetables, and had arbors where visitors could eat snacks or, as Pepys often did, entertain some congenial companion. The form in which we know Vauxhall best was given it in the early 1730s by Jonathan Tyers, whose family retained the ownership until 1792 and thus oversaw the heyday of the gardens. Now they were divided into larger sections by various cross-walks; there were pavilions, supper and music rooms, alcoves, an orchestra, and other exhibits dotted around the perimeter (fig. 2.1). By contrast, Ranelagh had a more restricted garden—opened in 1742 in the grounds of Lord Ranelagh's former house, its central feature was the huge, specially constructed Rotunda; but there were gravel walks, an octagonal lawn, a water basin, and a canal with its island and "Chinese" or "Venetian" temple (fig. 2.2).

These pleasure gardens have been much studied for their social and anecdotal interest and for the personalities connected with them.[3] But other topics have consequently been neglected. How, for instance, did Vauxhall and Ranelagh combine their gardenesque and their theatrical functions? Why, indeed, should such gardens be considered as theaters at all? What precedents for such an alliance existed in England or on the Continent? Such enquiries lead in their turn to questions about whether garden settings had special significance as stage designs. And then, finally, it is worth asking what light is thrown by these garden theaters at Vauxhall and Ranelagh upon the contemporary development of the landscape garden; did it, too, have theatrical implications which we now miss?

Vauxhall, from its earliest years, was obviously associated with a strongly theatrical dimension of social life, which was given, under Tyers's management, a visible and formal aspect. This was not, however, the clearly theatrical character of its nineteenth-century existence, when it became one stop on the London circuit for miscellaneous entertainers for whom stages and auditoriums were erected.[4] The mid-eighteenth-century gardens rather took their theatrical aspect from various architectural features, closely connected (albeit in muddled fashion) with actual theaters.

First, there were the three curving pavilions around the central grove (fig. 2.3). These constructions were "theaters" in that their apsidal shape echoed a standard feature of Renaissance garden architecture, itself indebted to many readings and misreadings of classical ruins including theaters like that of Marcellus in Rome as well as baths, libraries, and nymphaeums. John Evelyn, for instance, remarked upon the "theater

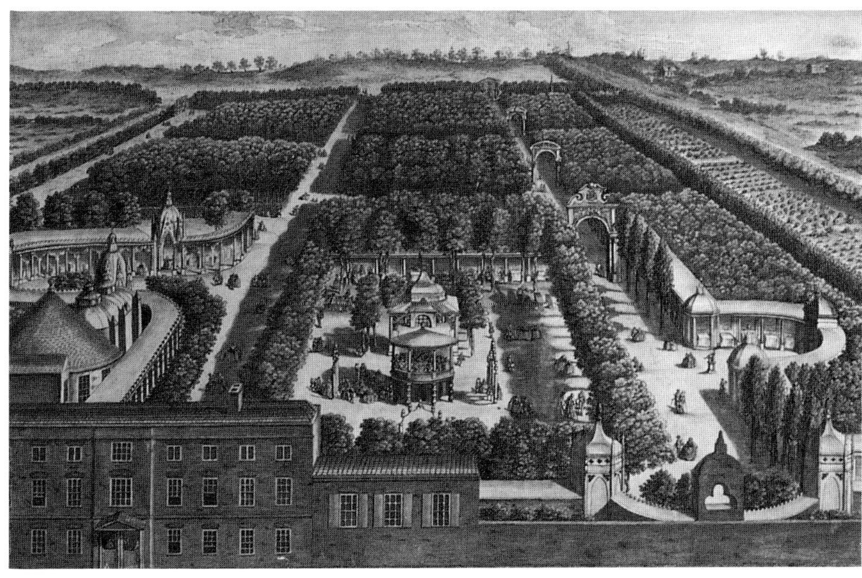

2.1. J. S. Muller after S. Wale, "A general prosepct of Vaux Hall Gardens . . .," from Stow's Survey of London, *1754. Robert Douwma (Print and Maps) Ltd.*

2.2. View of the canal, Chinese building, and Rotunda in Ranelagh Gardens, colored engraving, 1750s. Guildhall Library, London.

2.3. Thomas Bowles after S. Wale, Vauxhall, the Temple of Comus, c. 1751. British Museum, Grace Collection.

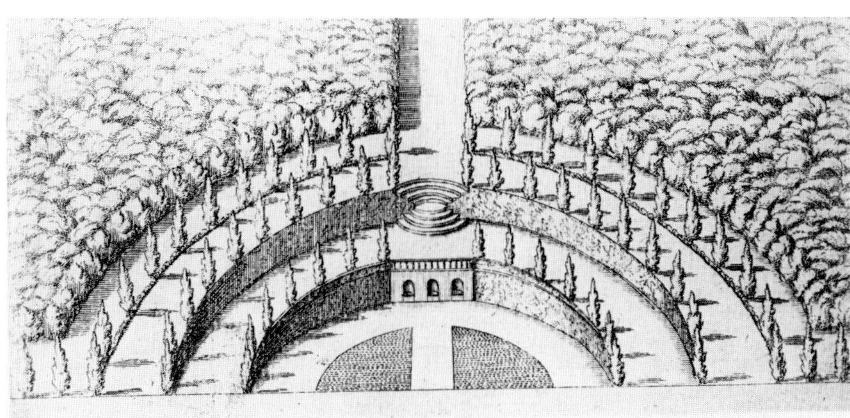

2.4. Engraving of the hillside amphitheater at Wilton, from Isaac de Caus, Le Jardin du Wilton, *c. 1645. Dumbarton Oaks, Trustees for Harvard University.*

for pastimes," when he visited Carlo Fontana's strikingly scenographic climax to the gardens of the Villa Mondragone at Frascati.[5] Such apsidal elements were a basic device in Italian garden design from Bramante's early *exedra* in the Belvedere Courtyard at the Vatican, itself copied from the Temple of Fortuna Primigenia at Palestrina, which it is now recognized was indeed used for various ritual performances.[6] The shape of a concave wall, perhaps with niches, or even an alcove cut into the hillside, sometimes mounted by a series of steps, became a permanent feature of seventeenth- and eighteenth-century garden design in France and England (fig. 2.4). But this is also the place to recall that courtyards, such as the Belvedere or that between the Pitti Palace and the Boboli Gardens in Florence, became spaces for theatrical and other entertainments; gardens were designed with amphitheaters, the Boboli again, for representations. The Italian garden, in short, made an essential contribution to what Jean Jacquot and his colleagues at the Centre National de la Recherche Scientifique have called, following Corneille, *le lieu théâtral*.[7]

Vauxhall undoubtedly absorbed this basic, but distinctly theatrical, form for its first major garden buildings in the 1730s. The curving pavilions declared themselves as "theaters" and cleared a space within their scope as an amphitheater. (Later, when Ranelagh had set a fashion with its Rotunda, originally described as an amphitheater,[8] Vauxhall established its own indoor arenas in various buildings: a rotunda, picture room, and supper room, all entered from one of the original curving pavilions.) These pavilions were themselves divided into innumerable niches, simply the adaptation to mass entertainment of garden alcoves, which derived ultimately from the classical *exedra* or conversation seats decorated with pictures that Cicero describes in his villa.[9] Such decorations were even adopted by Tyers at Vauxhall, where the booths were each supplied with a picture by Francis Hayman after his and Hogarth's designs.[10]

Now, such classical allusions—and we shall encounter more—are not of themselves likely to establish a specifically theatrical character. But the *exedra,* whether as intimate alcove or larger *frons scaenae,* had acquired an ambiguous status in garden design, and this Vauxhall manipulated with success. The scenographic garden at Mondragone, for example, was both stage—its statues and fountains viewed from the garden below—and auditorium or *cavea*—a rostrum from which to view the gardens (fig. 2.5). Less ostentatious *exedra* seats were both vantage

2.5. Water Theater, Villa Mondragone, Frascati, from Falda, Le Fontane di Roma *(Rome, 1675–1691).*

points whence to watch other events and stages where visitors themselves were made to feel they constituted the garden dramas.[11] For the Italian garden that most influenced France and England was one where the visitor was no longer a passive spectator; he was led, instead, as Sir Henry Wotton declared in a famous passage, "by several *mountings* and *valings,* to various entertainements of his *sent,* and *sight.*"[12] The expectation of a fine garden, whatever the formal means by which the effects were achieved, was that it work upon its visitor, involving him often insidiously as a participant in its dramas, which were presented to him as he explored its spaces by a variety of statues, inscriptions and (above all) hydraulically controlled automata.

It follows, I think, from these expectations of a fine garden that gardens also expressed some of the more complicated notions of the idea of *theatrum mundi.* Elizabethan audiences at the Globe Theatre had expected—the very scene they watched enforced this—to view a microcosm of the world. Gardens, too, were designed to include a conspectus of allusions. The words *theater* and *garden,* indeed, were used interchangeably to mean a collection or compendium: as in John Parkinson's *Theatrum Botanicum, The Theatre of Plants, or an Universall and Complete Herball* (1640) and Henry Peacham's *Minerva Britanna* (1612) which its subtitle explains as "a Garden of Heroicall Devises, furnished and adorned with emblems and Impresas . . ." Such titles, as Erwin Panofsky remarked to Herbert Weisinger, intimate a "world [that] becomes a grandiose spectacle, filled with floating images and a constantly changing scenery, rather than a structure clearly organized and intellectually penetrable."[13] The promise of a whole world of items which the words and arts of theater and garden held out was, as Panofsky suggests, not always redeemed in straightforward ways. If stage and garden dramatize the world, the world was also traditionally a theater, and the concepts were mutually endorsing and complicating. The simplest idea of *theatrum mundi* is that we are placed as admiring spectators in the theater of the world; but soon this slips into our being also actors, perhaps (as Plato implied) radically unsure of our true role in life's drama; from this it is another simple step into believing that "the very *mythos* of the play of life is itself a falsehood."[14] These shifting concepts were equally relevant to gardens as theaters—compendiums, that is, or stages where life's variety was made visible.

These ideas are rarely applied to garden design, despite the testimony of Henry Wotton and other amateurs. But it is evident that not only did seventeenth- and early eighteenth-century gardens promote the shifting perspectives of which Panofsky wrote but they were organized in order to ensure them. Vauxhall Gardens was a commercial exploitation of these garden traditions; if it catered largely to citizens with little experience of private gardens, its other clients from Pepys to Johnson certainly had that experience, and its very organization of visitors within the grounds subtly manipulated even the uninitiate into theatrical expectations.

Vauxhall and Ranelagh were designed to include various theatrical forms, like the curving pavilions, their niches and the rotunda amphitheaters. Furthermore, the gardens were provided with many other items quite specifically associated with the theater: there were the real vistas down the walks, assisted on the Italian Walk by a series of triumphal arches that accentuated the long prospect like wings; there were the illusionistic prospects, *trompe-l'oeil* scenes at the end of walks, like a painting of the ruins of Palmyra that closed the South Walk or the two arches of some Roman acqueduct at the end of the Cross Walk (these last made to seem real in an engraving after Canaletto [fig. 2.6]).

This repertoire of exotic backdrops was further augmented by various transparencies, sometimes actually hung in front of small stages: one of these depicted a Hermit pursuing his studies by the light of a fire and a brilliant moon, while another, immediately at the entrance to the gardens, represented an amphitheater through which was visible a garden perspective terminated with a pedestal. This mingling of garden and theater imagery—to the point where demarcations became blurred (Ranelagh's supper boxes *inside* the Rotunda opened at their rear into the actual gardens)—recalls many Renaissance theatrical events to which reference will be made later.

Confusions of art and reality, a staple feature alike of garden and theater, were further pursued at Vauxhall in *tableaux* or cinematic illusions, like the famous cascade which Tyers created to rival Garrick's at Drury Lane. It displayed a water mill, miller's house, and a foaming waterfall, made of tin. Its attraction, attested by Goldsmith's Mrs. Tibbs as by Fanny Burney's Evelina,[15] was the strong illusion of reality—the foam at the base of the cascade was especially admired—contrived out of the palpably unreal: the "switching-on" of this mechanism was actually announced by a warning bell to give people time to convene from all parts of the garden. In 1783 the cascade was replaced by a representation of a "mountainous view covered with palm trees and circumscribed by a rainbow" (quoted Southworth, p. 50).

Yet if the cascade's replacement by a "natural landscape" (ibid.) suggests that Vauxhall kept pace with contemporary picturesque taste, more of its garden theater entertainments continued to rely heavily upon earlier episodes of garden history. In 1791, to honor the Prince of Wales's birthday, fireworks heralded the drawing up of a curtain at the end of the South Walk to discover

> a Gothic temple of a splendid figure, having an artificial fountain playing in its center, and beautifully decorated with twisted columns and various ornaments formed by transparencies and lamps. The columns and the chief part of the temple was a piece of curious machinery which kept in constant motion and formed a pleasing coup d'oeil.
>
> (Southworth, p. 60)

This grotto is a late (and cheap) version of those innumerable Italian mechanisms that entertained visitors like Evelyn at Pratolino and other gardens.[16] Well into the nineteenth century Vauxhall even put on *trompe-*

2.6. E. Rooker (?) after Canaletto, Vauxhall, a view of the Centre Cross Walk, 1760s, from the grangerized History of Vauxhall Gardens *(1890), I, 78. Harvard Theater Collection.*

l'oeil naumachiae (see Southworth, pp. 60–61), yet another invocation of a Renaissance revival of classical entertainments, in pursuit of which the Pitti Palace courtyard was once flooded and which the lowest water terrace of the Villa Lante at Bagnaia wittily imitates in fountain sculpture. Some of the earliest entertainments in the New Spring Gardens were the hydraulic inventions of Sir Samuel Morland, who leased Vauxhall House after the Restoration; and according to Scott (p. 19) the name of the gardens derived from the water tricks or *giocchi d'acqua* which wetted unwary visitors; these devices had been an unfailing source of amusement to travelers in Italy from Montaigne to Evelyn.

To those who paid their entry fee to Vauxhall Gardens such spectacles were offered as entertainment and by many visitors their earlier associations with gardens were unnoticed. Other features of Vauxhall, presented to its clients by way of entertainment, were adapted from garden vocabulary generally available in the eighteenth century, at least until the influence of "Capability" Brown was felt. The most obvious items were the statues: the famous Roubiliac Handel[17] or the figure of Milton, seated on a rock in a listening posture in the area known as the "Rural Downs." At various times during the eighteenth century (the changes were simply commercial expedients to maintain the flow of visitors) the gardens were dotted with further items of a "readable" nature—an obelisk with a Latin inscription, the paintings in the supper boxes (subjects were mostly images of play and recreation, apt for the site), and further emblems and paintings in the rotunda and its extension, the picture room. Classical images were frequently invoked—for the historical allegories painted by Hayman in 1760–1761 and installed in the picture room, the casts of Diana, Apollo, Aurora (standing tiptoe on some "mountains" at the end of the Grand Walk), and even a copy of the Apollo Belvedere. That Tyers counted upon the "readability" of these images and considered a garden incomplete without a whole repertory of speaking pictures and statues is clear from the design of his own private gardens near Dorking. With their "labyrinth of walks, some descending, some ascending: in some parts easy, smooth, and level; in others, rugged and uneven" they must have put their visitors to much exploration. But the gardens were famed for their "moral sentences and admonitions," either inscribed on flags hanging "at every turn" or decorating the Temple of Death (thoughtfully provided with a desk for reading and meditation) or issuing out of two real human skulls at the entrance to the Valley of the Shadow of Death. Deep in this gloomy valley was Tyers's *pièce de résistance*: an alcove in two compartments,

> in one of which the unbeliever is represented dying in the greatest distress and agony, crying—"Oh, whither am I going?" . . . On one side, and above him, are his study of books, which buoyed him up in his libertine course, such as Hobbes, Toland, Tindal, Collins, Morgan, and others of the same stamp. In the other compartment, is the good Christian, or believer, in his dying moments, calm and serene . . . the Bible open before him, which, with several practical discourses upon it, and the sermons of our most noted divines, such as Clarke, Tillotson, and others of the kind, serve to make up his study.[18]

The whole representation was painted by Hayman, who had also decorated the Vauxhall supper boxes. Tyers's organization of his pleasure gardens, while shrewdly not putting off his clients with such strong moral injunctions, reveals him utilizing similar garden imagery and effects.

Vauxhall's theatrical forms and scope throw into relief the same, but generally neglected, aspect of English private gardens between 1650 and 1750. There is space here only for brief examples in lieu of a proper survey. We have seen how Wotton appreciated the theatrical excitements of an "incomparable" Italian garden and how Evelyn's visits to others elicited similar responses. Visitors to the Villa d'Este at Tivoli often responded to its series of events in language derived from the masque.[19] This highly manipulative aspect of Italianate designs was translated into French and English versions: the Earl of Arundel placed the magnificent head of Jupiter given him by Sir Dudley Carleton "in his *utmost* garden," that is to say, in a distant part of his sculpture garden besides the Thames, "so opposite to the Gallery dores, *as being open,* so soon as y^{u} enter into the front Garden y^{u} have the head *in yor eie all the way.*" Thus the visitor was drawn into the excitements of discovery among the rest of the sculpture collection. By chance some mutilated fragments from Arundel's garden were incorporated into another of the early pleasure gardens, Cuper's (corrupted quickly to Cupid's) in Lambeth, where "they received very ill usage from the Ignorance and Stupidity of those who know not their Value, and are still exposed to the open Air, and Folly of Passerby."[20] But the history of these particular Arundel marbles nicely illuminates the absorption by the popular garden theaters of ingredients from private gardens, themselves created in emulation of classical prototypes.

But as the visitor to Wotton's "incomparable" garden or to Arundel's was led among the entertainments he would be forced to stop occasionally in front of the grottoes, *exedras,* fountains, and other "theaters" to watch some extended spectacle. As the travel accounts of many Englishmen declare, these were the most attractive part of Italian garden art. The most sophisticated usually involved some display of automata, and as late a visitor as William Kent declared his appreciation of Pratolino's "very fine groto's adorn'd with shells and petrified stone with pretty water works as Galatea coming out of her Grotto drawn by Dolfini."[21] They contributed explicitly to the metamorphic world of Italian garden art, where one of the essential delights was the invitation to adjudicate continually the effects of art and nature. The seventeenth-century English and (early) French gardens readily copied such devices, as Evelyn's diary bears witness. Le Nôtre, the great French gardener to Louis XIV, disliked such frivolities, and they became less esteemed among the English. But the theatrical forms of Italian garden survived, even where their detailed exhibitions did not. So Le Nôtre's superb gardens at Vaux-le-Vicomte, for example, lead us down to the grand, double, water theater, with river gods and their attendants as huge *tableaux* in niches, and the woods, in one of which Moliere's *Les Fâcheux* was performed in 1661, with designs by Giacomo Torelli. Yet it did not need actual representations to organize a garden's theatrical form and ambience: two surviving gardens designed by John Evelyn at Wotton and Albury in Surrey make this clear. The rear of the house at Wotton gives upon a wide walk and circular pool backed by an arcade, above which a terraced hillside rises; from these terraces, which form the backdrop when viewed from the house, the house and other gardens become the vista and the terraces a rostrum for the spectator. At Albury, though the scale is larger, the same change of role takes place as we move from the site of the house, down into the valley and up the terraces. But in addition the highest terrace is broken in the center with a water theater, like those Evelyn admired in Frascati.[22]

The design of gardens, at least before "Capability" Brown, would continue to invoke structures which collected and composed some "entertainments" for visitors. At Lord Burlington's Chiswick gardens there were paths in the *patte d'oie* (goose foot) formation established in the gardens on both sides of the river (see fig. 4.3 for one of these). This, it has been plausibly argued, is a derivation from the stage of Palladio's Teatro Olimpico in Vicenza—the *trompe l'oeil* city streets of Palladio being translated into the alleys of vegetation terminated with buildings and obelisks.[23] This doubtless learned allusion derived from Burlington's crusade to naturalize Palladian architecture in England, but its effect was to theatricalize the garden scenery.

As the landscape movement grew, other "theatrical" shapes and experiences would be introduced into more "natural" scenery, as happened at Stowe and Rousham. But the Temple of Venus or the Temple of British Worthies at Stowe (see fig. 3.2) and the Vale of Venus or Praeneste Terrace at Rousham all detain and focus for visitors visual and verbal dramas, often engaging them as participants in understanding or even physically maneuvring themselves so that stage and auditorium might exchange places. One of the earliest landscape designers to work at both Stowe and Rousham was Charles Bridgeman, one of whose most distinctive "signatures" was the garden theater.[24] These probably owe their largest debt to Le Nôtre's work, but the famous theater at Claremont (fig. 2.7) derives directly from Serlio's codification of the Vatican Belvedere *exedra* in his *Cinque Libri d'Architettura*. But the main point that Bridgeman's work enforces is that theatrical forms continued to be a dominant feature of garden design at least until the mid-eighteenth century even where no evidence exists for actual dramatic representations. But that they continued to exercise some control over behavior and thinking in gardens is clear. Bolingbroke's famous remark to Pope on the "multiplied *scenes* of your little garden,"[25] Pope's own delight in the entertainments of his garden and grotto, his iconographical representation (perhaps by Kent) in the cave or *cavea* of making, all testify to a theatrical dimension which we are inclined to neglect. Horace Walpole, who also acknowledged the dramas of moving through Pope's garden, was attentive elsewhere to these garden theaters: at Stowe in 1770 he reported that "a small Vauxhall was acted for us at the Grotto in the Elysian Fields, which was illuminated with lamps, as were the thicket and two little banks on the lake."[26] His use of "Vauxhall" as a generic noun (not by any means an isolated example) points to close relationships between garden, theatre and garden theater.

There is one magnificent visual example of a private garden, organized in a series of theatres, though doubtless Pope would not have appreciated its topiary. Balthasar Nebot's set of views of Hartwell House,[27] painted in the late 1730s, shows the immediate vicinity of the house laid out in various theaters which utilize pavilions and obelisks as termination points for perspectival scenes contrived in yew (fig. 2.8). Further, he shows the garden's owners and their friends responding, if undemonstrably, to the theatrical context, just as the very points of view he selects from which to paint declare the ambiguity of those theaters, which are sometimes stages and sometimes stations from which to observe the larger theater of the new garden.

The grounds of Hartwell House are made by Nebot to resemble seventeenth-century stage sets with garden scenery—they even suggest, though in fact this may not have been so, that the perspective tricks of stage scenery (whereby, as Serlio put it, "a man in a small place may see . . . a thousand fayre things") have been rendered in yew. Gardens like these at Hartwell figured often in stage designs. One can only conclude that the two arts of perspective theater scenery and garden design, first flourishing together in the Cinquecento, sustained and

2.7. Claremont amphitheater, engraving by J. Rocque, 1734. London Borough of Lambeth Archives Department.

2.8. Balthasar Nebot, topiary arches and "shutters" to the George II column, Hartwell House, Buckinghamshire, 1738. Buckingham County Museum, Aylesbury.

mutually inspired each other's endeavors then and later. Gardens not only incorporated theaters, but came to be planned *in toto* as theaters; while gardens featured prominently as dramatic locations in intermezzi, operas, and plays.[28] Indeed, the exchanges between the arts were carried on occasions to subtle extremes: an opera performed in the Barberini Palace in 1656 had a row of fountains across the proscenium opening for which real water was piped from the gardens, while painted gardens appeared on the curtain.[29] A theater constructed at the Buen Retiro Palace in Madrid in 1640 had a rear wall which parted to show real gardens beyond the illusionist ones.[30] We have already seen how Vauxhall Gardens continued to mix real and illusionary scenery, while a rival pleasure garden, the Apollo, painted the end of its spacious indoor room with a landscape "which concealed the orchestra from the public view" and presumably aided the illusion that the music came from out-of-doors.[31]

The parallel and sometimes joint endeavors of garden and theater design introduce other considerations, perhaps of more importance to the English literary historian. Granted that gardens occurred often as settings (by the later seventeenth century they were standard equipment for London theaters[32]) and granted that scenery in theaters and Italian-derived garden art were still new and exciting developments, did gardens have any special significance in dramatic representations? Did such scenery have its own visual codes or language upon which the verbal text depended? Undoubtedly it did, though the sheer incidence of garden settings inevitably meant they were sometimes used in a token, unstrenuous fashion. But from the masques of Inigo Jones (a prime witness, since he knew Italian stage and garden art), through some Restoration plays, to *Arsinöe,* the special significance of gardens as dramatic setting is clearly, if variously, announced.

In Jones's masque designs gardens play two roles.[33] They may be the locale of ideal states, either political ("the beautiful garden of the Britanides," *Luminalia*) or seasonal ("spacious garden with walks, parterras, close arbours and cypress trees . . . all which figureth the spring," *Florimène*). This was, of course, a traditional significance of the garden, as in the Fount of Vertue and the Garden of Plenty depicted on the triumphal arches which greeted James I's entry into London. Yet equally traditional was the garden as trap and deceit, often associated with Circe, whose garden appeared in *Tempe Restored* as it had in earlier, Continental entertainments like the *Balet comique de la Royne* of 1581.

Above all, gardens were uncertain territory, partly because of this double role they enjoyed. We must recognize the essential, exciting insecurity of a spectator's confrontation with a garden at an actual villa as in the masquing hall. The developments of Italian garden art that emphasized surprises and metamorphic play lent their authority to all such dramatic ambiguities as well as contributing much more of their imagery than has been allowed. The opening rocks which disclosed Oberon's palace in 1611 recreate theatrically our experience of walking toward Buontalenti's grotto in the Boboli Gardens, where the distant sight of an architectural feature changes into a recognition of "natural" stonework which finally, inside, completely surrounds us. Jones's mechanism simply reversed the experience.[34]

The scene from *Oberon* is typical of the masque's thematic and technical reliance upon transformation. In this, too, garden experience played an important part, for its essence was movement, often a carefully prepared sequence of events and discoveries, as the spectator was led onward. The verbal texts of masques often emphasized this garden quality even in their descriptions of the static back-shutter designs; though Jones's design for "A Garden and a Princely Villa" (II, plate 281) manages to convey a fine sense of our having arrived at the top of a flight of steps which lead into the excitements of a new garden. In *Lord Hay's Masque* we are told of "two ascents," which as in any steeply terraced site force choices upon the visitor, "that on the right leading to the bower of Flora, the other to the house of Night" (I, 116). *Tempe Restored* has a palace "seated on [the] side of a fruitful hill . . . with an open terrace before it and a great stair of return descending into the lower grounds" (II, 480). Sometimes the invocation of this garden movement is economical—*Luminalia's* "further part of the garden opened" (II, 708); but sometimes, as in *Coelum Britannicum,* much more elaborate:

> the scene again is varied into a new and pleasant prospect clean differing from all the other, the nearest part showing a delicious garden with several walks and parterr as set round with low trees, and on the sides against these walls were fountains and grots, and in the furthest part a palace from whence went high walks upon arches, and above them open terraces planted with cypress trees, and all this together was composed of such ornaments as might express a princely villa [fig. 2.9].[35]

2.9. Inigo Jones, garden backdrop for a masque, drawing of 1630s. Trustees of the Chatsworth Settlement (photograph: Courtauld Institute of Art).

Such passages both work to ensure that the scene is "read" correctly and depend upon a knowledgeable response. Most other references to gardens emphasize how much the new dramaturgy of the masque, as Stephen Orgel and Roy Strong have explained it, also constituted a garden's drama—"annihilating the barrier between the ideal and the real" and requiring the active participation of the audience whose "wit and understanding made the miracles and metamorphoses possible" (I, 1 and 13).

Wit and understanding could hardly be counted upon to the same extent in the Restoration theatre; nor were the technical resources as sophisticated. But audiences were probably expected to "read" garden settings as part of a comedy's full meaning. No longer, of course, were these villas and princely gardens, but public ones like Mulberry and Vauxhall (still known as New Spring Gardens); however, what an audience expected of experiences in them seems to have differed very little. It is their dramatic ambiguity that is invoked and involved in the plays: places of pastoral perfection, accentuated by their "gardenhood" (as Walpole called it in 1769 when he thought it threatened), where Valentine and Christine may plight their troth at the end of *Love in a Wood*; but also places of intrigue, duplicity, play, and consequent confusions.

The Mulberry Garden by Sir Charles Sedley (1668) uses both expectations. The eponymous setting authorizes the pastoral heroics of Forecast's children as well as libertine intrigue generally throughout the play. But two scenes are actually set there. In one (I.iii) the country girls, Olivia and Victoria Everyoung, prefer its intricate diversions to the "long walk at home" and enjoy rather innocently its amorous excitements ("the air of this place is a great softener of men's hearts"). In another (IV.i) it is the intrigues and play that dominate; those gallants like Estridge and Modish who like to work the gardens are outmaneuvered by Olivia and Victoria in conjunction with Wildish, who was taken there by the other two men to see if they could make him fall in love. In the setting of two adjacent arbors the hidden and masked girls are the audience of a double bill—Wildish's charade with the other two men and theirs with him. But the encounters of the gardens foil the gallants' performance and when they seek to ease their discomposure by turning to the neighboring ladies in masks Olivia and Victoria reveal themselves. The garden theater rewards those who will not spend too long in disguise and the rather extreme revenge that Modish and Estridge take upon Wildish, who marries Olivia, is to lure to the Mulberry

Garden a widow for whom Wildish was arranging a match, kidnap her, and marry her to Estridge. Thus do garden intrigues issue for better and for worse in real rather than feigned relationships.

Other comedies manage to mediate between the two garden ambiences more subtly than Sedley, even making this the mainspring of an action. Lady Brute in Sir John Vanbrugh's *The Provoked Wife* (1697) is quite certain that "[New] Spring Garden" is the ideal location for her plot with Bellinda and she associates it with both "surprise . . . the most agreeable thing in the world" and doing a "good turn" (III.iii). In *She Would If She Could* by Sir John Etherege (1668) the Mulberry Garden and the New Spring Garden are where the libertines exercise their skills, but are outmaneuvered by Ariana and Gatty, who thereby affirm the pastoral potential of such places. The libertines fall, as Peter Holland has noted[36] and as the treacherous world of gardens has always contrived; but their fall is in part and a little uneasily redeemed by those who play the gardens less gratuitously: indeed, as Courtall tells Freeman at the very start of II.i, "the fresh air" of the Mulberry Garden does expel the vapors of wine drunk elsewhere. The two scenes that Etherege sets in the Garden involve the audience's recognition not only of its contemporary significance (acknowledging at once Ariana's "you seldom row to Fox Hall without some such plot against the city" (IV.ii)), but of their potential as meaningful, even symbolic, settings. The stage designs may have been recognizable and "realistic,"[37] but there were aspects of the actual gardens which the stage could not reproduce: namely, crisscross walks, spatial deceits and discoveries, and the opportunities afforded to schemers to make topography work on their behalf. Yet II.ii clearly anticipates an audience's comprehension of how Ariana and Gatty, masked, exploit the garden walks (*The Women go out, and go about behind the scenes*) to corner Courtall and Freeman even while making the men believe the opposite has happened (*Enter the Women, and after 'em Courtall at the lower door, and Freeman at the upper on the contrary side*). The stage directions simply invoke theater geography which the audience must read as that of gardens.

As the gallants admit to each other as that scene gets under way, such garden encounters are always problematic ("I have been so often baulked with these vizard-masks"). Dramatists seem to use the pleasure gardens as settings which register and promote discovery, disconcertion, and confusion: the New Spring Garden of *She Would If She Could* (IV.ii) and the end of IV.iv of *The Provoked Wife,* also set there. But

Vanbrugh illustrates how the fluid, if not problematical, roles of actor and audience in the garden theaters could also serve a playwright's turn. Lady Fancyfull and her maid use an arbor in New Spring Garden from which to watch the others, who are themselves actors (Lady Brute and Bellinda) and audience (Constant and Heartfree), the deceiving and the duped, until Sir John's drunken intrusion upon the scene forces a reorganization of roles. Bellinda and Heartfree go off to pry into the "secrets of the Garden," released as innocent spectators, while Lady Brute and Constant rehearse an old act. Illusion, discovery, reaction, and realignment are the staple of Restoration dramatic action; but this theatrical dimension of life is thrown into strong relief by scenes set in gardens which endorse and actively encourage such sequences.

Thomas Clayton's opera, *Arsinöe, Queen of Cyprus,* performed at the Theatre Royal, Drury Lane, in 1705, had garden sets designed by Sir James Thornhill which have exercised theater historians for the light they throw upon stage conditions at the time. But the significance of the settings has been ignored; indeed, one historian states that a design's subject "has little to do with this opera."[38] Peter Motteux's libretto, published in 1707, does however yield some evidence that the gardens, de rigueur perhaps in fine productions, signaled some of the meanings we have already discovered in Restoration comedy and Inigo Jones's masques. With *Arsinöe* we are back with a princely villa, but its message continues to be both the heroic, ideal paradise of love and the stage of love's confusions and despair. Thornhill's well-known sketch for the first scene (fig. 2.10)—clipped hedges and arbors as wings, steps descending from the terrace of the stage into an illusionary parterre beyond, replete with fountains and *exedra*—is the setting for the Queen's slumbers and Ormondo's astonished discovery of her ("what heavenly Fair"). His servant, stumbling around in the darkness, heralds the confusions that follow as Ormondo prevents the murder of Arsinöe, pursues the attacker, and leaves the Queen to flee in fright from the garden. Gardens recur twice in the opera, reminders of an idyllic world of sleeping beauty and love at first sight; but the set of II.i is a *Great Hall looking into a Garden*—affairs of state, resulting in Ormondo's fight with Feraspe, have pushed that world away into a distant prospect. Act II, scene viii brings the action outside once more (*Arsinöe alone. A Garden*); but it is her warring passions that she sings of and the garden's unstable paradise changes into despair and death as Ormondo is finally led off to prison.

2.10. *James Thornhill, sketch of a set for* Arsinoë, Queen of Cyprus, *c. 1704. Victoria and Albert Museum.*

It would be indeed surprising if the rise and progress of garden art in Italy, France, and England, unlike anything seen there before, did not have profound implications for that culture at large. As always with the translation of ideas from the Continent, England's response and contribution were both delayed and consequently liable to be more eclectic. Vauxhall and Ranelagh in the eighteenth century illustrate this clearly. Jonathan Tyers's management of the former gave the theatrical potential of the Restoration pleasure gardens shapes and opportunities drawn from a long history of garden and theater. Significantly he democratized garden art, at a time when it was still largely a rich family's pastime, and he maintained its links with theater at a time when "Capability" Brown's designs were eliminating not only "readability" from a landscape but various theatrical forms and opportunities as well. And in this connection it is worth noting that reactions to Brown's style, whether William Chambers's, the picturesque proponents', or Humphry Repton's, all put these elements back into the landscape.[39]

It is this ineluctable theatricality of Vauxhall and Ranelagh that was so fascinating at the time and is interesting now. That these gardens maintained close connections with the legitimate theater and benefited from an exchange of personnel is not, however, any satisfactory explanation of the phenomenon.[40] There was in increasingly larger sections of society (a fact upon which foreigners remarked)[41] a taste for theatricality which discovered at places like Vauxhall and Ranelagh increased scope for both fantasy and role playing. These garden theaters readily accommodated the fête champêtre and the masquerade, both of which were naturalized in England in the eighteenth century. The essence of masquerade, of course, was the chance to disguise one's everyday self and play with and in new, temporary roles; these in their turn, as Boswell remarked, required "a great flow of Spirits and a Readiness at Repartee."[42] If one did not know one's lines, they had to be improvised. This connects the vogue for masquerade, I think, with the conversation piece: both derived from the *fête champêtre,* both concern the art of living with people in society, with all the role playing that involves,[43] and both made theaters out of their locations at Ranelagh or some country house. For the masquerade may have started in such arenas as the Haymarket Opera House, organized by the Swiss Heidegger (Master of Revels to George II), pleasure gardens during the summer months, and, during the winter, Carlisle House in Soho Square (though it is interesting that even this indoor site was given distinctly gardenesque imagery with a grotto, elegant walks, and trees);[44] but the masquerade's theatricality quickly left precise arenas and permeated the whole town. Pope's *Dunciad* gives "Stage and Town" interchangeable status and his last chapter of *Peri Bathous* ironically anticipates the whole city becoming one vast theater. Max Byrd reminds us, too, that the theater is at the heart of London in James Thomson's *Winter* ("The Comic Muse / Holds to the world a picture of itself").[45]

Reactions to these developments, as in Pope's case, were mixed. I discount simple complaints of immorality; especially before Tyers's management, Vauxhall had a very *louche* reputation, as Pope's obscene interpretation of his own lines on Stowe makes clear in *A Master Key to Popery*.[46] But Tyers was at pains to clean up the image of Vauxhall, and the London magistrates as well worked to make such places safer and more decent. The complaints, nevertheless, continued and were, I suspect, unconscious or covert protests at the whole spread of theatricality itself. At its most extreme this allowed a Captain Watson to attend a masquerade as Adam in "an unavoidable indelicacy of dress" or Elizabeth Chudleigh to appear at Ranelagh in 1749 as Iphigenia ready for the sacrifice, her dress or undress provoking Mrs. Montagu to remark that the "high priest might easily inspect the entrails of the victim."[47]

Lydia in Tobias Smollett's *Humphry Clinker* conducts herself in a more seemly fashion, but Matthew Bramble's irascible view of Vauxhall is an oblique commentary upon the stagey intrigue of his niece, who is not surprisingly delighted by the gardens.[48] The novel ends with the conventional but scarcely casual analogy of *theatrum mundi*: "The comedy is near a close; and the curtain is ready to drop." Yet throughout Smollett explores human playfulness and attitudes toward role playing, which are aptly focused during the visit to Vauxhall early in the novel. Lydia's enthusiasm stresses the complete range of diversions and people—the very microcosm which we have seen was expected of garden and theater; she writes breathlessly of "the variety of beauties . . . wonderful assemblage of the most picturesque and striking objects," not forgetting Vauxhall's approximation of the music of the spheres. Even those who resented or were sceptical of Vauxhall and the widespread theatricality (Mat Bramble's complaints are a grumbling reversal of his niece's enthusiasm) noted this completeness of life, like Fielding's "here, in one confusion hurl'd, / Seem all the nations of the world."

Concordia discors evidently found fresh fields to exploit at Ranelagh, where in 1749 an anonymous versifier allowed as how

> *Here the whole world in Miniature we see,*
> *This scheme makes even Contraries agree.*[49]

So the gardens played the world, and the world, as Pope obsessively charted, played at theater. Hogarth, who satirized these developments in his 1724 engraving *Masquerades and Operas or the Taste of the Town,* moved in his paintings from actual theater scenes of Gay's *The Beggar's Opera* to subjects where private theatricals alert one to the ambiguous status of actor and audience and finally to the theater of life itself and the roles played there by harlot, rake, and apprentice. Fielding, similarly, deserted the theater for the novel without leaving the stage. For an artist's resources and insights were undoubtedly extended by the current theatricality. Vauxhall and Ranelagh may have been the "Two Grand Seminaries of Luxury" that a 1769 edition of Defoe's *Tour* announced them as being,[50] but their curriculum was more extensive and more absorbing. Pope himself, however much he disliked the raging theatrical fever of the metropolis, always viewed it with mixed feelings, while his Horatian or Twickenham poems depend for their subtlety upon the dramatization of their poet and his setting. The eighteenth century sees a fresh potency accruing to the conventional metaphors by which such heroines as Evelina are introduced "upon the great and busy stage of life." Evelina's history is itself a chronicle of her own education in the complex human arena of role playing, and her visit to Vauxhall a key scene in that drama.

Places like Vauxhall, with their contrived rurality and pastoral theaters, were not popular simply because, as one historian has claimed, "the Englishman has ever had a genuine love for the country" (Scott, p. II). Even Sir Roger de Coverley (*Spectator,* 383) appreciated the contrivance, the pastoral *art* of Vauxhall. These garden theaters expressed and encouraged a theatricality which eighteenth-century society and its arts adopted with enthusiasm and insight. Boswell was often at Vauxhall himself, as Rowlandson's famous watercolor testifies, and he is no mean witness to the art of playing various parts in life; so we should pay him special attention when he tells us that Vauxhall "is peculiarly adapted to the taste of the English nation."[51]

12
A
b
c
b
b
c
b
d
d
c
e
e
22
22
24
15
15
18
23
16
21
20
4
y
z
i
i
1
1
2

3 EMBLEM AND EXPRESSION IN THE EIGHTEENTH-CENTURY LANDSCAPE GARDEN

The progress of landscape gardening in the eighteenth century is, as everyone knows, closely connected with literary history. Their relationship is celebrated in Horace Walpole's apophthegm: "Poetry, Painting, and Gardening, or the Science of Landscape, will forever by men of taste be deemed Three Sisters, or the *Three New Graces* who dress and adorn nature."[1] Their cooperation certainly established a new style of landscape gardening. But what is rarely recognized are the consequences for the "sisters" themselves of their joint enterprise. The fresh ideas they promoted were subject to modification and revision and one particular development—that from *emblematic* to *expressive* gardening—determined parallel movements in literary history.

It will be useful to begin with a late and retrospective account of the history of landscape taste, because it probably offers a clearer, sharper version of certain changes than ever, of course, actually occurred in a park or garden. In 1770 Thomas Whately published his *Observations on Modern Gardening*; at the center of his thinking about landscape is the distinction he makes between the emblematic and expressive character of a garden:

> Character is very reconcileable with beauty; and, even when independent of it, has attracted so much regard, as to occasion several frivolous attempts to produce it; statues, inscriptions, and even paintings, history and mythology, and a variety of devices, have been introduced for this purpose. The heathen deities and heroes have therefore had their several places assigned to them in the woods and the lawns of a garden; natural cascades have been disfigured with river gods, and columns erected only to receive quotations; the compartments of a summer-house have been filled with pictures of gambols and revels, as significant of gaiety; the cypress, because it was once used in funerals,

> has been thought peculiarly adapted to melancholy; and the decorations, the furniture, and the environs of a building, have been crowded with puerilities, under pretence of propriety. All these devices are rather *emblematical* than expressive; they may be ingenious contrivances, and recall absent ideas to the recollection; but they make no immediate impression, for they must be examined, compared, perhaps explained, before the whole design of them is well understood; and though an allusion to a favourite or well-known subject of history, of poetry, or of tradition, may now and then animate or dignify a scene, yet as the subject does not naturally belong to a garden, the allusion should not be principle; it should seem to have been suggested by the scene; a transitory image, which irrestibly [sic] occurred; not sought for, not laboured; and have the force of a metaphor, free from the detail of an allegory.[2]

Whately is not alone, nor is he the first, to argue in this way: as we shall see, Joseph Warton's poem, *The Enthusiast,* begins in exactly the same way and specifically identifies Stowe with its "gilt alcoves, [and] marble-mimic gods, / Parterres embroider'd, obelisks, and urns" as a garden uncongenial to the enthusiastic taste.

Stowe was and continues to be a fine example of an emblematic landscape that requires "reading"; in Whately's words, it "must be examined, compared, perhaps explained, before the whole design . . . is well understood." It is a necessary element in his fairly tendentious argument that he should insist upon this complicated process of understanding an emblem. It is not easily determined to what extent this process was ever instinctive or how much the recognition of emblematic devices depended upon a highly trained intellectual capacity. As late as 1709 an edition of Cesare Ripa's *Iconologia: or Moral Emblems* was issued in London, "wherein are Expressed Various Images of Virtues, Vices, Passions, Arts, Humours, Elements and Celestial Bodies." Its readers were further advised that "these images are the representatives of our Notions; they properly belong to Painters, who by colours and shadowing, have invented the admirable secret to give body to our thoughts, thereby to render them visible." The edition was directed at "Orators, Poets, Painters, Sculptors" in the hope that it would aid invention. Yet these "lovers of ingenuity" were provided with the customary alliance of image and explanatory legend, without which very few of the emblems were properly understood.[3]

The gardens at Stowe, begun only a few years after the publication of that edition of Ripa, provide constant examples of visual exhibits, often accompanied by inscriptions or mottoes, the full meaning of which depends upon the exact encounter of word and image that we find in the emblem book. No part of Stowe provides a more concentrated exercise in mental agility than the valley known as the Elysian Fields. As its name suggests, this oblique glade is fraught with poetic and mythic meaning. Its very style is crucial: when it was created in the 1730s, the still largely formal pattern of the main park was deliberately abandoned for a natural style that evidently carried its own implications (fig. 3.1).[4] For it appears that images of a golden age—whether classical or Christian—eschewed the self-consciously formal or geometric visions that fallen man imposed upon nature. Milton's picture of Eden, according to Walpole,[5] rightly omitted topiary, for such ingenuities were unworthy of that first, archetypal gardener, the Lord God. Other images of the golden age—even such an early example as Heyns's emblem of Tempe in his *Emblemata* of 1625—always seem to offer us ideally natural landscape compositions.

The water that flows through Stowe's Elysian Fields appears first through the mouth of the Grotto, recently restored; like that at Stourhead, it was a place to enter and, like Pope's grotto, to which we shall return, a focus for meditation. In classical mythology natural caves with springs (rare and treasured events in a dry climate) were honored by the supposition that they were the home of nymphs and the Muses. The most renowned of such *nymphaeums* was that which in Roman times was reputed to have been the haunt of the nymph Egeria, a name of particular resonance because, as Livy and Plutarch testify, Egeria, the wife of a legendary philosopher-king, Numa, "entertained familiar conversation with the Muses" in her cave and to those visitations "ascribed the greatest part of (their) revelations."[6]

Renaissance villas often included a *nymphaeum* as a cool retreat for hot Roman days, but in the English climate such practical exigencies were less relevant (as we are reminded by the confrontation of the Lincolnshire lady showing off her grotto to a distinguished visitor: "Would it not be a pretty cool habitation in summer, Dr. Johnson?" "I think it would, madam,—for a toad"). So it was inevitable that the mythical rather than the pragmatic considerations of English grottos would be emphasized. The grotto at Stowe shares with many others the allusion to Egeria and her inspiration by the Muses; only at Stowe,

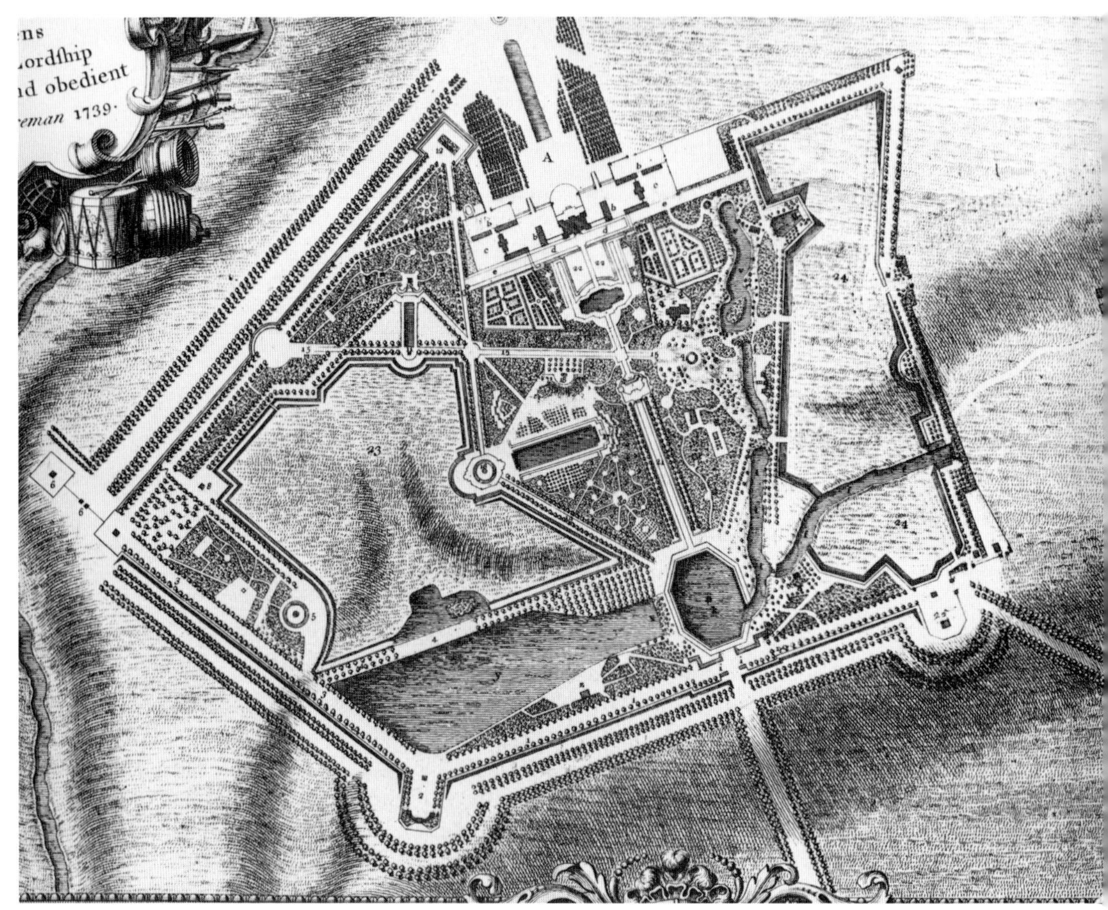

3.1. Plan of Stowe, 1739. The valley of the Elysian Fields may be seen at the right edge of the central garden, its waters eventually emerging into the Octagonal Pond. Dumbarton Oaks, Trustees for Harvard University.

like much else in this incredibly learned and witty garden, the allusion is introduced at exactly the right point.

From the grotto and toward our right down the Elysian Fields is the monument to Captain Thomas Grenville. It was added after 1747—a vestral column in the Roman manner—to honor a member of Lord Cobham's family who was killed aboard his ship, the *Defiance,* fighting the French. Its addition observes the decorum of the whole emblematic contrivance; on the top of the column the figure of Heroic Poetry fingers a scroll with the words *Non nisi grandia canto*: her face is turned toward the Temple of British Worthies.

This Temple, halfway down the Elysian Fields, is seen first from the Temple of Ancient Virtue; both were designed by William Kent (figs. 3.2–3). The authors of the modern guide to the gardens tell us that although the Elysian Fields were to be hidden from the main park they had somehow to be linked with it,[7] accordingly the Rotunda already in the western part of the garden was to be balanced by another circular building on the eastern side, terminating the Great Cross Walk. This piece of architecture—the Temple of Ancient Virtue, built about 1734–is as emblematic and as complicatedly so as anything in the Elysian Fields upon which it looks down. It is a temple with Roman authority, like the Egerian grotto, the figure of Heroic Poetry and (to leave the Elysian Fields for a moment) the statue of George I in Roman armor (by John van Nost about 1717–1720) on the north front of the house.

But as with so much English Augustanism it was a matter as much of assimilation as of imitation, of making "Homer speak good English" as of just translating him; of "putting Horace into a more modern dress than hitherto he has appear'd in."[8] The Roman armor had to fit George I, or, in satire, be seen not to fit. So the Temple of Ancient Virtue is indeed a copy of the Temple of Vesta at Tivoli (with columns changed from Corinthian to Ionic); but it is equally authorized by a magnificently bold version of such a temple already gracing an English landscape—Hawksmoor's Mausoleum at Castle Howard, under construction at that time (see fig. 1.16). Kent would certainly have seen plans for it at Lord Burlington's, whose judgment on the Mausoleum had been solicited.

A further speculation concerns the conjunction of a vestal temple with a tomb. Stowe's Temple is dedicated to and sustained by the purest of standards—Ancient Virtue; yet, as the name implies, those values are past and it is therefore a temple of remembrance, a tomb of

3.2. Stowe: the Temple of British Worthies, from the slope below the Temple of Ancient Virtue (photograph: author).

3.3. Stowe: the Temple of Ancient Virtue from the Temple of British Worthies (photograph: author).

fallen ideals. But just as Hawksmoor's building contains a magnificent surprise, so does this emblem at Stowe. At Castle Howard the massive and rather awesome building beckons somberly across the fields; yet once inside the tone changes marvelously to a serene lightness, the Christian point of which is fairly obvious, taking us from the gloom of death to its transcendence. At Stowe a similar *double take* occurs in our reading. Beside the Temple of Ancient Virtue, but now unfortunately lost, was another building, satirically in ruins: a Temple of Modern Virtue (fig. 3.4). So, the conjunction of the Temple of Ancient Virtue with Hawksmoor's Mausoleum might suggest only dead ideals; but alongside the rubble of the present how much better is even a historical commemoration than nothing at all. This point is made again in another way. Inside the Temple of Ancient Virtue were statues of the greatest lawgiver, philosopher, poet, and general of the ancient world. Across the valley are modern figures, commemorated among the British Worthies. Perhaps we are meant to register the continuing British efforts at emulating the ancients. But then again, the simple statement of the four statues from the past seems more eloquent, more poised and truly heroic than the sixteen busts across the valley, ranged a little grotesquely—as if surprised at their resurrection in the Elysian Fields—in the curve of small niches.

It may be worth quoting here William Gilpin's account of these opposing yet complementary temples. We shall return again to Gilpin's *Dialogue on the Gardens . . . at Stowe,* published anonymously in 1748, for it is a crucial document in establishing the change of taste from emblematic to expressive gardening. But in the passage on the statues of Ancient Virtue Gilpin is firmly orthodox in his appreciation of the emblems and the panegyric does recreate for us the nostalgia and atavistic mood of Kent's Temple:

> There stands Lycurgus; there Socrates; there Homer; & there Epaminondas. Illustrious chiefs, who made Virtue their only Pursuit, and the Welfare of Mankind their only Study; in whose breasts mean Self-interest had no Possession. To establish a well-regulated constitution; to dictate the soundest Morality, to place Virtue in the most amiable Light, were Ends which neither the Difficulty in overcoming the Prejudices, and taming the savage Manners of a barbarous State; the Corruptions of a licentious Age, and the Ill-usage of an invidious City; neither the vast Pains of searching into Nature, and laying up a Stock of Knowledge sufficient to produce the noblest Work of Arts; nor popular

3.4. Stowe: engraving of the Temple of Modern Virtue. Collection of Dr. and Mrs. Peter Willis.

> Tumults at Home, and the most threatening dangers abroad, could ever tempt them to lose Sight of, or in the least abate that Ardency of Temper with which they pursued them.[9]

Gilpin's character, Callophilus, a learned *virtuoso,* demonstrates exactly the manner of reflective, even labored, reading of a garden's emblems that Whately was to condemn.

Across the valley, then, from this "assembly of great men" is the Temple of British Worthies, which is "gloriously filled . . . with the greatest wits, Patriots, and Heroes, that are to be met with in our Chronicles" (p. 28). But, significantly, Gilpin with his interest in expressive features of landscape fails to read this emblematic construction properly—he produces a similar panegyric to that inside Ancient Virtue, an insufficient response, as we shall see, to this ideological building.

For its construction in about 1735 Kent removed eight busts from Gibbs Building elsewhere in the garden (see fig. 4.4) and fitted them into this curiously naive structure, designed to hold a further eight busts, which were added later. The message of these ranged figures is anti-Stuart, anti-Catholic, pro-British. The best account of the emblematic purpose of these patriotic presences is by a modern historian of the garden:

> Among the eight Worthies were two sovereigns, and you might suppose that one of them would have been Queen Anne, for whom Lord Cobham had fought so stoutly and who had promoted him from colonel to lieutenant-general. But no, with all her virtues Queen Anne was a Stuart. She was left out. The sovereigns were the great patriot, Elizabeth, last before the Stuarts, with her poet Shakespeare; and William III, supplanter of the Stuarts, with his philosopher John Locke. Between was John Hampden, the local patriot from Aylesbury, who had drawn his sword against the Stuarts and died for the Parliament. There were also Bacon and Newton, who had clearly shown that Truth, though not of course its Divine Origin, was to be found by intellectual process and not by listening to what the priests had to say.[10]

The eighth figure is Milton, who besides writing the last great epic poem in English worked for Oliver Cromwell and disliked priests. This particular religious hostility is reinforced by a quotation from the sixth book of the *Aeneid,*[11] also transferred from Gibbs's Building, in which a line praising the priesthood is omitted on both buildings—such is the learned subtlety of this architecture that we must not only identify our Virgil but recognize how and why it is incomplete.

The Temple of British Worthies is a curious emblem, both architecturally and ideologically, and I suspect that the two are related. Although its celebration of British worth is undeniably sincere, the sequence of flat points over the niches and the gathering of busts seem a little naive and gauche, a diminished glory, in comparison with the accoutrements of Ancient Virtue. Our skepticism is reinforced by the memorial on the rear of British Worthies to one Signor Fido, whose innumerable virtues are recorded in a long and enthusiastic inscription:

He hunted not after Fame,
yet acquired it,
regardless of the Praise of Friends,
but most sensible of their Love.
Tho' he lived amongst the Great,
he neither learnt nor flatter'd any Vice.
He was no Bigot,
Tho' he doubted of none of the 39 Articles.
And, if to follow Nature,
and to respect the Laws of Society,
be Philosophy,
he was a perfect Philosopher;
a faithful Friend,
an agreeable companion,
a loving Husband,
distinguish'd by a numerous Offspring.[12]

Alas, Signor Fido turns out to have been only a greyhound. So much for the British Worthies?

The whole emblematic construction of these Elysian Fields, with British and Ancient worth separated by the waters that flow in what was known as the Styx, has been compared to, even traced in part to a suggestion by, Alexander Pope.[13] In Pope's Horatian imitations and in his *Dunciad* there is the same address to allusion and cultural reference and yet the same need to identify the modern, satiric manipulation of sources that we have found in the landscape at Stowe. Above all, and this goes far to substantiate the debt to Pope at Stowe, the emphasis in the Elysian Fields is upon inspiration and heroic song. From the Egerian grot where the Muses may be supposed to lurk, past the figure of Heroic Poetry (added later, it is true, but the family has maintained too neatly for coincidence the dominant leitmotif), to the satiric juxtaposition of Ancient and Modern Virtues, and finally, to the declension of epic achievement from Homer and Milton to an unambiguous absence of any Stuart poet—these are all Pope's interests, canvassed in the landscape architecture with something of the same skill and subtlety that he contrived in his couplets.

The gardens at Stowe outside the Elysian Fields are equally allusive and richly emblematic. Congreve's Monument wittingly offers a monkey gazing at itself in a mirror to celebrate the satirist's art. The Pebble Alcove accommodates the Temple arms picked out in colored pebble, perhaps an allusion to Horace's gladiator ("Vejanius Armis / Herculis ad postem fixit, latet abditus agro") and to Pope's version of it that seems, in passing, to take up the skepticism already encountered in the British Worthies:

Our Generals now, retir'd to their Estates,
Hang their old Trophies o'er the Garden gates,
In Life's cool evening satiate of applause,
Nor fond of bleeding, ev'n in Brunswick's cause. (IV, 278–279)

For Stowe was only developed as a landscape garden when Sir Richarad Temple, afterwards Lord Cobham, was dismissed from Queen Anne's army. And not far beyond the Pebble Alcove is Gibbs's Temple of Friendship, dedicated to the group of opposition Whigs: Gilpin notices the "Emblem of Friendship above the Door, those of Justice and Liberty, and those other ornaments upon the Walls," which included busts of Cobham's political colleagues. On the ceiling was a satiric painting: "There you see sits Britannia; upon one side are held the Glory of her Annals, the Reigns of Queen Elizabeth and Edward III; and on the other is offered the reign of ———, which she frowns upon, and puts by with her hand" (p. 34). These imperial themes of the Cobham circle are reflected yet further on at the Palladian Bridge, which was decorated with portraits of Raleigh and Sir William Penn and with a relief depicting Britannia receiving produce from the four corners of the earth.

Among the less strenuously political devices in the garden were allusions to *The Aeneid* in Dido's Cave and to Virgil's other influential poem, *The Georgics,* for such would seem to be the significance of devoting a substantial section of the garden, called Home Park, to agricultural purposes.[14] The traditional retirement of the hermit fathers is recalled at St. Augustine's Cave, and at the Hermitage. The emblematic pan-pipes decorate this building with a somewhat inappropriate flourish, but their call is answered from across the park by Vanbrugh's Temple of Bacchus (since destroyed, with exquisite emblematic tact, to make way for Stowe School chapel). Both Bacchus and Venus, divinities particularly to be celebrated in gardens,[15] have their temples; in the Palladian structure that Kent provided for Venus at the southernmost point of the landscape were lascivious paintings of Spenserian subjects.

Kent had a special penchant for *The Fairie Queene*: he illustrated it before his death and the engravings depict several of the temples that Kent had earlier designed for patrons' landscape gardens.[16] The references to Spenser at Stowe are an important illustration of Whately's point that allusions to favourite poems may animate a scene. But Kent's most learned reference, I believe, to *The Fairie Queene* occurs at Rousham. This exquisite, miniature landscape garden beside the Cherwell also has its emblematic character. But the centerpiece of the garden was and is Kent's Vale of Venus. So delightful is this descending series of ponds presided over and graced by the goddess's meditative form that its charm has disarmed further inquiry. But the shepherds and satyrs who spy upon Venus from the surrounding bushes have surely some meaning. Perhaps it is a reworking in gardenist form of some painterly vision of nymphs and satyrs, like that by Rubens in the Prado. But a more exciting theory and one supported by Kent's evident delight in Spenserian theme is that the Vale of Venus recalls that eloquent vision in the sixth book of *The Fairie Queene* where the poet, in the person of Colin Clout, presents and explains to Sir Calidore the dance of the Three Graces:

> *Handmaids of Venus, which are wont to haunt*
> *Upon this hill, and dance there day and night:*
> *Those three to men all gifts of grace do grant;*
> *And all, that Venus in herself doth vaunt,*
> *Is borrowed of them. . . .*
>
> *These three on men all gracious gifts bestow,*
> *Which deck the body or adorn the mind. . . .* (VI. x. 15–23)

And for the properly equipped and learned mind this encounter with Venus among the glades of Rousham would bring back with suitable propriety Spenser's discussions of courtesy and its connections with the countryside.

But as Rousham itself, despite its compactness, makes perfectly plain, there is room for other characteristics than the emblematic. Just as important a feature of Kent's plan are the walks and winding paths that link and circle the various items that require (in Whately's words) to be examined and explained. At Stowe this provision was made rather more dramatically in the late 1740s. Perhaps initiated by Kent and more likely carried on under the supervision of Capability Brown, that doyen of the naturalistic, unemblematic landscape, the Grecian Valley was established to the northeast of the main garden.

It is, I imagine, a perfect example of Whately's expressive landscape: for one thing, it no longer encourages the social intercourse that seems to dominate every prospect in Sarah Bridgeman's views of Stowe (see fig. 4.4), especially that of the parterre where a figure intriguingly like Pope bends to talk to Cobham in front of a garden that is peopled with further guests and decorated all around with statues and emblems of Apollo, the Muses, the Liberal Arts and Sciences.[17] The Grecian Valley no longer requires the learned attention to detailed meaning; it makes no claim upon our intellect. The subtle varieties of the valley afford a landscape that seems to answer our moods, that allows a unique and individual response by each visitor to its unobtrusive character. It expresses us and our changing moods, or such is the illusion that it encourages. And as if to accentuate this deliberate escape from the emblematic activities of the main garden, in 1764 the Gibbs Building that had once housed the busts of the British Worthies was rebuilt deep in the tangles at the head of the Grecian Valley and renamed the Fane of Pastoral Poetry: an eloquent emblem of a displaced taste for a learned genre of verse and a learned type of gardening.

One of the last niches to be filled in the Temple of British Worthies at Stowe was honored by Alexander Pope. He is there undoubtedly for his part in the creation of the landscape at Stowe and its invocation as the epitome of fine landscaping in the *Epistle to Burlington*:

> *Still follow Sense, of ev'ry Art the Soul,*
> *Parts answ'ring parts shall slide into a whole,*
> *Spontaneous beauties all around advance,*
> *Start ev'n from Difficulty, strike from Chance;*
> *Nature shall join you, Time shall make it grow*
> *A Work to wonder at—perhaps a STOW.* (*III.ii. 143*)

It is also mischievously appropriate that the declensions of heroic poetry that I traced should be extended by Pope's presence; for not only had he translated Homer, but his ironic allusions to *Paradise Lost* in the great epic on the Dunces were a substantial part of his sense of the incompatibility of his modern world with the proper pretensions and effects of epic verse.

But there is yet a further meaning in Pope's addition to the British Worthies. Perhaps only an accident, it is nevertheless exactly relevant to a discussion of the changing taste in gardening from the emblematic to the expressive. For although Pope is firmly fixed in the "readable" structure of the Elysian Fields, he in fact looks north toward the new, expressive extension of Stowe into the Grecian Valley. And this is curiously apt. For I believe that we must sufficiently enlarge our sense of his role in the landscape movement to register his prophetic grasp of the possibilities of expressive gardening. And these possibilities he went some way to realizing in his own garden and grotto at Twickenham.

There is considerable evidence now on Pope's house[18] and grounds, and I shall not be producing any more. But there are rival interpretations of that evidence, and these are my concern. Professor Maynard Mack has admirably demonstrated the emblematic nature of Pope's landscape, dotted with urns, statues, inscriptions, and culminating in the memorial to his mother. Perhaps the most elaborate example of this iconography that Professor Mack offers to explain is Pope's design for the grass plot at the river's edge, an account of which is given by Joseph Spence:

> His design for this was to have a swan, as flying into the river, on each side of the landing-place, then the statues of two river gods reclined on the bank between them and the corner seats, or temples with
>
> Hic placido fluit amne Meles
>
> on one of their urns, and
>
> Magnis ubi flexibus errat Mincius
>
> on the other. Then two terms in the first niches in the grove-work on the sides with the busts of Homer and Virgil, and higher, two others with those of Marcus Aurelius and Cicero.

This elaborate contrivance, properly read, would lead the spectator to recall the birth of Homer from Politian and the poetic conquest of Greece from Virgil and so Pope's own role in rededicating this classical literary heritage to his own age.[19]

But we have evidence of alternative modes of gardening in Pope's landscape. Serle's plan of the garden in 1745 (fig. 3.5) shows that around

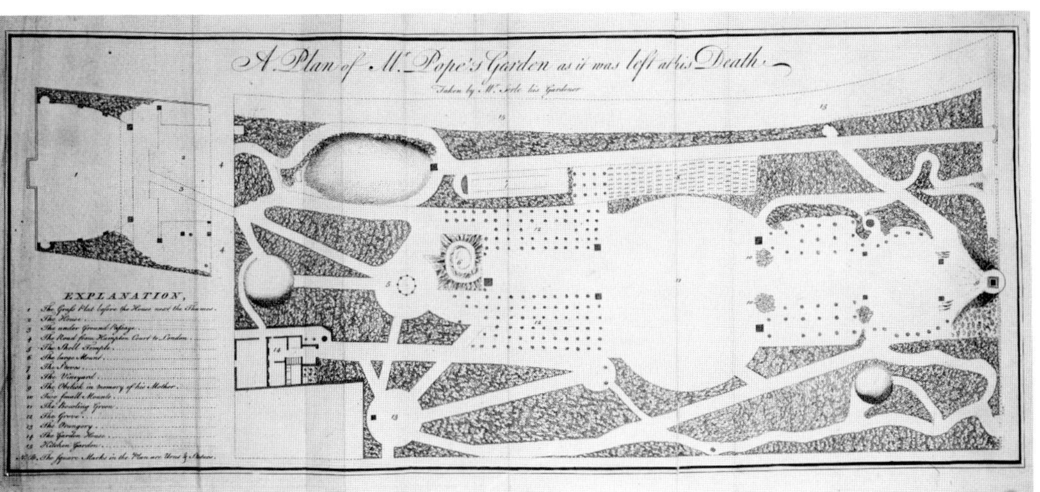

3.5. John Searle, engraved plan of Pope's Garden at Twickenham, 1745. British Library.

the perimeter Pope has allowed some informal, meandering paths that recall the requirement of Stephen Switzer that a garden should preserve examples of what he calls "a private and natural turn."[20] The phrase acknowledges, as Pope's paths seem to practise, some important congruence between privacy and an absence of human ingenuity in landscape design. We can see this connection better in an engraving of Hammels (fig. 3.6): the largely formal, old-style garden has been retained near the house and a very self-conscious example of the new informality established on the hillside above.[21] But, their extravagance apart, the "private and natural" turns allow, even promote, the solitary and introspective walk. Within the far smaller area at Pope's disposal the same indulgence has been allowed. Indeed, we have ample testimony of this particular feature of the Twickenham estate. Bolingbroke begins a letter to the poet with a promise to communicate his thoughts "just as they pass through my mind, just as they use to be when we converse together . . . when we saunter alone . . . among the multiplied scenes of your little garden."[22] The solitary perambulations of the two friends among the exquisite varieties of the little garden suggest that—undisturbed in places by the emblematic devices that call and challenge and direct the mind—thought could be subtly conditioned by the changing contexts. This is surely akin to Whately's expressive quality, where

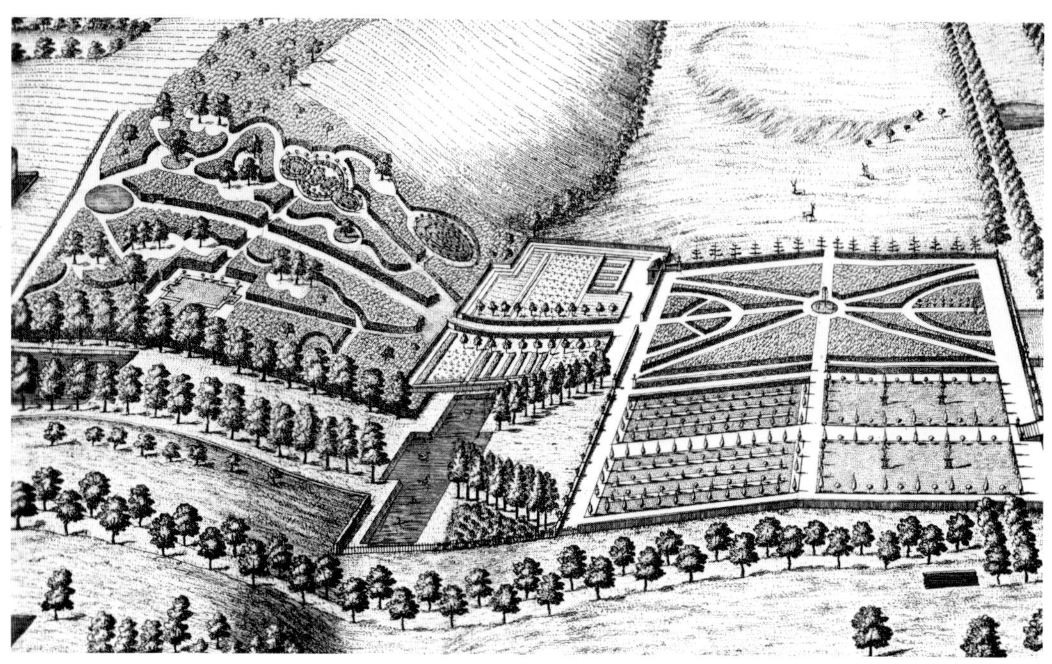

3.6. Detail from T. Badeslade's engraved view of Hammels, Hertfordshire, 1722. British Library.

"ideas should *seem* to have been *suggested* by the scene" (my italics). And Pope himself begins the *Essay on Man* with an exactly similar testimony to the congruence of idea and landscape:

Let us (since Life can little more supply
Than just to look about us and to die)
Expatiate free o'er all this scene of Man;
A mighty maze! but not without a plan;
A Wild, where woods and flow'rs promiscuous shoot,
Or garden, tempting with forbidden fruit.
Together let us beat this ample field,
Try what the open, what the covert yield;
The latent tracts, the giddy heights explore
Of all who blindly creep, or sightless soar. (III.i. 11–13)

The passage employs a various landscape as a metaphor of the human condition; yet the force of the verb "expatiate" (i.e. talk freely and literally wander about) establishes a covert equation between the mind's activity and the contexts it visits during a philosophic stroll.[23]

That Pope certainly acknowledges this equation is evident above all in his grotto. Maynard Mack tells us that it was a "setting that expressed him" (p. 8), citing Thomas Fuller's adage that "As is the Gardner, so is the Garden" (p. 4)—in his explanation of Pope's construction of a landscape that emblemizes with elaborate detail Pope's image of himself. But the grotto, like the garden, had its private and natural turns; the variety of its rooms has not been sufficiently stressed, nor its essentially private iconography. Pope's poetry, for reasons we shall explore, gives us generally the public image of the grotto's visitors:

There, my retreat the best companions grace,
Chiefs, out of war, and Statesmen, out of place.
There St. John mingles with my friendly bowl,
The feast of reason and the flow of soul. (IV, 17)

But we have other testimony to its intricately private meaning for Pope. As a prime exhibit, of course, there are the sketches by William Kent or the Countess of Burlington of this solitary, self-styled "hermit of Twickenham."[24] And just as the hermit fathers surrounded themselves with various memorials of their spiritual life, so this solitary philosopher of the English Enlightenment contrived appropriate contexts for himself. There is, for example, Pope's own design for the philosopher-poet of his *Essay on Man,* meditating among a landscape of time's emblematic repertoire. For the exercise of his more private meditations Pope designed the grotto.

Maynard Mack has discussed the Christian emblems—the Crown of Thorns and the Five Wounds—that decorated the river entrance to the grotto (pp. 63–64). They are the most accessible of the allusions. Serle's account of the full range makes a further point: the highly personal allusiveness of the geological ingredients that Pope collected. In the first room, Serle lists "Several fine Fossils and Snake-stones, with petrified Wood, and Moss in various shapes, from the petrifying Spring at Nasborough in Yorkshire" alongside "Fine Verd Antique from Egypt"; in the third room are pieces from Kent, Bath, Plymouth, Cornwall; and in the fourth

> Fine sparry Marble from Lord Edgcumb's Quarry, with different sorts of Moss. Several fine Pieces of the Eruptions from Mount Vesuvius, and a fine piece of Marble from the Grotto of Egeria near Rome, from the Reverend Mr. Spence; with several fine Petrifactions and Plymouth Marble, from Mr. Cooper; Gold Clift from Mr. Cambridge in Gloucestershire; and several fine Brain-Stones from Mr. Miller of Chelsea.[25]

Serle, who was Pope's gardener, had presumably a unique opportunity to understand this collection of materials. But really only Pope himself would fully appreciate the rich associations with friend and geological place that the materials of the grotto offered. They may, in one sense, be like Whately's emblems that require assiduous reading; but in a more important one they are expressive features, "transitory images," that irresistibly occur only to the one man capable of grasping them.

This private scene goes far towards establishing the extent and scope of Pope's romanticism.[26] We certainly need not argue that the grotto betrays an advanced taste for natural settings in which Pope (here we would have to cite his claim that the grotto "ressemble[s] Nature in all her workings")[27] suddenly becomes a precursor of the Lake poets. We can (and must) assent to Mack's insistence upon Pope's "Augustan convictions about Art . . . that 'nature' is discovered in (and also brought to) her perfection only by means of art" (p. 60). Yet that does not preclude an equally important sense of Pope's use of such traditional notions in the interests of his meditative penchant.

The grotto has further evidence to offer. Its variety of rooms is made particularly important by Pope's development of the natural spring he was lucky enough to discover there. We know he was fully aware of the mythic force of a cavern with water.[28] But we also know that he worked equally hard to diversify the water into different forms; in fact, into different "characters" that Thomas Whately was later to claim made water a peculiarly successful feature of the expressive garden. Here, first, is part of Whately's description:

> So various are the characters which water can assume, that there is scarcely an idea in which it may not concur, or *an impression which it cannot enforce*: a deep stagnated pool, dank and dark with shades which it dimly reflects, befits the seat of melancholy. . . . A gently murmuring rill, clear and shallow, just gurgling, just dimpling, imposes silence, suits with solitude, and leads to meditation; a brisker current, which wantons in little eddies over a bright sandy bottom, or babbles among pebbles, spreads cheerfulness all around; a greater rapidity, and more agitation, to a certain degree are animating; but in excess, instead of wakening, they alarm the senses; the roar and the rage of a torrent, its force, its violence, its impetuosity, tend to inspire terror. (63–64).

If we turn back to the various aquatic effects in Pope's grotto, their variety will be surprisingly similar to those of Whately's catalogue.

Some notes of Pope's own in a sketch now in the Municipal Library at Penzance suggest his desire not only to vary the architectural character of each scene but to diversify the water into "a spring of water," "a basin receiving the small waterfall," an underground stream, and finally a "bagnio."[29] Elsewhere he speaks of "three falls of water" and of the additional image of water afforded by the view toward the Thames with "the Sails on the River, passing suddenly and vanishing."[30] A visitor to the grotto soon after the poet's death was especially impressed with the variety of water effects:

> Here it gurgles in a gushing Rill thro' fractur'd Ores and Flints; there it drips from depending Moss and Shells; here again, washing Beds of Sand and Pebbles, it rolls in Silver Streamlets; and there it rushes out in Jets and Fountains; while the Caverns of the Grot incessantly echo with a soothing Murmur of acquatick Sounds.

Yet the resourcefulness of Pope's grotto did not end there. For the same writer goes on to describe a contraption that enlarged this aquatic imagery into the one kind that the small grotto could not otherwise have achieved—namely, a Salvator Rosa–like torrent, savage and terrifying:

> This is effected by disposing Plates of Looking glass in the obscure Parts of the Roof and Sides of the Cave, where a sufficient Force of Light is wanting to discover the Deception, while the other parts, the Rills, Fountains, Flints, Pebbles, etc. being duly illuminated, are so reflected by the various posited Mirrors, as, without exposing the Cause, every Object is multiplied, and its Position represented in a surprising Diversity. Cast your Eyes upward, and you half shudder to see Cataracts of Water precipitating over your Head, from impending Stones and Rocks, while salient Spouts rise in rapid Streams at your Feet: Around, you are equally surprized with flowing Rivulets and rolling Waters, that rush over airey Precipices, and break amongst Heaps of ideal Flints and Spar.[31]

The artificiality of these devices is not disputed. But the significance of the whole elaboration of this grotesque underworld of Pope's private study is its creation of a machinery of meditation, various landscapes where the expressive character of water determines mental activity by the subtle manipulation that Whately was to identify as the peculiar quality of expressive rather than emblematic gardening—having "the force of a metaphor, free from the detail of an allegory."

The freedom is equally and importantly that the poet is the master of his associative patterns of thought—the emblematic gardens at Stowe, for example, fairly strictly determine the direction and kind of reflections; equally, they can be shared by all who are learned enough to read them. In Pope's grotto—an early exemplum, I suggest, of the expressive garden—the "hermit" discovers his own mode and line of meditation, choosing by instinct the room where the combination of water and private geological architecture suited his reflective mood. Pope himself acknowledges this crucial element of personal control over his mental activity: in the famous, often quoted, description of his grotto he explains that the varieties of image which the camera obscura recreates for him are invoked precisely "*when you have a mind to light it up*."[32]

This account of the expressive potential of Pope's Twickenham landscape would be of little consequence in itself: an accident of cultural history. But Pope's private landscape occupies an important place in his poetic career and we know that as early as 1722 when Sir Godfrey Kneller painted his portrait Pope adopted the traditional pose of the reflective and meditating man, *il penseroso*. It is an image that acquires fresh meaning during the mid-eighteenth century, especially in literature, and there are some interesting, if generally unobserved, connections between those developments and the place in his public career as poet that Pope chose to give to his private world at Twickenham.

Pope began his career with firm convictions and resolutions about the status of art and the function of a poet. Like Dryden before him, he aspired to a public poetry that transcended merely personal inclinations and beliefs and offered to treat large contemporary events, like the Treaty of Utrecht, or large philosophical issues, like those of his *Essay on Man*. Pope also shared the traditional notion of art as offering permanent visions of a transitory world: "The Muse shall sing, and what she sings shall last." In his first *Dunciad* of 1729 he saw the forces of dullness, bad verse, and worse scholarship threatening civilization, but his mockery of their puny efforts which he held in ironic contrast to the usual matter of heroic poetry is not despairing. In the years that follow he continues to work on the first section of his *Magnum opus,* "a system of Ethicks in the Horatian way," apparently confident still of his own strengths and resolutions. But during these same years (1731–1735) he is also composing the *Epistles to Several Persons,* another section of the great work, but one in which new interests are conspicuous. Their tone, like their title, suggests greater intimacies. Although the poems identify and satirize public figures, they locate their values in personal friendships, individual virtue and, above all, the private elysiums that the poet's friends—often with his help—were creating in their landscape parks. And if they came to share Pope's confidence in the virtues accessible through landscaping ("Gardening is . . . nearer God's own Work, than Poetry"[33]) they would in their turn have confirmed the poet's scepticism about his public role.

The isolated commendations of private worlds in his poetry and letters retrospectively gain in significance. He had told the Earl of Strafford in 1725 that he had "long been convinced that . . . [no] publick Professors of Gardening (any more than any publick Professors of Virtue) are equal to the Private Practisers of it" (*Correspondence,* II, 309).

And a few years later he opposes the private world of gardening to the scribblers of Grub Street—"every stick you plant, and every stone you lay, is to some purpose: but the business of such lives as theirs is but to die daily, to labour, and to raise nothing" (ibid., II, 522). What he himself raised at Twickenham had, as we have seen, a very personal resonance. He was in his own way imitating his father of whose rural retirement he had written:

Stranger to Civil and Religious Rage.
The good Man walk'd innoxious thro' his Age.
No courts he saw, no Suits would ever try,
Nor dar'd an Oath, nor hazarded a Lye:
Un-learn'd, he knew no Schoolman's subtle Art,
No Language, but the Language of the Heart. (IV, 126)

A "language of the heart," like that "flow of soul" which he identifies as pervading his grotto, can only find expression in a flexible landscape, fully susceptible to mood and personal impression.

On his own confession Pope was drawn to a contemplative life and even on occasions succumbed to a vision-filled indolence.[34] Even in the poetry of the early 1730s there is a fascination with theories of psychology that would refute his own celebration of the "ruling passion." He seems increasingly to acknowledge the complexities of the human mind:

Our depths who fathoms, or our shallows finds,
Quick whirls, and shifting eddies, of our minds?
Life's stream for Observation will not stay,
It hurries all too fast to mark their way.
In vain sedate reflections we would make . . . (III.ii. 17–18)

The quirks and inconsistencies, susceptible to no easy scheme, are amusingly and readily acknowledged when he writes on the characters of women. And his own "personal" verses in imitation of Horace depend equally upon a flexible response to mood and mental complexities.[35]

Pope's interest in mood had always been linked with his notions of landscape. In an early *Spectator* essay of 1712 he distinguished between two human inclinations by invoking two kinds of garden:

> Some men, like pictures, are fitter for a corner than a full light; and I believe such as have a natural bent to solitude, are like waters which may be forc'd into fountains, and exalted to a great height, may make a much nobler figure and a much louder noise; but after all run more smoothly, equally, and plentifully, in their own natural course upon the ground.

Not the formal Bridgemanick theatre, but a natural rill like that he found and channeled through his own grotto. Moreover, his aphorism "All gardening is landscape-painting"[36] provides another link between mood and landscape. It is the paintings of Claude Lorrain and Salvator Rosa that are customarily taken to be the visual influence on much landscape gardening and their paintings are distinguished above all by the manipulation of mood. Two of the former's pictures that we know to have been in England during Pope's lifetime are exciting examples of this: *Landscape with Psyche at the Palace of Cupid* (sometimes known as *The Enchanted Castle*) provides its central figure—and she is emblematic of the soul and its meditations—with a marvelously expressive landscape of feeling. Similarly, the *Pastoral Landscape with Apollo and Mercury* is an illustration of the story taken from Ovid, an exploration of its mythic or emblematic meaning, as well as a visualizing of mood in landscape. So when landscape gardeners attempted to recreate Claude pictures they were also involved in realizing his moods in their parks. And we know from an incident at Woburn Farm that Pope was perfectly aware of this effect in landscape:

> When I [Joseph Spence] told Mr. Southcote that the sight of his ground near his house was always apt to lead me into a pleasing smile and into a delicious sort of feeling at the heart, of which I had nothing when I was in his much nobler views along the brow of the hill, he said that Mr. Pope had often spoke of the very same effect of it on him.[37]

It is time to draw together these, admittedly sometimes speculative, ideas on Pope and to make some final suggestions about his influence on the joint course of landscaping and poetry in the years after his death. He displays—this is no surprise with Pope—a tantalizing ambiguity in his ideas on both. He encourages, probably even plans, the emblematic gardening of the Elysian Fields for Lord Cobham, ensuring that their "readability" requires as much learned attention as the poetry of his own *Dunciad*. Yet he reveals himself equally susceptible to moods in a landscape and to the expressive potential of all contexts for solitary meditation. It's possible that Pope would not have chosen to distinguish as sharply as Whately did in 1770 between the rival kinds of garden; and further it is true, as we saw at Rousham, that one landscape could provide opportunities for both "allegorical" and "metaphoric" meditations.

But as his career advances he grows less confident of the public role of poetry and by the final version of *The Dunciad* in 1743 quite appalled at the prospects for poetry. Yet by some quite uncanny insight his denunciation of the bad poets and indifferent critics seems to make most fun of those elements in mid-eighteenth-century writing that were to draw upon the expressive features of the landscape taste. Did he recognize that the concerns and habits of poetry would change yet was (quite rightly) disconcerted by the early manifestations of these new poetics? Or did the disillusionment with a public role for poetry blind him to the consolations that a different sort of poetry could draw from his own meditations in the expressive landscapes of Twickenham?

In 1742 Pope had added to *The Dunciad* his vision of the total disintegration of civilization. The Augustan poet fends off the darkness of unreason as long as possible:

Yet, yet a moment, one dim ray of light
Indulge dread Chaos, and eternal night

. . . .

Suspend a while your force inertly strong,
Then take at one the Poet and the Song.

The generalizing effect of "the Poet and the Song" implies not merely Pope's own annihilation by darkness but the total intellectual death "when Wit and Humour are no more":

Nor public flame, nor private, dares to shine;
Nor human spark is left, nor glimpse divine!
Lo thy dread Empire, Chaos is restored;
Light dies before thy uncreating word:
Thy hand, great Anarch, lets the curtain fall;
And universal darkness buries all.

That final engulfing darkness is Pope's great enemy and he attacks all the dunces' activities that promote it: their taste for bardic trance ("In lofty madness meditating song; / Her tresses staring from Poetic dreams" [V, 321]); their predilection for opiate-induced dreams and the visionary worlds released by sleep; their love of the Gothick past (V, 324), of the gloomy, private realm of enthusiasm and night thoughts.

Pope certainly knew the enemy he was attacking and the opening to his final book seems to allude explicitly to Edward Young's *Night Thoughts,* a long, rambling poem dedicated to exactly those visions that Pope denounced. Young actually invites the fate, in his case propitious for poetry, to which Pope condemns the dunces: "Canst thou, O Night! indulge one labour more? / One labour more indulge; then sleep my strain." In a further passage Young apostrophizes the world of sleep which had that very year gathered Pope's dunces to its depths:

While o'er my limbs sleep's soft dominion spread,
What though my soul fantastic measures trod
O'er fairy fields; or mourn'd along the gloom
Of pathless woods; or down the craggy steep
Hurl'd headlong . . .
Or scaled the cliff; or danced on hollow winds,
With antic shapes, wild natives of the brain?

My song the midnight raven has outwinged,
And shot, ambitious of unbounded scenes,
Beyond the flaming limits of the world
Her gloomy flight.[38]

What is immediately striking not only about Young's indifferent poem but about much of the new poetry that it represents is that it reaches its best moments in such visions of expressive landscapes that emerge as metaphors of the poet's meditations.

But this imagery is no longer offered by landscape gardens. Warton's *Enthusiast or the Lover of Nature* specifically rejects the "gardens deck'd with art's vain pomps" and leaves Stowe for the expressive countryside beyond. Warton published his poem in 1740 and, as we know, ten years later the Grecian Valley had been added, perhaps to accommodate this new taste. In other ways, too, Stowe had anticipated these developments. The Temple of Liberty or Gothick Temple, designed by Gibbs and begun in 1741 in a natural setting (fig. 3.7), was a reminder of Britain's Anglo-Saxon past before the shackles of classical tradition were fastened upon her—though it works admittedly in a rather old-fashioned, emblematic way. Around the Temple at one time were a set of sculptures by Rysbrack of the Saxon deities that gave their names to the days of our week. These had first stood as early as

3.7. Stowe, the Gothick Temple, or Temple of Liberty (photograph: author).

1731 in a Druidical grove of oak trees ("another emblem there!")[39] near the house.

But these anticipations and even concessions to the tastes which Pope attributed to his dunces could not really save the landscape garden as the suitable context for the new style of meditative poet. William Gilpin's visit to Stowe in 1748 is eloquent. As his response is dramatized in the *Dialogue* we see that he is clearly competent in reading the emblematic messages of the various buildings, statues, inscriptions. But both in his enthusiastic identification of the expressive elements at Stowe (especially pp. 58–59) and his celebration of natural scenery in Scotland (pp. 23–25) Gilpin testifies already to the psychological emphasis of his illustrated tours of British scenery. Already in the mid-1750s Thomas Gray had written his ode on *The Bard,* an image of the new poet and his scenery that was quickly adopted by Warton as a criterion by which to judge Pope's poetry.[40] Gray's subject is taken from the legendary Druid past and provided—it is Gray's addition to his source material—with suitable Snowdonia scenery:

> *On a rock, whose haughty brow*
> *Frowns o'er old Conway's foaming flood,*
> *Robed in the sable garb of woe,*
> *With haggard eyes the poet stood;*
> *(Loose his beard and hoary hair*
> *Streamed, like a meteor, to the troubled air)*
> *And, with a master's hand, and prophet's fire,*
> *Struck the deep sorrows of his lyre.*
> *"Hark, how each giant-oak and desert cave*
> *Sighs to the torrent's awful voice beneath!"*

Gray's admiration for this new landscape of inspiration was matched by a contempt for landscape gardening:

> the Mountains are extatic, and ought to be visited in pilgrimage once a year. none but those monstrous creatures of God know how to join so much beauty with so much horror. a fig for your Poets, Painters, Gardeners, and Clergymen, that have not been among them: their imagination can be made up of nothing but bowling-greens, flowering shrubs, horse-ponds, Fleet-ditches, shell-grottoes, and Chinée-rails.[41]

But this disappointment with the resources of meditative pattern in landscape gardens had been anticipated even by those who did most to promote them. Addison recognized that "the beauties of the most stately garden or Palace lie in too narrow compass, the Imagination immediately runs them over, and requires something else to gratify her; but in the wide fields of nature, the sight wanders up and down without confinement and is fed with an infinite variety of images."[42] And Pope, with whom I must end, also seems to have recognized that emblems had equal force as flexible, expressionist imagery. In his early poem of 1717, *Eloisa to Abelard,* he borrows from the two rival traditions: the emblematic representation of melancholy by Ripa; and the expressive, mood-landscapes of Salvator Rosa that the gardenists were realizing in their English parks. There is no doubt at all which imagery succeeds best in identifying Eloisa's melancholy:

The darksome pines that o'er yon rocks reclin'd
Wave high and murmur to the hollow wind,
The wandering streams that shine between the hills,
The grots that echo to the tinkling rills,
The dying gales that pant upon the trees,
The lakes that quiver to the curling breeze;
No more those scenes my meditation aid,
Or lull to rest the visionary maid:
But o'er the twilight groves, and dusky caves,
Long-sounding isles, and interrupted graves,
BLACK MELANCHOLY sits, and round her throws
A death-like silence, and a dread repose:
Her gloomy presence saddens all the scene,
Shades every flower, and darkens every green,
Deepens the murmur of the falling floods,
And breathes a browner horror on the woods.

4 *UT PICTURA POESIS, UT PICTURA HORTUS*, AND THE PICTURESQUE

In 1807 Robert Southey confirmed what had been apparent for some years, that "a taste for the picturesque has sprung up." He noted that a "course of summer travelling is now looked upon [as] essential" and its main purpose was "to study the picturesque, a new science for which a new language has been formed, and for which the English have discovered a new sense in themselves, which assuredly was not possessed by their fathers."[1] Southey was certainly right about the modishness of picturesque taste, a fashion upon which Jane Austen was also commenting more satirically at about the same time in *Northanger Abbey*.[2] He was, however, less accurate about the newness of the "science" and its language, even wrong to claim that earlier generations had possessed no picturesque sense. His historical errors nevertheless highlight an aspect of the picturesque which has never been studied: the reason for its popularity at that precise point in the history of taste. The "picturesque moment," as Martin Price has called it,[3] cannot simply be explained by the coincidence of increased opportunities for travel and for the appreciation of visual art, although these undoubtedly contributed to the vogue. For as Southey aptly remarks, the picturesque was a *language*, and a language apparently needed with some urgency at that "moment." It is to the explanation of the historical origins of that picturesque language that this essay addresses itself. At the start it may be helpful to state, somewhat baldly, that the picturesque seems to have come to its special prominence at precisely the time when the traditional maneuvers of *ut pictura poesis* were moribund and under attack and that the picturesque should be understood as a reformation and adjustment of those old Renaissance strategies to serve new ideas, attitudes, and adventures of the human spirit.

I

One of our difficulties with "picturesque," a term which in 1849 John Ruskin considered the vaguest of any except "theological expressions," is that it has served the turn of various parties.[4] In use for at least a century before Southey thought it "new," it was invoked at different moments to explain different aesthetic experiences. It began by having a very general application, but Southey's time was used almost exclusively about landscape, and if it is remembered how quickly and radically landscape taste changed in Europe during the eighteenth century the elasticity of the term cannot be surprising. To chart its progress it will be useful to focus precisely upon its use by landscape (including landscape garden) theorists and practitioners, for that is the context in which it seems to have yielded most to the demands for a new language.

Early writers who directly or indirectly supported what we have come to know as the English landscape garden often invoked the art of painting in their discussions of garden layout. Addison and Pope, it is well known, thought painted representations of landscape subjects apt models for the design of gardens:

> Fields of Corn make a pleasant Prospect, and if the Walks were a little taken care of that lie between them, if the natural Embroidery of the Meadows were helpt and improved by some small Additions of Art, and the several Rows of Hedges set off by Trees and Flowers . . . a Man might make a pretty Landskip of his own Possessions.[5]

> All gardening is landscape-painting. Just like a landscape hung up.

> You may distance things by darkening them and by narrowing the plantation more and more toward the end, in the same manner as they do in painting.[6]

Yet it should be noted that the word *picturesque* is not used in these remarks upon garden design. This suggests (what should perhaps be obvious)[7] that neither Addison nor Pope has in mind the aesthetic to which we now refer with the word. Both make their remarks casually, throwing out analogies in passing to illustrate a particular point. Yet precisely because their gestures toward painted landscapes are so readily, if briefly, invoked, we must ask exactly what structure of ideas and assumptions underlies these casual allusions to pictures.

Neither Addison nor Pope sees the garden as anything but an artificial creation, so they seize upon painterly analogies to signal that assumption as well as some of its practical consequences. It is equally clear that both writers were thinking of the formal lessons which a landscape painting could teach gardenists, techniques of organizing real, three-dimensional space by translating from illusionary painted surfaces. But formal aspects of landscape painting—the disposition of a various terrain, the handling of lights and shades, the perspective—are by no means the only aspects of the genre that Addison and Pope would have acknowledged. For them painting involved matters of theme and meaning. Pope makes this much clearer in his actual use of the term *picturesque,* which occurs four times in annotations to his Homer translations, although two of these are the same casual throwing-off of analogies already encountered.

Of the other two the most illuminating comes in the headnote to Book XVI of *The Iliad*:

> We see Patroclus touch'd with the deepest Compassion for the Misfortune of the *Greeks,* (whom the Trojans had forc'd to retreat to their Ships, and which Ships were on the Point of Burning) prostrating himself before the vessel of *Achilles,* and pouring out his Tears at his Feet. *Achilles,* struck with the Grief of his Friend, demands the Cause of it. *Patroclus,* pointing to the Ships, where the Flames already began to rise, tells him he is harder than the Rocks or Sea which lay in prospect before them, if he is not touch'd with so moving a Spectacle, and can see in cold Blood his Friends perishing before his Eyes. As nothing can be more natural and affecting than the Speech of *Patroclus,* so nothing is more lively and Picturesque than the Attitude he is here describ'd in.[8]

That use of *picturesque* has little if anything to do with landscape. Pope took the word to be a French term, denoting what was proper or typical for a painting, and he applies it here—strictly—to the dramatic moment of Patroclus's address to Achilles. We are invited to see this as if it were the subject of some heroic history painting by Raphael, Nicolas Poussin, or the Carracci, and the invitation draws automatically upon seventeenth-century theories of *ut pictura poesis* and the parallels between the arts. Painters of historical subjects took their incidents from such writers as Homer and would expect the Homeric text to be used in its turn by those who viewed such paintings.[9] Pope's note on Book XVI implies that we should read the scene in painterly ways, whereby the rocky background and the burning ships provide a setting which, however excitingly rendered by the imaginary painter, is also a visual simile for Achilles's obduracy and his friend's passion, an equivalence to which Patroclus's gesture draws attention; the central event of this "picture" is human action, and its landscape is ancillary.

The context of Pope's commentary and therefore the full and proper meaning of the term *picturesque* may conveniently be found in Dryden's "Parallel of Poetry and Painting" of 1695, a text which Pope knew; Dryden's essay was reissued in 1718 with his own *Epistle to Jervas.*[10] The "Parallel" was composed as a preface to Dryden's translation of Du Fresnoy's *De arte graphica,* one of several French academic exegeses of *ut pictura poesis* which themselves drew upon Italian commentaries by Alberti, Daniello, and Dolce. Dryden affirms the strongest possible bond between poetry and painting, not in their emulation of each other's effects, but in their necessary imitation of some significant and unified human action. The parallel is developed further in terms of rhetoric's *inventio, dispositio,* and *elocutio,* which had been long assimilated into literary theory. Among the aspects of *inventio* which Dryden discusses is decorum:

> The composition of the painter should be conformable to the text of ancient authors, to the customs, and the times. And this is exactly the same in Poetry; Homer and Virgil are to be our guides in the Epic; Sophocles and Euripides in Tragedy: in all things we are to imitate the customs and the times of those persons and things which we represent.

Similar expectations of painting inform Pope's identification of imaginary pictures in Homer's text. Just as Dryden thought nothing should go into a poem or a picture which was not what he calls "convenient to the subject," so Pope wondered whether some of Homer's "descriptions and similes [were not] too exuberant and abounding in circumstances."[11] Just as a painter (in Dryden's words) will reject "all trifling ornaments" so will a "poet refuse all tedious and unnecessary descriptions." The pictures which Pope identifies in the Homeric text are characterized by a central human action, the setting of which is apt, consonant, and subservient. This decorum of setting is clear from another of his *Iliad* notes:

> I cannot conclude the Notes to this Book without observing, that what seems the principal Beauty of it, and what distinguishes it among all the others, is the Liveliness of its Paintings:

> the Reader sees the most natural Night-Scene in the World. . . . We see the very Colour of the Sky, know the Time to a Minute, are impatient while the Heroes are arming, our Imagination steals out after them, becomes privy to all their Doubts, and even to the secret Wishes of their Hearts sent up to *Minerva*. . . . We are perfectly acquainted with the Situation of all the Forces, with the Figure in which they lie, with the Disposition of *Rhesus* and the *Thracians,* with the Posture of his Chariot and Horses. The marshy Spot of Ground where *Dolon* is killed, the Tamarisk, or aquatick Plants upon which they hang his Spoils, and the Reeds that are heap'd together to mark the Place, are Circumstances the most Picturesque imaginable. And tho' it must be owned, that the human Figures in this Piece are excellent, and disposed in the properest Actions; I cannot but confess my Opinion, that the chief Beauty of it is in the Prospect, a finer than which was never drawn by any Pencil.[12]

In the sequence of imaginary "Paintings" of heroic action it is the aptness of the landscape which he emphasizes, its part in the pictorial ensemble of human action. That, too, is Pope's evident emphasis in a letter of December 1712 to John Caryll, where he observes that a couplet by Ambrose Philips seems "to me what the French call very *picturesque*."[13] The couplet in question—

> *All hid in snow, in bright confusion lie,*
> *And with one dazzling waste fatigue the eye*

—comes from an *Epistle to the Earl of Dorset from Copenhagen,* and what seems "very *picturesque*" is its aptness as a setting for the writer of an epistle thus entitled. In just the same way, perhaps, the audience of Purcell and Dryden's *King Arthur* (1691) would have found the winter scenery of its Act III, scene 2 appropriate for the dramatic tableau in which Cupid thaws the frozen Genius of the Isle. So when in the "Postscript to the Odyssey,"[14] focusing on the diction of natural description in the "imaging and picturesque parts," Pope says that their "character" is "simplicity and purity," what he implies is that they do not distract from, but rather give support to, the actions for which the descriptions provide a setting. So that "Circumstances the most Picturesque imaginable" in the note to *Iliad* X previously quoted will be those which contribute most to the central human action of the imagined picture.

II

Pope's singling out of "Prospect" in *Iliad* X is certainly of a piece with his wish to elevate the status of landscape in his own poetry, in his own gardening, and in his commentaries upon Homer's imaginary pictures. But in his own or in others' "pictures" he never lost sight of the need to attend to significant human action (usually with some appeal to classical texts) and to contrive for it the proper "ornaments." This is abundantly clear in the development both of his poetic career and in his gardening activities. From his earliest poetic composition, the "Ode on Solitude," to the last satires and the fourth book of *The Dunciad* Pope makes setting, prospect, and natural description subservient to the whole human picture, its action measured against the scale of classical epic or the norms and forms of Horatian retirement. So it would hardly be likely that in his gardening endeavors he would abandon such attitudes. Indeed, he hints at faults in Homer precisely by suggesting that a successful epic must share with an "order'd Garden" the satisfactory subservience of parts to a whole.[15]

This is not the occasion for a detailed review of early eighteenth-century gardening in the light of the traditions of *ut pictura poesis.* But a few instances of Pope's *picturesque* in its garden application are necessary. In his own garden at Twickenham and in those of his friends he admired or helped to form, human action was central and formal, painterly techniques were used to highlight it. The human action, whether contemporary or historical, usually contained ingredients derived from classical culture and required some verbal commentary upon the visual experience to enunciate the whole garden episode. *Ut pictura hortus.*

Twickenham was focused in several "history" paintings.[16] Formal elements were organized to emphasize temples, statues, obelisk, or urns which contributed most to the "action"; Pope makes this quite clear in the remark already quoted in part: "You may distance things by darkening them and by narrowing the plantation more and more toward the end, in the same manner as they do in painting, and as 'tis executed in the little cypress walk to that obelisk." The obelisk (fig. 4.1) was placed at the end of his garden in 1735 as a memorial to his mother, and with its carefully controlled setting formed the culminating picture of his little garden. He made exactly the same point about the centrality of human action in his own history by placing a passage about his father at the climax of the *Epistle to Dr. Arbuthnot,* published also in 1735.

4.1. Pope's obelisk to his mother's memory in his gardens at Twickenham, Middlesex. Engraving from Edward Ironside's History and Antiquities of Twickenham *(London, 1797), reprinted in John Nichols,* Miscellaneous Antiquities, *in* Continuation of the Biblioteca Topographica Britannica, *X, facing p. 40.*

Other scenes of the Twickenham garden were designed to form public rather than private history pictures. Two in particular, planned but never executed, suggest that throughout his career Pope saw his garden as the locale for his own special kind of historical subject, namely the acknowledgment of the classical past as a model for contemporary England, although this was always attended by an alert sense of both the absurdities and the adjustments which the use of classical culture enjoined upon eighteenth-century Englishmen.[17] His garden necessarily took up classical ideas of retirement and garden design, mediated through Renaissance forms since no Roman gardens existed, just as his Horatian imitations and *The Dunciad* focus upon literary matters. His proposals for a statue of a sleeping nymph and his scheme for river gods besides the Thames are evidence of his eagerness to provide significant and unifed "action" for his garden pictures. The first, which was implemented by Henry Hoare at Stourhead some years later, recalled both a specific statue in the sculpture gardens of the Vatican Belvedere and a literary topos;[18] the second, which involved temples and terms besides the Thames in conjunction with two reclining river gods and inscriptions from Virgil and Poliziano, would have had the same meaning vis-à-vis Pope's role in the history of gardening as Maynard Mack has argued for his literary career.[19] Sleeping nymph with her inscription and the river gods with theirs would have declared Pope's contribution to the traditions of villa life and secured for the Thames a place in the distinguished roll call of rivers from classical Tiber to Medicean Ambra. These themes constituted the significant action that Pope planned for his garden; every indication is, too, that the scenes would have been organized in ways that answered painterly notions of decorum in order to "rien omettre des circonstances necessaires dans la composition d'une histoire."[20] Pope's scorn of Timon's villa in his *Epistle to Burlington* is precisely for compositions so random and so lacking in the art that arranges how details contribute to a whole *histoire*.

We tend to lose sight of the essential role of some significant human action in early eighteenth-century gardens when we begin to consider them simply as designs. But that formal aspects were subservient to subject matter cannot be forgotten, as other gardens which Pope admired and may have had a hand in, such as Stowe or Rousham, testify. At two strategic locations in the latter were placed sculptural and architectural items, the correct understanding of which established the action or history of the garden pictures in which they figured. On the top of the steep bank above the river, from which the visitor gazes over Oxfordshire countryside, was sited a copy of Scheemakers's *Lion Attacking a Horse;* this probably aludes to the same sculptural subject placed in the Fountain of Rome of the Villa d'Este at Tivoli. Initially its placement at Rousham echoes a similar experience at Tivoli, for from the Fountain which depicts ancient Rome one may view the real, modern Rome on the horizon; but the whole point of the allusion is that at Rousham neither classical nor modern Rome is anywhere to be seen, except obliquely and by studied imitation. A few steps away at the Praeneste Terrace a similar comparison incorporating a contrast enacts another cultural history scene: the name of the terrace in this case provides the "plot," for William Kent's elegant little terrace was named after the ancient town now known as Palestrina; it imitates its famous elevation above the campagna, and in miniature it mimics the arcading of the ruined Temple of Fortune for which the town was celebrated. But once again the visitor is expected to attend to the diminution of the classical past when it is imitated in the England of the 1730s. When we reach the end of the garden at Rousham and look back to its Praeneste framed by the sides of the great alley, formal picturing devices are magnificently used to highlight one of the garden's central pieces of "action."[21]

Similarly, at Stowe in the 1730s Cobham created the ensemble of temples in the valley known as the Elysian Fields. One contemporary is recorded as saying that the "Elysian Fields . . . is the painting part of his gardens."[22] It is clear that this could *not* have referred to modes of pictorial composition in a garden in the late eighteenth-century sense of *picturesque,* if only because the temples are such a striking and meaningful part of the scenery. William Gilpin himself visiting Stowe as a young man in the late 1740s grasped immediately that there was some significance in juxtaposing a Temple of Ancient Virtue, a handsome classical building modeled probably upon the so-called Temple of the Sybil at Tivoli, with a deliberately ruined structure, the Temple of Modern Virtue.[23] What Gilpin did not remark was an extension of that historical comment: inside the Temple of Ancient Virtue were full-length statues of four exemplary ancients, which were in striking contrast to sixteen busts of British Worthies placed in a curious structure, half classical yet somewhat squat and Gothic, apparently inaccessible across the River Styx. It is as if that Temple of British Worthies, elaborately provided with inscriptions, is offered in only partial competition with its classical counterpart across the river of death. The meanings of this triangular arrangement are appreciated by the garden visitor largely through perspective, an essentially pictorial structuring of their action in which form and content cooperate.

This capacity of gardens to present some significant human action in the manner of a history painting may be approached in another way, which also demonstrates how the traditions of *ut pictura poesis* played a vital part in garden picturesque. It is clear that early eighteenth-century gardenists saw their designs in terms of the theater: Pope and visitors to Twickenham referred to the "scenes of [his] little garden," while Pope on his travels saw the actual topography of the Avon Gorge at Bristol as "the broken Scenes behind one another in a Playhouse."[24] Imaginary landscapes in his poetry are also "scenes." Such comparisons are invoked as casually as those with landscape painting, but the very fact that such analogies "have been constructed and [were] received on a largely unconscious level only makes an attempt to comprehend them all the more imperative."[25]

Not only were gardens organized in perspectival views like stage sets, but like those in the theater their *scenes* were unthinkable except as stages for human action. We have to try and envisage this theatrical aspect of gardens not in terms of James Thornhill's famous designs for *Arsinöe* in 1700, empty of dramatis personae, but with human action centrally displayed, as in Hogarth's theater paintings or engravings of garden entertainments during the reign of Louis XIV. By the end of the seventeenth century gardens and the drama shared with painting a theory of representation and presentation of action that was one of the final flowerings of Renaissance doctrines of *ut pictura poesis.* The audience at a Corneille tragedy, the spectator of Marly's sculpture, or the visitor to Versailles saw imagery and heard or read words which were mutually involved, not so much in imitating each other's modes, but in jointly promoting what Dryden, interpreting these ideas for his countrymen, termed human nature and the representation of the passions. In France dramatic theory sustained the ideas and imagery of painters, sculptors, and gardenists just as it provided examples of formal structure.[26] The distinction tends to be ours; but when Poussin used a model theater to organize his paintings he was arranging an idea. Actors' gestures and the postures and expressions of figures in painting both utilized an elaborate vocabulary for the *expression des passions.* So

Félibien's discussion of the Poussin painting now known as *Landscape with a Man Killed by a Snake* (fig. 4.2) stressed how all its effort was directed to express "des passions que peu d'autres Peintres sçû figurer aussi dignement que lui."[27] This language of bodily gesture, which Pope evidently knows when he discusses Patroclus's "attitude" in *Iliad* XVI, was both visual and verbal. As the English translator of the *Conference of Monsieur Le Brun,* the most famous and influential of French exponents of what has been called the "legible body," explained in his dedication to Sir Godfrey Kneller,

> though Painting speaks all Languages, and the Heads in the following Book [heads displaying different passionate expressions] are the same in all places, they yet want to be supplied and illustrated by the Pen; being as imperfect without the Descriptions, as a Mathematical Demonstration without the Problem.[28]

Thus by Pope's time *picturesque* or what was proper for a painting involved a cluster of endeavors, theories, and techniques which drew the arts into community. For the purposes of this enquiry the most crucial of these theories were that a painting—whether it took the form of framed picture or ceiling decoration, a drama or a garden—should represent some significant human action; that all the parts or ornaments of that painting should contribute to the whole; that verbal commentary was needed not only to amplify the visual but to make explicit either literary sources or a body of literary theory (such as the expression of the passions) or the full resonance of some terrace in an Oxfordshire garden named Praeneste.

III

There were, however, some considerable problems with a garden's attempt to duplicate the significant human action of the drama or history painting. In the first place there was the simple fact that, as a medium, the garden cannot function like a picture or the stage. The role of the garden visitor in its scenes highlights this particular awkwardness of the garden picturesque, and in doing so it alerts us to a second. If (as Dryden explained) painterly decorum required that the artist "imitate the customs and times of those persons and things" which he represents, it was by no means clear what were apt compositions for gentlemen's gardens in early eighteenth-century England. The sa-

4.2. *Nicolas Poussin,* Landscape with a Man Killed by a Snake. *National Gallery, London.*

tiric alertness to discrepancies between the classical world and modern times which underpins the elements at Rousham and Stowe previously discussed suggests that there was some uncertainty as to what subject matter was appropriate to Georgian gardens.

A history painting by Poussin depicts humans at the center of the action; landscape, including architectural elements, is often a vital but subsidiary feature. In a garden responsibility for the action rests with the temples, statues, inscriptions, and other such devices, for the human has no permanent place in the design; the "action" of a garden's painting is supplied by the visitor, stimulated by the scene and its allusions; the garden visitor becomes a protaganist by his act of reading these devices. In practice, the garden visitor is both spectator of the elements in its design and an actor in its dramas. This is clear in all of the contemporary visual evidence.

Jacques Rigaud's drawings of the gardens at Chiswick (fig. 4.3) give prominence to the humans who seek to understand what they contemplate. Inasmuch as they are actively engaged in "reading" the garden they may be seen as actors in its drama; they are even given the language of gesture familar from history painting and the drama. Rigaud successfully makes explicit what is only implied in verbal accounts: they note what may be observed ("Every walk terminates with some little Building, one with a Heathen Temple, for instance the Pantheon, another with a little villa"),[29] Rigaud shows the act of observation. The same is true of his drawings of Stowe, where the contemplation of such garden "ornaments" as the busts which eventually were installed in the Temple of British Worthies preoccupies some of the visitors (fig. 4.4). Pope, too, in having himself painted by Jonathan Richardson with the garden obelisk to his mother's memory in the background, recognized the role that was played in all garden history painting by the human actor.[30] And in William Kent's more finished landscape drawings, as befits the work of somebody trained as a history painter, the human involvement in the scene is stressed.

But Rigaud's drawings also reveal that the garden visitor is a spectator as much as an actor. Of course, the very presence of such an audience confirms the centrality of human action in a garden's picture. And it is by no means inconsistent with the parallels of *ut pictura hortus* that some central event in a painting is represented as being watched by less involved bystanders. Nevertheless, where a history painting and a garden differ is precisely in the relationship of their viewers with the

4.3. Jacques Rigaud, drawing of the Great Obelisk in Chiswick Gardens. Devonshire Collection, Chatsworth, Trustees of the Chatsworth Settlement (photograph: British Museum).

4.4. Jacques Rigaud, detail from drawing of visitors at Gibbs's Building in the grounds of Stowe, Buckinghamshire. Metropolitan Museum of Art, New York; Harris Brisbane Dick Fund, 1942.

scene that is viewed. We must work to "read" a painting by Poussin, as he himself advised; but it is also clear that this involvement is physically of a very different order than when we stand in a garden and view a scene which, however pictorially contrived and separated from us like Pope's obelisk seems to have been at the end of his garden, still makes us part of it in ways that a painting cannot. A painting represents significant human action; but a garden rather provides the materials and the scenario for its visitors to complete by partaking in the action. Yet they must also be spectators, above all of their own involvement. In just the same way Pope requires readers of his *Dunciad* and his *Imitations of Horace* (fig. 4.5) to appreciate parallels he is drawing between modern and classical culture, to delight in the discrepancies, and to become actively involved by the very quality of their response in the moral-literary action which is the poem's subject.

But a dunce or Grub Street hack would not be able to participate in reading *The Dunciad* in the same way as, say, Lord Cobham or Lord Burlington; that is precisely what the poem is about. Garden pictures, too, depended upon what their visitors who wished to become part of the action could contribute. If they were learned and witty, then places like Rousham, Stowe, and Pope's Twickenham yielded a full and intricate action in which they were necessarily involved. But it was equally possible to visit gardens without that cultural sophistication—Rigaud's drawings suggest that there were as many "idle" as "involved" spectators—just as there must have been gardens without the high density of reference and allusion that could be found at Chiswick or Stowe. It is precisely as a result of these cultural variations that the garden picturesque which Pope championed came to be challenged.

The significant human action which Poussin or Corneille presented was historical or mythical. Insofar as a garden involved living people as its actors, its action was contemporary and could not readily or easily observe the rules that had been elaborated for painting or drama. The decorums needed for early eighteenth-century garden pictures were not as automatically available as for painters and dramatists; indeed, even for those the treatment of contemporary life and manners posed problems, as perhaps Arthur Devis's conversation pictures sometimes suggest. These could be solved by making the search for decorum and for a plausible translation of historical into contemporary material the centre of the action, often with satirical emphases: *The Beggar's Opera* or Hogarth's comic history paintings would be examples. Gardens, too, could invoke satire, as has been suggested; but their success rested

(16)

Scilicet [31] UNI ÆQUUS VIRTUTI ATQUÆ EJUS AMICIS.

[32] *Quin ubi ſe a* Vulgo & Scena, *in* Secreta *remorant*
Virtus Scipiadæ, & *mitis* Sapientia Læli;
Nugari cum illo, & diſcincti ludere, donec
Decoqueretur olus, ſoliti.
—— *Quicquid ſum ego, quamvis*
Infra Lucili cenſum, ingeniumque, tamen me
[34] *Cum* magnis vixiſſe *invita fatebitur uſque*
Invidia, & fragili quærens illidere dentem,
Offendet ſolido; ——————

Niſi

(17)

I will, or periſh in the gen'rous Cauſe.
Hear this, and tremble! you, who 'ſcape the Laws.
[31] TO VIRTUE ONLY and HER FRIENDS, A FRIEND,
The World beſide may murmur, or commend.
Know, all the diſtant Din that World can keep
Rolls o'er my *Grotto,* and but ſooths my Sleep.
[32] There, my Retreat the beſt Companions grace,
Chiefs, out of War, and Stateſmen, out of Place.
There *St. John* mingles with my friendly Bowl,
The Feaſt of Reaſon and the Flow of Soul:
And He, whoſe Lightning pierc'd th' *Iberian* Lines,
Now, forms my Quincunx, and now ranks my Vines,
Or tames the Genius of the ſtubborn Plain,
Almoſt as quickly, as he conquer'd *Spain.*
[34] *Envy* muſt own, I live among the Great,
No Pimp of Pleaſure, and no Spy of State,
With Eyes that pry not, Tongue that ne'er repeats,
Fond to ſpread Friendſhips, but to cover Heats,
To help who want, to forward who excel;
This, all who know me, know; who love me, tell;
And who unknown defame me, let them be
Scriblers or Peers, alike are *Mob* to me.

E This

4.5. Alexander Pope, The First Satire of the Second Book of Horace . . . Imitated *(London, 1733), 16–17. Folger Shakespeare Library, Washington, D.C.*

fundamentally upon the appreciation of learned visitors. Where such learning was not displayed in a design or available in its actors and spectators, then the garden picturesque which Pope envisaged was bound to change.

Picturesque declensions were, of course, part of much larger cultural patterns. Assumptions about what was proper for a painting came to be challenged during the eighteenth century for a series of complicated reasons. The challenge was particularly strong from those who were interested in landscape, either inside or outside a garden; so it is in that area that the transformations of what may be called the academic picturesque may be studied in sharpest focus. The traditions of *ut pictura poesis* were under review, and landscape itself was both contributor to and beneficiary of such revisions.

IV

Five factors which helped to work these changes in picturesque expectations of landscape may be isolated; it must, however, be stressed that they are enunciated here with far more coherence and sense of pattern than they would have enjoyed in practice. There was, firstly, a shift in the patronage of artists and gardenists from the aristocracy and upper gentry for whom the Grand Tour, the heritage of Rome, and its attendant verbal/visual languages were axiomatic, to far less learned gentry and bourgeoisie; or, if still equally learned, as many of the new patrons were, far less concerned to parade that learning or make it a central concern in their landscapes. Secondly, this new patronage looked rather to Dutch art for its collections than to the classical modes and subjects of Poussin or Claude—and Dutch art was not primarily associated with the traditions of *ut pictura poesis*.[31] Thirdly, the territory of the British Isles was explored and looked to for subject matter, as the Dutch countryside itself had been; and the language of classical let alone neoclassical scenes was not endemic to Britain. As long before as the time of Inigo Jones, his friend Edmund Bolton declared of Stonehenge that "The dumbness of it . . . speakes; that it was not any worke of the ROMANS. For they were wont to make stones vocall by inscriptions."[32] Fourthly, travel increasingly familiarized men with the great mountainous areas of Europe—the Alps, Snowdonia, the English Lakes, the Scottish Highlands: not only did these seem far less susceptible to translation into neoclassical languages, but Edmund Burke actually defined their sublimity largely in terms of the inexpressible.[33] Travel, too, subtly and slowly undermined one of the key concepts of traditional aesthetics: the imitation of nature for Dryden meant human nature; increasingly now it meant nature. The pull of the term is discernible even in Pope: we have seen him singling out prospect in Homer, and he himself added "a few Epithets or short hints of Description" to the Greek. Fifthly and finally, the theatre of action in a garden involved the mind of the spectator himself. Locke's epistemology and its development by his English eighteenth-century successors gave to the individual mind an enormous power, power to shape itself—even if the shaping was sometimes fairly mechanical—in unique ways. How one mind interpreted and used images which its sight provided was potentially quite unlike any other mind; certainly, there were conservative rearguard actions fought to preserve a universal and general map of human experience, but paths were opened to the authority of the individual sensibility.[34]

Pope's aesthetics had been traditional, and this obviously affected his notions of *ut pictura hortus*. But elsewhere, especially in circles that were less conservative, the old ideas were, not so much under attack, as dying of inertia and lack of understanding. Above all the centrality and comprehensibility of classical languages were called in question. Addison, for instance, in his *Dialogue on . . . Medals,* posthumously published in 1721, rejected as preposterous the learned significances which Renaissance artists and writers, drawing on Seneca and others, had given to the dance of the Three Graces. The Abbé Du Bos in *Reflexions critiques sur la poésie et sur la peinture* of 1719 attacked what he considered an overclever *esprit* among modern artists and took Rubens to task for introducing allegorical figures into his historical series on Marie de Médicis: such devices were "des chiffres, dont personne n'a la clef, et même peu de gens la cherchent." An English author, Joseph Spence, argued in his *Polymetis* that Rubens's Whitehall ceiling was unintelligible since it was not clear why "cupids . . . [should] conduct a triumphant sort of car, drawn by wild lions." Now, as the late D. J. Gordon showed in a pioneering article entitled "Ripa's Fate," what Spence neglected was one of the many Renaissance handbooks of *ut pictura poesis,* in this case Alciati's *Emblems,* which showed the power of love as a cupid taming the wildest of animals by driving them in a chariot.[35] Spence's ignorance of emblematic codes suggests a substantial decline in the fortunes of *ut pictura poesis*. Published in 1747, *Polymetis'* subtitle declares that it is "An Enquiry concerning the Agreement Between the Works of the Roman Poets and the Remains of the Ancient

Artists." Spence's basic point about such verbal/visual traditions is that we have lost virtually all understanding of classical imagery. He had his leading, eponymous character propose a means of collecting and collating all the verbal and visual documents available about each of the Roman deities so as to preserve that knowledge. The passage is too long to quote in full, but some selections will make the point:

> The deities of the Romans (says Polymetis) were so numerous, that they might well complain of wanting a Nomenclatour to help them to remember all their names. Their vulgar religion, as indeed that of the heathens in general, was a sort of Manicheism. Whatever was able to do good or to do harm to man, was immediately looked on as a superiour power; which, in their language, was the same as a deity. It was hence that they had such a multitude of gods, that their temples were better peopled with statues, than their cities with men. It is a perfect mob of deities, if you look upon them all together: but they are reducible enough to order; and fall into fewer classes, than one would at first imagine. I have reduced them to six; and considering their vast number, it was no little trouble to bring them into that compass.
>
> You see that Rotonda, with a Colonnade running round it, on the brow of the hill? Within that, are the great celestial deities; as the milder ones relating to the human mind and civil life, (Fidelity, Clemency; Peace, Concord; Plenty, Health; all the Mental or Moral Deities, of the better sort;) are placed in the Colonnade about it; one in each opening between the pillars. That temple, lower down the hill to the right, contains the beings which preside over the element of fire: which, according to the antients, had its place next to the supream mansion of the gods. You may call this, if you please, the temple of the Sun and Stars. There I have lodged all my antiques that relate to the Sun, to the Planets, to the Constellations; and to the Times and Seasons, as measured by the former. That Octogon, opposite to it on the left, is the temple of the Winds, and of the imaginary beings of the air. Those two temples on either hand below them contain, one the deities of the Waters, and the other the deities of the Earth: and if I had a temple for the Infernal beings, with the Vices of men round it, in the same manner as their Virtues are placed round the celestial one, I question whether you could name any one imaginary being in all the theology of the ancients, that might not properly enough be placed in one or other of these six repositories. . . .

> The statues are placed in niches made for them; and ornamented with copies of such antient relievo's or pictures as relate to them. In their pedestals, I have contrived drawers, to put in the medals, gems, prints and drawings, I have been so long getting together: such under each, as have any reference to the deity they are placed under: much in the manner as the books of the Sibyls were kept by Augustus in the base of the Palatine Apollo. And thus I have disposed of all my collection, with somewhat more of regularity and order, than is observed generally in much better collections than I am master of.
>
> You, Philander, know that my principal view in making this collection was to compare the descriptions and expressions in the Roman poets that any way relate to the imaginary beings, with the works that remain to us of the old artists; and to please myself with the mutual lights they might give each to the other. I have often thought when in Italy, and at Rome in particular, that they enjoy there the convenience of a sort of contemporary comments on Virgil and Horace, in the nobler remains of the antient statuaries and painters. When you look on the old pictures of sculptures, you look on the works of men who thought much in the same train with the old poets. There was generally the greatest union in their designs: and where they are engaged on the same subjects, they must be the best explainers of one another.[36]

What is above all crucial in *Polymetis* is that Spence enjoyed his classical learning, especially its visual/verbal configurations, at the same time as he realized that it was fast becoming a lost language. This double response presumably also explains the book's popularity: there were further editions in 1775 and 1774 as well as a school version of 1764 which went into six editions. Evidently there was the need as well as the wish to learn the languages of classical mythology. And what makes Spence's attempt to fill an educational vacuum particularly relevant to a discussion of the decline of *ut pictura poesis* is that as a passionate gardenist he was far less eager to invoke the detailed and specific language which his *Polymetis* explains. Even Polymetis tells his guests that the gardens where his collections are displayed are "rather wild than regular." That is the style of garden design favored by Spence and his gardening friends and patrons whose casual remarks and apothegms on the subject he assiduously collected. These gardening observations do not suggest as firm a commitment to learned gardening as we might expect from the author of *Polymetis*.

Many of the remarks Spence collected and evidently agreed with attend to the formal lessons to be learnt by the garden designer from paintings. In 1758, for instance, he noted:

> The general aims: to follow "beautiful Nature" (as Raphael, and not Caravaggio and the Dutch painters);—to vary the scenes, lights and shades, colours of leaves, etc.—to hide what is disagreeable near you and take in what is agreeable:—to extend the appearance of your ground, call in the country, and make as much of the circle round you subservient to your design as you can.[37]

That suggests that he subscribed to the ideas of decorum and to making parts serve the whole. He drew the correct analogies with dramatic theory, too: "As a probable falsehood is fitter for drama than an improbable truth, so the appearance to the eye is to be followed in gardening rather than the fact."[38] In all, much of his garden aesthetic accords with the literary and painterly theory we have surveyed: the formal aspects are designed to support the ideas, the action; there should be a unity of action—"a view of the whole and all its parts," which in their turn should exhibit a propriety in their ornament—statues of Flora and zephyrs are apt for parterres, but Pomona and Vertumnus for orchards; the principal view in a garden is as the principal object in a painting; gardens, like other great art, have a moral function.[39] These ideas are all implicit in Spence's presentation of Horatio's garden in his *Essay on Pope's Odyssey,* including the last dialogue:

> When they alighted, Philypsus order'd his Servant before them to the Dome of Apollo, with a Book or two he had brought in the Coach; whilst He and *Antiphaus* walk'd on gently to enjoy the Freshness of the Air, and the Beauties of the Place. The Sun (which now began to be in its decline) as it shot thro' the Trees, made a thousand wavering Mixtures of Light and Shade: The Birds, on all sides were answering one another in their little natural Airs: every thing look's Fresh about 'em; and everything was Agreeable.[40]

Everything seems to be there: the centrality of human action, the painterly qualities of light and shade, apt for the scene, the books to supplement images, above all the propriety of proceeding with books to the Temple of Apollo when the sun is beginning its descent; each element contributes to the whole.

But there is another side to Spence's academic picturesque, namely his scepticism with the old iconographical languages it usually employed. In the eighteenth dialogue of *Polymetis* a character singles out the garden statuary at Versailles, the "collections in Rome itself," and Ripa's emblems as examples of inventions which "we are frequently at a loss to know what they mean."[41] *Polymetis* and its eponymous character are learned in the old languages, but Spence is no longer satisfied with them. Of Apollo, for instance, we learn in the eighth dialogue from Polymetis that above all he exemplifies beauty, but that there are different Apollos depending upon their imagery: the Apollo Venator, the sun god, the president of the Muses, Apollo Vates or Lyristes, the Action Apollo, and so on.[42] But the scene in Horatio's garden has none of these precise significations: Apollo's Dome at most contributes a general appropriateness to the beautiful sunset and to an evening devoted to books. Spence, in short, does not seem to bother with precise mythology in his gardens: in *Polymetis* he even argues that "the figures of the things themselves speak . . . the clearest language," which is therefore to be preferred to allegorical devices.[43]

Spence may well have been influenced by the type of gardens with which he was involved, smaller and less ambitious than the grand "history paintings" of Stowe and Rousham. But it was also clear that others with similar classical skills nevertheless shared his lack of interest in learned gardens: Joseph Warton wrote,

> *Lead me from gardens deck'd with art's vain pomps.*
> *Can gilt alcoves, can marble mimic gods,*
> *Parterres embroider'd, obelisks, and urns*
> *Of high relief; can the long spreading lake,*
> *Or vista lessening to the sight, can Stow,*
> *With all her attic fanes, such raptures raise*
> *As the thrush haunted copse . . .* [?][44]

This reaction was set out more systematically by Thomas Whately some twenty or so years later, when he distinguished between emblematic and expressive gardens and opted for the latter which yield "transitory" images that are "not sought for, not labored, and have the force of a metaphor, free from the detail of allegory." Whately, in fact, argues energetically that what serves well in paintings need not or will not be apt in gardens.[45] But as early as the 1720s Jonathan Richardson's discussions of European landscape pictures showed him on the one hand hard put to understand the ensemble of figures and setting in Poussin's

Landscape with the Body of Phocion or the *Landscape with a Man Killed by a Snake* (see fig. 4.2) and on the other hand inclined to read landscapes in terms only of their affective qualities. Even Pope felt and responded to the expressive potential of place.

V

The retreat from an academic picturesque, where the decorum of subject and setting, parts and whole, was primary and where learned verbal/visual references to literary and historical sources as well as to a repertoire of expressive gesture were expected, may be traced in the work of both the landscape designer "Capability" Brown and the painter Richard Wilson. Their work highlights and helps to explain the movement from a learned and universally translatable picturesque to one much more hospitable to the language of forms and to the vague, the local, the sentimental, and the subjective, all of which characterize the new picturesque of Gilpin and Price.

When Claude Lorrain sketched the Muses he was proposing to use in his *Landscape with Apollo, the Muses and River God* (fig. 4.6), the figures were identified with little captions borrowed from the text of Cesare Ripa's *Iconologia.* In the finished painting (fig. 4.7) those verbal tags were of course eliminated, and viewers were presumably expected to make their own identifications on the basis of knowledge shared outside the pictorial frame of reference. To a later eighteenth-century viewer of the painting the figures may well have been purely incidental, *staffage* in a beautiful landscape which was the main object of admiration and study. In the absence of any documentation of such an attitude, that must be speculation only; but exactly the same elimination of readable subject matter, historical or mythological, from a landscape can be demonstrated in the designs of "Capability" Brown.

Brown's especial skill was to shape the forms of landscape into an attractive whole. With a keen eye, no doubt, to clients' expectations and with a keen ear for contemporary declensions of old formulae, he gestured to the old picturesque when in 1774 he advised the Earl of Scarbrough that he could manage the grounds at Sandbeck and Roche Abbey "with Poet's feeling and with Painter's Eye." But the phrase is actually in parentheses, a rhetorical touch, with no purchase upon the *ut pictura poesis* to which it distantly alludes. Brown's work, moreover, played down the readable elements in landscape; at most, his place making was exactly fitted to a new sensibility which liked to speak directly and personally to its surroundings in what Spence had called

4.6. Claude Lorrain, drawing of the Muses (preparatory study for figure 4.7). Thomas Agnew & Sons Ltd, Bond Street, London.

4.7. Claude Lorrain, Landscape with Apollo, the Muses, and River God. *National Galleries of Scotland.*

"the clearest language of things themselves."[46] Where he still betrayed his allegiance to one fundamental neoclassical attitude was in his search for an ideal Nature in its unchanging and permanent forms beneath all local accidents and superficial variations. It was this classicism of form that the picturesque exponents of the 1770s, 1780s, and 1790s could not understand, preferring to return to a landscape either its readable structures and busy associationist clutter or to submerge its forms beneath fussy and local "texture" (fig. 4.8).

In contrast to Brown, whose presentation of *la belle nature* he obviously respected, Richard Wilson seems to have been a fairly well read, even intellectual man. He favored or sought the favor of patrons who would for various reasons appreciate his ambition to produce landscape paintings in the style of the classical French and Italian landscapists in Rome, where in 1750 Wilson himself went to study. His Italianate paintings aspire to many of the older traditions of *ut pictura poesis* which we have already traced; they represent significant human action, not only in such obvious instances as *The Destruction of Niobe's Children,* but in his views of *Villa of Maecenas at Tivoli* (fig. 4.9) or the *Landscape Capriccio on the Via Aemilia.* In both of these the historical association and the readable items—the Roman sarcophagus, the ruins of the bridge built at Narni by Augustus, the imagery of antique religion in the so-called Sybil's Temple—all contribute to the representation of some idea, to which the Claudian allusiveness of Wilson's handling contributes an apt arcadian scenery. Wilson aspires to elevate these landscapes into the category of history paintings, though the human figures have dwindled in them to merely decorative details; at most they are our surrogates within the landscape, experiencing and reading it.

Wilson was visualizing the same sense of Italian landscape instinct with historical associations and moral lessons that Joseph Addison had celebrated at the beginning of the century. In his catalogue of the 1982–1983 Wilson exhibition David Solkin aptly quoted some lines from Addison's *Letter from Italy, to the Rt. Hon Lord Halifax* which make this clear:

For wheresoe'er I turn my ravish'd eyes,
Gay gilded scenes and shining prospects rise.
Poetick fields still encompass me around,
And still I seem to tread on Classic ground;
For here the Muse so oft her Harp has strung,
That not a mountain rears its head unsung,
Renown'd in verse each shady thicket grows,
And every stream in heavenly numbers flows.

4.8. François Vivares, engraving of a waterfall in Bolton Park, Yorkshire, 1753.

4.9. Richard Wilson, Distant View of the Villa of Maecenas at Tivoli, *c. 1757. The Tate Gallery.*

Addison insists several times upon the *scenes* he visits, empty stages of Roman history which he brings his wide reading to fill. (Pope imagined the same process in his *Epistle to Mr Jervas:* "Or seek some ruin's formidable shade; / While fancy brings the vanish'd piles to view, / And builds imaginary *Rome* a-new"). In his prose *Remarks on Several Parts of Italy* Addison announces its ambition to compare "the natural face of the country with the Landskips that the Poets have given us of it;" in other words, he extrapolates pictures (*landskips*) out of classical poetry, as Pope would do with Homer, and proposes to read them into the actual Italian topography.[47] It is that process of *ut pictura poesis* that Richard Wilson may be said to reverse when he offers landscape imagery informed by the classical texts which will give it meaning—those, for instance, which celebrated Maecenas and the luxury which was his country's eventual downfall (fig. 4.9).[48]

Such significant human action, even if only articulated by empty or ruined scenery, required correspondingly grand treatment. "Greatness of idea," to quote a contemporary reaction to Wilson, finds its proper formulation in "beautiful composition."[49] It is what Reynolds, writing in *The Idler* in 1759, identified as the Italian style, which

> attends only to the invariable, the great and general ideas, which are fixed and inherent in universal Nature: the Dutch, on the contrary, to literal truth and a minute exactness in the details, I may say, of Nature, modified by accident. The attention to these petty peculiarities is the very cause of this naturalness so much admired in the Dutch, which if we suppose it to be a beauty, is certainly of lesser order, that ought to give place to a beauty of a superior kind, since one cannot be obtained but by departing from the other.[50]

But as Solkin has shown, Wilson often modified his high Claudian mode by invoking precisely those Dutch compositions and details.[51] Such concessions to a less serious brand of landscape art were apparently his response to the necessity of appealing to a less learned clientele. But it is possible to see even his Roman landscapes in the grand style, instinct with historical reference and literary allusion, as evidence of this shift in taste and learning. We may be able to furnish them with an elaborate and translatable iconography, but it is clear from contemporary reactions that the meanings they conveyed were essentially vague. They suggest, as Jonathan Skelton put it in 1758, "many pleasing reflexions" with their "venerable Relicts of ancient Roman Grandeur."[52]

Like contemporary verses on the subject, the communication of Wilson's action is in the most general terms, which we may flesh out in our own way or, equally, ignore with no real loss of pictorial enjoyment. The onus of reading the action of these paintings derives far less from their own requirements than from habits of mind ("See prostrate Rome her wondrous story tell")[53] which spectators chose to bring to bear upon them.

It is a switch of emphasis from what is there to be read to the reader's act of reading, from inherent meaning to the potentialities of readership. Doubtless some new clients wished to be less intellectually challenged—Wilson found this, and so did "Capability" Brown; but equally, they wanted to be left to their own devices as spectators. Lockean psychology and the rise of sentiment fostered individual responses, which in their turn neglected the universal languages of *ut pictura poesis.* So William Shenstone in 1760 saw in contemporary writing "ye voice of Sentiment, rather y^n the Language of *Reflexion;* adapted particularly to strike ye Passions, which is the only merit of Poetry that has gained any regard of late."[54] The movement is from representation of passions in action to the record of the passions struck; from public languages to private sensibilities; from what is clearly translatable by educated people to the provision of hints and directions for private responses; from invariable, great, and universal ideas—say *genius loci* or *concordia discors,* both of which are themes Addison canvasses in his Italian verses—to more vaguely defined "character" of ground where our impressionistic moods or our delight in formal excitements of light and shade are gratified; execution takes the place of event.

VI

The seeds of such declensions had been sown at least half a century before Wilson left to study painting in Italy, and his is just one of many examples that could be offered to show how the neoclassical picturesque was undergoing revision. A writer in the *Analytical Review* of 1784 welcomed Lessing's *Laocoön* and its challenge to some of the traditional melding of words and images:

> in the foremost rank of technical criticisms are those that aim at ascertaining the boundaries, and setting the limits, of the different modes of imitation; or at discriminating in each art the nature and properties of those materials and modes of conduct, which,

> from being closely connected among themselves, have hitherto been confounded with each other. From long bigotted deference to the old maxim, that poetry is painting in speech, and painting dumb poetry, the two sisters, marked with features so different by nature, and the great masters of composition, her oracles, have been constantly confounded with each other by the herds of mediocrity and thoughtless imitation. Hence that deluge of descriptive stuff, which overwhelms by a rhapsody of successive sounds what can only be represented by figure, and the less frequent but equally absurd attempt of combining moments and subdividing expression.[55]

This celebration of what the writer also called "The futility of such mutual inroads of poetry and painting on each other" was occasioned by a review of Uvedale Price's *Essay on the Picturesque*. The picturesque flowered in these ruins of the sisterhood of poetry and painting, yet remained curiously faithful to both verbal and visual languages.

The cooperation of subject matter with form gave way to an art and an aesthetic in which handling became all-important, for it was responsive to objects which were "rough, rugged, and broken, with various marks of age and decay."[56] When Allan Ramsey traveled to Italy in 1736 his companion recorded "many fine picturesque views of ancient ruins," including "a fine Pictoresque view at Tivoli of the great Cascade, and the temple of the Sybils, likewise from the place where formerly Mecaenas and Horace's Villas stood, are delightful falls of water and Grott's all grown over with Ivy and evergreens."[57] Clearly, the meaning of ruins was of far less value to those travelers than the formal delights of rough and broken surfaces which pencil and palette could recreate. By 1797 those aspects had complete priority: John Thomas Smith's *Remarks on Rural Scenery* thought the "neglected fast ruinating cottage" yielded "far greater allurements to the painter's eye."[58]

William Gilpin's picturesque tours contributed to this vogue, though his earlier *Essay upon Prints* had reiterated something close to the old aesthetic of *decorum,* since for him design meant "a proper time, proper characters, the most affecting manner of introducing those characters, and proper appendages."[59] He disliked "all the Dutch masters," too, precisely those models whom Price and Knight valued for the encouragement they gave to what Gainsborough called "business for the eye."[60] Intricacies of texture in landscapes, real or painted, seemed to fill the vacuum which the departure or neglect of subject had created.

Wordsworth thought "Historical subjects shd. never be introduced into Landscape but when the Landscape was to be subservient to them—Where the Landscape was intended principally to impress the mind, figures, other than such as are general . . . are injurious to the effect."[61]

This celebration of the formal aspects of scenery, however, was not really divorced from its old cooperation with subject matter. But the central and significant human action, to which Wordsworth alludes, was now outside the picture; it was located in the picturesque connoisseur him or herself. Sensibilities, moods, feelings, associations, ideas were all integral to the picturesque experience and they needed words for their articulation. J. H. Pott in his *Essay on Landscape Painting* of 1782 declared that the "meanest object in nature, a stone, the stump of a tree, a piece of broken ground, if imitated most exactly, will immediately affect the mind with pleasure," just as Robert Morris in 1739 had urged how "Every Country, has its peculiar Enchantments of Situation . . . to allure our Eyes or Attention and fill us with agreeable Ideas."[62] To express these ideas and pleasures, words were still needed; hence that outpouring of verbal commentary during the picturesque movement. So that it was perfectly apt, a reformulation of an old alliance, for Gilpin to be hailed as the "*ne plus ultra* of pen and pencil united." It was also eloquent of new adjustments to traditional collaborations that as late as 1825 Wordsworth himself planned "to make Snowdon the scene of a Dialogue upon Nature, Poetry, and Painting—to be illustrated by the surrounding imagery."[63]

5 SENSE AND SENSIBILITY IN THE LANDSCAPE DESIGNS OF HUMPHRY REPTON

The special place of Humphry Repton in the history of English landscape gardening is only beginning to be recognized.[1] For too long he has been either indistinguishable from his predecessor, "Capability" Brown, or simply dubbed "picturesque." Furthermore, it has also seemed that until very recently it was hard to say anything very strenuous about his work; it was as if the satiric putdown of Thomas Love Peacock's *Headlong Hall* had wholly conditioned our attitudes toward Repton, who appears in that novel thinly disguised as Marmaduke Milestone. It is Milestone himself who is made, unwittingly, to belittle the achievements of his art:

> One age, sir, has brought to light the treasures of ancient learning; a second has penetrated into the depths of metaphysics; a third has brought to perfection the science of astronomy; but it was reserved for the exclusive genius of the present times, to invent the noble art of picturesque gardening, which has given, as it were, a new tint to the complexion of nature, and a new outline to the physiognomy of the universe![2]

The imputation of intellectual poverty is extended later when Peacock mocks both the absurd ideas that the "noble art" promotes and the unstrenuous formulations of its aesthetics: when the possible improvements to the grounds of Headlong Hall are the occasion for Mr. Escot's encomium of the "wild man of the woods," or when it is gravely debated whether Lord Littlebrain driving a four-in-hand along gracefully curving gravel is a more acceptable prospect than an "ass and four goats" characterizing "a wild, uncultured scene."[3]

The association of Repton/Milestone with "picturesque gardening" continues to this day, with little attention to either Repton's contribution to the picturesque debates or their sequence—Repton's involvement in these preceded by twenty years Peacock's satire. Thus David Watkin, for example, lumps Repton with Uvedale Price and Richard Payne Knight among the "Picturesque theoreticians,"[4] while Alistair Duckworth has explained how the "radical improvements of the kind Repton made were not improvements at all but 'innovations' or 'alterations' of a destructive nature" as opposed to the more naturalistic styles of Price and Knight."[5]

Such adjudications, with less justification than Peacock into whose satiric field are indiscriminately drawn various landscape gardening practitioners, neglect two important and related aspects of Repton's career. First, that while he certainly began by wishing to emulate Brown's success, Repton was too attentive to the current needs and sites of his patrons to perpetuate aesthetics irrelevant to their situations.[6] Second, that he proves to have been fundamentally more conservative than Duckworth, for example, perhaps taking his cue from Jane Austen's *Mansfield Park,* would allow.

Repton was as eager as anyone in the late eighteenth century to contribute to the aesthetics of landscape. But that desire was firmly held in check by his recognition and assumption of a professional role. He worked, after all, at the beginning of what *The Architecture Review* referred to as "the brass tacks period" of gardening history,[7] a time marked by the rise of the professional—Brown, Repton, then J. C. Loudon—after a period of interventions by talented amateurs. Joseph Addison, Alexander Pope, and William Kent, together with the noble gardening lords like Carlisle, Cobham, and Burlington, had been fascinated with the ideologies and aesthetics that sustained what they saw as their pioneer efforts in garden design; but their professional successors necessarily had to attend more carefully to the practical exigencies of a client's topography or temperament.

Repton, indeed, begins the first chapter of *Observations on the Theory and Practice of Landscape Gardening* (1803) by noting that theory and practice "have seldom fallen under the consideration of the same author; because those who have delivered their opinions in writing on this art have had little practical experience, and few of its professors have been able to deduce their rules from theoretical principles."[8] It was because he could acknowledge the wide range of "opinions" embodied in both the practice and the theory of his predecessors that Repton gradually came to translate the mindless visual taste which Peacock justly mocks into a more strenuous aesthetic of designs closely related to their social functions. It is this which is the topic of this essay.

Repton's decision, after a sleepless night in 1788, to turn his attention to landscape gardening was explained to friends, if a little portentiously, as nevertheless the commitment to a profession with a history:

> I have been advised to render my leisure proffitable [*sic*] by a profession which since the loss of Brown and Richmond has been understood by no one so well as by yourself [Reverend Norton Nicholls]. . . . Mason, Gilpin, Whatley [*sic*] and Gerardin have been of late my breviary, and the works of Kent, Brown and Richmond have been the places of my worship.[9]

His ambition to be venerated in the same pantheon involves, above all, his professional appraisal of changing tastes in gardening and habits among his clients.[10] While he can attest to his historical perspectives by frequent and admiring invocations of Alexander Pope's judgments upon landscape, he is yet perfectly aware of new developments that preempt the emblematic and iconographical apparatus of Pope's era from contemporary gardens. For not only do his writings not discuss, for instance, garden statues, but he joins Thomas Whately's attack on allegorical gardening by identifying "statues, vases, basso-relievos, sculpture, etc." as having "no use."[11]

Repton's sense of this change was displayed very early in his career, as can be focused by contrasting his Red Book for Babworth (1790) with an engraving of Stowe of 1739.[12] In both we can observe that the garden is a place for social encounters and discourse; whereas at Babworth it is a private, family affair (fig. 5.1), that Repton cleverly offers in the painterly idiom of a sentimental genre picture, the scene at Stowe is a larger social gathering, concerned to promenade and appreciate the statues of the Muses and Sciences in their niches around the parterre (fig. 5.2). The earlier engraving also invokes an appropriate visual idiom, the celebratory print of large estates where the collection of antique statues is prominently displayed. What we see at Stowe is a landscape of learned allusion that Gilbert West describes in his poem on Stowe:

> *Phoebus, and th'attendent Virgin Train,*
> *That o'er each Verse, each learned Science reign,*
> *And round embellishing the gay Parterre,*
> *Unite their sacred Influences here.*[13]

Though professionals had certainly been engaged to work for Lord Cobham, his garden and park are essentially the work of cognoscenti,

5.1. Humphry Repton's proposed scene for Babworth, from the Babworth Red Book. Private collection.

5.2. Engraving by B. Baron after J. Rigaud of the parterre at Stowe, Buckinghamshire, published by Sarah Bridgeman, 1739. Dumbarton Oaks, Trustees for Harvard University.

View of the Perterre *from the* Portico *of the* House. *Veüe du* Partere *prise sur le* Perron *du* Chateau.

an intimate circle of amateurs to whose landscape interests and schemes Pope refers when he expresses his conviction that "no publick professors of gardening (any more than any public professors of virtue) are equal to the Private Practisers of it."[14] In contrast, Babworth is a delightful amenity, rescued from its original windswept state by a professional, who has provided his clients with comfort and happy visual prospects over the neighboring countryside. Though the family is certainly cultivated, its intellectual needs are not obviously served by the garden, as the Cobhams' had been at Stowe.

We may register Repton's professional obligations toward his clients and the changes in landscape philosophy by comparing other parts of the gardens at Stowe with further Repton designs. At Stowe during the 1730s and 1740s the use of the rival architectures of Grecian and Gothic was always in the service of ideas.[15] The Temple of Ancient Virtue, placed in the Elysian Fields, contained statues of four exemplary classical figures; ironically placed beside it was the ruined Temple of Modern Virtue. The architecture of Ancient Virtue revived memories of classical precedents—notably the so-called Sybil's Temple at Tivoli—and their renaissance in modern times—perhaps Hawksmoor's mausoleum at Castle Howard. Its authority was contrasted with the Gothic suggestions of the Temple of British Worthies across the valley. Ten years later the more eloquent Gothic of the Temple of Liberty was established on the hill behind; surrounded as it once was with busts of the Nordic deities whose names gave us the days of our week, it was a visual emblem of a rival tradition—the sense of England's own Gothic history, its early freedom from classical rules and restriants. By Repton's time this symbolic use of architectural styles for political and cultural "messages" has surrendered to other contingencies: the need to allow clients to choose their preferred style, and the solely visual or formal basis of that choice.

Early in his career Repton displays what Sir Nikolaus Pevsner has called a "crazy visual single-mindedness."[16] At Welbeck (first Red Book, 1789) he explores the virtues of horizontal or perpendicular lines in Grecian-Roman or Gothic architecture respectively. Even earlier at Wembly he speculates upon the "picturesque effect . . . produced by the mixture of Gothic buildings with round-headed trees," while "those of the Grecian will accord either with round or conic trees; but, if the base be hid, the contrast of the latter will be most pleasing."[17] It was finally left to the client's choice (fig. 5.3).

5.3. Humphry Repton, Sketches and Hints on Landscape Gardening, *1794, facing p. 18. Dumbarton Oaks, Trustees for Harvard University.*

The contrasts at Stowe were not, of course, without their visual delights; but what was seen should have promoted what was thought and what the eye enjoyed also nourished the mind. And it is also worth stressing that this readable garden vocabulary was presumably available as a shared culture to most of Cobham's visitors. Repton's garden designs, by contrast, lack any attention to such readable structures. Only once, at Langley Park, where the owner insisted that an "unsightly" house be retained because his mother had liked it and that Repton dress it up with a Doric facade, does he argue rather unctiously that the building, "thus ornamented, may be considered as a temple sacred to filial piety."[18] Otherwise he seems guided at first by purely visual tastes, and then increasingly by social considerations. It is the pleasure and effects, not the meaning, of an architectural style that concern him, as in his reflections on Wyatt's Gothic Sheffield Park in Sussex.[19]

Repton's early affinities were obviously with the picturesque cult. Certainly William Mason was not alone in placing Repton firmly in the picturesque traditions, and he did so in a letter to none other than William Gilpin.[20] Repton's own remark, quoted earlier, about the base of a house being hidden betrays his thinking of garden design in terms of a picture. He was later to realize that a house and garden were seen by people who move around and for whom bases are not always hidden. Though this sense of his clients' perspectives and needs led him to revise his picturesque tastes, the traces of his early visual thinking linger throughout his career. Thus the discussion of Grecian and Gothic architecture in his last publication, *Fragments on the Theory and Practice of Landscape Gardening* (1816), still attends to their visual merits.

> In the quiet, calm, and beautiful scenery of a tame country, the elegant forms of Grecian art are, surely, more graceful and appropriate than a ruder and severer style; but, on the contrary, there are some wild and romantic situations, whose rocks, and dashing mountain-streams, or deep umbrageous dells, would seem to harmonize with the proud baronial tower, or mitred abbey, 'embosomed high in tufted trees,' as tending to associate the character of the building with that of its native accompaniment.[21]

But the passage issues from a discussion of the "relative *effects* of the two styles" and some sensible attention to the demands of "a British climate" upon merely picturesque possibilities.[22]

The picturesque theorists with whom Repton came to disagree were still conditioned, as he had been, by the presiding notion of eighteenth-century landscapists that painting, together with poetry, had contributed most to the development of the English garden. Hence his retort to Knight's picturesque improvement of a Brownian park (fig. 5.4) is that it revealed more of a taste for Salvator Rosa than for real nature. Repton, in fact, grew to mistrust the tangled thickets of the dialogue between Art and Nature that flourished throughout the eighteenth century and especially around the idea of the landscape garden. In the "Advertisement" for his *Observations* of 1803 he lamented how difficult was the "application of any rules of Art to the works of Nature."[23] To recognize his particular solution to that difficulty some brief excursion into its history must be undertaken.

Except in such a garden as Stourhead, where the influence of Claude Lorrain may be an undeniable presence, it is difficult to see in practice what these painterly influences had forced designers to do that they would not also have learned from, say, Italian gardens or theater designs. But the expectation that landscape designs would borrow from painterly structures was as much part of the mental assumptions of visitors to gardens as of their creators. From Vanbrugh, who had advised the Duchess of Marlborough to send for a landscape painter to design the grounds at Blenheim, to Pope, who deemed it axiomatic that "all gardening is landscape painting"; from Walpole, who spoke of the "multiplied scenes" of Pope's little garden at Twickenham, to the young William Gilpin at Stowe in 1747, his eye conditioned to discover Salvator Rosa–like compositions in a "fine Rock, beautifully set off in Claro-obscuro, and garnished with flourishing Bushes, Ivy, and dead Branches," gardens were read as if they were pictures. Yet by mid-century it was precisely this picturesque aspect of garden design that seemed to please least; Joseph Warton's Enthusiast begged to be led

> *from gardens deck'd with art's vain pomps.*
> *Can gilt alcoves, can marble-mimic gods,*
> *Parterres embroider'd, obelisks, and urns,*
> *Of high relief; can the long, spreading lake*
> *Or vista lessening to the sight; can Stow . . .*

in short, satisfy as much as the world beyond its ha-ha.[24] And while visiting and appreciating the pictured effects of the gardens at Stowe in 1747 Gilpin is yet prophetic of the new taste in his commendation of northern scenery.[25] It is certainly his preference for "real" Nature over

5.4. Two contrasting etchings by B. T. Pouncy after Thomas Hearne, from Richard Payne Knight's The Landscape, *1794. Dumbarton Oaks, Trustees for Harvard University.*

the contrived prospects in a landscape garden that—at least among the literary and aesthetic avant-garde—dominates the second half of the century. Such is Thomas Gray's judgment in a letter to William Mason of 1765:

> the Mountains are extatic, and ought to be visited in pilgrimage once a year. none but those monstrous creatures of God know how to join so much beauty with so much horror. a fig for your Poets, Painters, Gardeners, and Clergymen, that have not been among them: their imagination can be made up of nothing but bowling-greens, flowering shrubs, horse-ponds, Fleet-ditches, shell-grottoes, and Chinée rails.[26]

In its turn such taste imposed upon landscape designers the task of emulating what Warton called "unfrequented meads, and pathless wilds." This required the elimination of both a learned and emblematic garden and any obvious debts to painterly structures in its composition. An early example of such "naturalistic" tendencies is the Grecian Valley at Stowe, begun at the end of the 1740s. If not the work of "Capability" Brown, who started his career at Stowe, it is certainly prophetic of it. The picturesque self-consciousness of Stourhead or other parts of Stowe is largely absent in what appears to be a "natural" valley. By the 1760s, the Grecian Valley seems to have extended its influence to other parts of the gardens. These increasingly informal or more "natural" tastes that Brown fostered turn the contrived landscapes of his predecessors—one might think of Kent's Vale of Venus at Rousham—into parkland where, though the ingenuity of man has evidently been exercised, his art is concealed. The organization of natural phenomena in Brown's plans for Heveningham, for example (fig. 5.5), is surely designed to provide images of what Repton (speaking of Brown) called "the ground [in] its original shape"; Brown had shown—again according to Repton—that "more variety might be introduced [into gardens] by copying Nature, and by assisting her operations." As a consequence, we "were taught that Nature was to be our only model."[27]

By the time Repton came to assume Brown's place in the gardenist profession the naturalism of the latter's designs was already under attack. It came most energetically from those, like Uvedale Price and Richard Payne Knight, who invoked their ideas of a wilder and even more "natural" landscape outside gardens to demand a revision of Brownian design. Yet one of the complex ironies of this debate, of

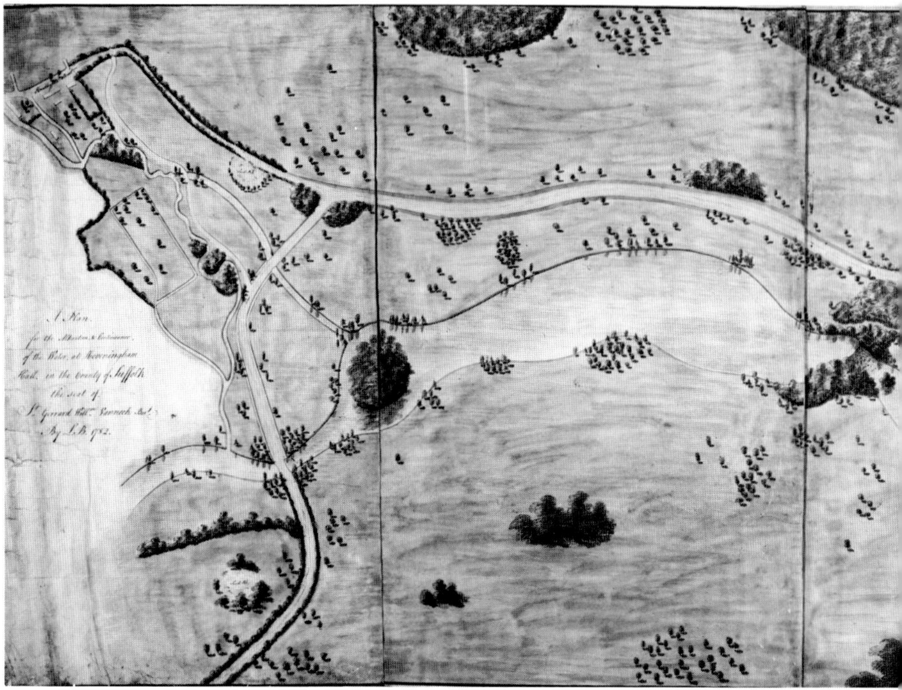

5.5. Lancelot ("Capability") Brown, plan for Heveningham Hall, 1762. Heveningham Hall (photograph: Country Life).

course, is that Knight's objections to Brown's landscapes for their lack of real or natural beauty invoked an experience of nature that a very limited range of prints and paintings had taught him. Once the artificial contrivances of landscapes at Stowe, Stourhead, or Hagley Park had been exhausted or outgrown and it was the turn of other landscapes outside the garden—in the Wye Valley, the Lakes, or the Peak District—they were still explored with an eye, like Gilpin's, nurtured upon prints and paintings. So lovers of "nature," like Warton's Enthusiast, found in the unorganized scenery outside the garden the hidden manifestations of achieved artistry because they "read" or saw them only in terms of previously encountered artifact. For throughout the whole cycle of these changing tastes it is evident, in E. H. Gombrich's words, that no artist can discard all conventions and "paint what he sees" or, rather, garden as he sees.[28] Even Repton's claim that Brown took nature as his "model"

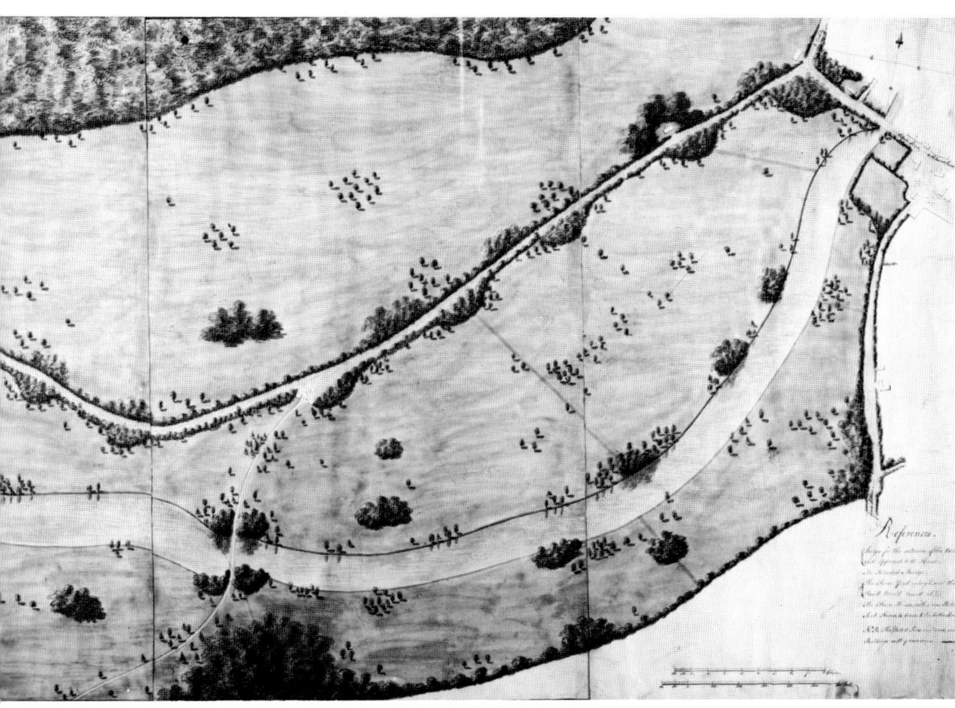

betrays in its painterly metaphor the recognition of a carefully controlled relationship that is *not,* however, mere identity between the source of an artist's ideas and the works he produces.

Repton certainly shared Knight's skepticism with some of Brown's more obvious mannerisms—serpentine water, belts and clumps of trees, smooth lawns right up to the house walls. But in his quarrel with Knight and Price over what revisions were required in landscape design after Brown he reveals a surer grasp of the intricacies of the aesthetic debate. He seems to me, therefore, less the "man of compromise" that Pevsner terms him,[29] than an original contributor to the development of English landscape gardening, in both its theory and its practice. And this originality derives from Repton's recognition of the mediating force of both painterly conventions in landscape design and the social needs and conventions of his clients.

Responding to Knight's comparison of a Brownian park with a picturesque improvement of it, Repton accused him of only appreciating scenes that were "fit object[s] for the representation of the pencil" and of "no delight but in the scenes of Salvator Rosa."[30] Accordingly, one of his rather facetious modes of attack in the quarrel with Knight and Price was to suggest that they should invoke a wider range of painterly precedent and rigorously apply their picturesque theory. This sometimes took the form of ridicule: "Our kitchens may be furnished after the designs of Teniers and Ostade, our stable after Woovermans, and we may learn to dance from Watteau and Zuccarelli."[31] On another occasion he invokes Watteau to make a more serious point: "In forest scenery, we trace the sketches of Salvator Rosa and of Ridinger; in park scenery, we may realize the landscapes of Claude and Poussin: but, in garden scenery, we delight in the rich embellishments, the blended graces of Watteau, where nature is dressed, but not disfigured, by art."[32] Painterly habits of seeing are perhaps more honored there, but Repton is principally concerned to make one of his fundamental points: namely, that there are different kinds of landscapes (for which we may well draw upon our painterly connoisseurship to appreciate), and that different kinds of topography require different treatments from a designer. It is Pope's "Consult the genius of the place" rescued and brought up to date for Repton's clients.

Repton's main territory for improvement tended to be around the house; this was either because he was called in at places where Brown had worked before him in the park, leaving less scope for fresh work, or because many clients were, like Mr. and Mrs. Simpson at Babworth, owners of more modest estates. Accordingly it is the authority of Watteau rather than Rosa that is invoked, not only because he supported Repton's preference for thickly wooded landscapes in the background, but also because his paintings endorse the garden as a locale for social activity.[33] It quickly became Repton's guiding principle that a modish sensibility for "scenes of horror, well calculated for the residence of Banditti"[34] consorted neither with the needs of his clients nor with the demands of the terrain where he worked. He notes himself that such opinions were not generally accepted when he first began to express them.[35]

Repton is acute enough and generous enough to praise Knight's estate at Downton Vale for its apt realization of visual structures learnt of Salvator Rosa:

> A narrow, wild, and natural path sometimes creeps under the beetling rocks, close by the margin of a mountain stream. It sometimes ascends to an awful precipice, from whence the foaming waters are heard roaring in the dark abyss below, or seen wildly dashing against its opposite banks; while, in other places, the course of the river Teme being impeded by natural ledges of rock, the vale presents a calm, glassy mirror, that reflects the surrounding foliage. The path, in various places, crosses the water by bridges of the most romantic and contrasted forms; and, branching in various directions, including some miles in length, is occasionally varied and enriched by caves and cells, hovels and covered seats, or other buildings, in perfect harmony with the wild but pleasing horrors of the scene.[36]

It is obvious to Repton that at Downton Vale Knight's preferred visual taste and the topography coincide happily. Equally, he notes that Price's place at Foxley, being less romantically situated than Knight's, admitted "some little sacrifice of picturesque beauty to neatness, near the house";[37] this in its turn was obviously responsible for the "shade of difference betwixt the opinions of Mr Price and Mr Knight."

But the design elements that between them Price and Knight endorsed were ill suited for the work Repton was called upon to do. He argues, rightly, that if they "were introduced in the gardens of a villa near the capital, or in the more tame, yet interesting, pleasure-grounds which I am frequently called upon to decorate, they would be . . . absurd, incongruous, and out of character."[38] His judgment is quickly confirmed by looking at the topography in which most of his work was executed. The very first Red Book which Repton prepared (though, in fact, for his third commission) dealt with Brandsbury in Middlesex in 1789. Lady Salisbury's villa was in sight of the city of London, views of which Repton retained (fig. 5.6); but he also registered his appreciation of the valuable grazing land by deliberately refraining from introducing "plantations," concentrating instead—in a way that would become his forte—upon the area immediately adjacent to the villa itself. The overall effect marks Repton out very early as a designer with a different aesthetic, a different attitude toward fashion, and above all a different clientele than Price and Knight or even Brown.[39]

Similarly in other of Repton's commissions, Knight's favorite repertoire would have suited neither the open spaces around Cobham Hall in Kent, nor the downland of Uppark, West Sussex, with its back cloth

5.6. Repton's proposed view of London from the grounds of Brandsbury, Middlesex. Brandsbury Red Book, 1789, folio 13. Dumbarton Oaks, Trustees for Harvard University.

of beech woods. Equally typical of the countryside in which Repton seems to work at his best is the whole of what he himself called "the beautiful valley from Welwin to Hertford"[40] that came to include his landscapes at Tewin Water and Panshanger. Even the potentially more picturesque scenery around Wyatt's Gothic house at Sheffield Park, that included a wooded lakeside already shaped by Brown, would not really have lent itself to the Gothic fantasies of Knight. Repton, in fact, introduces a terrace in front of the Gothic building, acknowledging that "real comfort, and . . . ideas of *picturesqueness,* are incompatible."[41] As he was to ask in 1816, though the "subjects represented by Salvator Rosa, and our English Mortimer, are deemed picturesque," are they therefore "fit objects to copy for the residence of man in a polished and civilized state?"[42] So around Lord Sidmouth's house in Richmond Park he replaces the picturesque idiom with symmetries of a more commodious and formal, if visually less attractive, garden design.

In some ways, as Repton is well aware, these revisions of picturesque gardening theory entail the revival of ideas from Pope's generation and even earlier. He urges upon his contemporaries what Pope had praised Lord Burlington for explaining to theirs:

'Tis Use alone that sanctifies Expense,
And splendor borrows all her rays from Sense.

It is accordingly the human criterion that is looked to in all designs. As early as his Red Book for Welbeck (1789) Repton offers an analogy, reminiscent of conservative aesthetics from Pope to Reynolds's *Discourses,* between history painting and landscape painting on the one hand and park scenery and forests on the other: parks and history painting "have a higher place in the scale of arts" because they concern themselves with men.[43] It is then hardly surprising that Repton greets so mirthfully various passages of Knight's poem, *The Landscape,* in which long neglected quarries, moldering abbeys, ruined castles, and antiquated cottages seem to be offered as suitable habitations for human beings. In their place, for reasons of "common use," "utility," and "convenience" Repton urges "close-mown grass, or firm gravel walks."[44] If these smack too much of art's interference, Repton would have retorted with Pope's injunction about Nature:

But treat the Goddess like a modest fair,
Nor overdress, nor leave her wholly bare.

It is a couplet that he seems to evoke in his praise of Watteau's gardens where "nature is dressed, but not disfigured, by art."

An excellent early example of Repton's tactics in adjudicating between the extreme picturesque demands of a site and human exigency is contained in the Red Book for Blaise Castle, upon which he drew only briefly for his publications.[45] The folly from which Blaise Castle took its name (fig. 5.7) was obviously a prime picturesque and romantic exhibit; it is the occasion of an enthusiastic flight of fancy by Catherine Morland in *Northanger Abbey:*

5.7. Humphry Repton, inside front cover of the Red Book for Blaise Castle, showing his trade card in the middle, with sketches of the new entry lodge he designed (above) and the folly or "castle" from which the estate took its name (below). Bristol City Museums.

"Blaise Castle!" cried Catherine, "what is that?"
"The finest place in England; worth going fifty miles at any time to see."
"What! is it really a castle—an old castle?"
"The oldest in the kingdom."
"But is it like what one reads of?"
"Exactly; the very same."
"But now, really, are there towers and long galleries?"
"By dozens."[46]

She never gets to see it, only dreaming of "narrow winding vaults" and a "low grated door." It would be nice to think that Jane Austen knew and even expected her readers to know that the Gothic fantasy built by Thomas Farr at Blaise in 1766 was neither old nor extensive enough to include all those towers and galleries and winding vaults. Repton, like Catherine, certainly responds to "this Romantic place," but, unlike her, tempers his enthusiasm at once with the sensible reflection that the folly itself would be "wholly inapplicable to a family residence." His task is consequently to respect and "preserve or heighten" its "native beauties," while allowing its owner his comfort and convenience.

Repton's major problem was to provide a landscape that honored the romantic associations of a "castle," yet was equally appropriate to the fine neoclassical house that William Petty had designed (fig. 5.8) and upon which work must obviously have started before Repton's visits to Bristol. He first removed the entrance from Henbury village, where already "a number of Villas or large country houses seem to dispute with each other by their size and cumbrous importance." The new and more isolated entry lodge was then designed in the Gothic taste (see fig. 5.7) after much deliberation, which the Red Book explains:

> Some difficulty occurs with respect to the name of Blaise Castle, and as the house neither does nor ought to partake of the castle-character, there may perhaps appear a little incongruity in making the entrance in that stile, yet I cannot propose an entrance-lodge of Grecian architecture to a house which is no where seen from the road, while the Castle, both from its giving name to the place and from its conspicuous situation, seems to demand a very different stile of entrance.

5.8. Humphry Repton, the "effect of a new house" in the landscape, Blaise Castle Red Book. Bristol City Museums.

The gatehouse also seemed in keeping with the new approach road that Repton arranged to pass an extravagantly rustic house already in the grounds and wind its way along the "shapes of the ground of this Romantic Place." Lest his excessively serpentine approach—a feature that in theory he detested—should be misunderstood, he explained at length how he had first been forced by the exigencies of a ravine to wind the road about and then had chosen to submit himself to the "genius of the place":

> I trust however that the line of road will be found perfectly easy and accessible on the ground, however violent it may appear on paper, and that when Time has thrown its ivy and creeping plants over the rawness of new walls and fresh hewn rocks, the approach will be in strict character with the wildness of the scenery, and excite admiration and surprise without any mixture of that terror which tho' it partakes of the sublime, is very apt to destroy the delights of romantic scenery. The gate being in character with the castle to which it is the prelude, introduces us to a wood with which it is in harmony, and I expect the stranger will be agreeably surprised to find that on quitting this wood, he is not going to a mouldering castle whose ruined turrets threaten destruction, and revive the horrors of feudal strife; but to a mansion of elegance, cheerfulness, and hospitality where the comfort of neatness is blended with the rude features of nature, without committing great violence on the Genius of the Place.

We should note Repton's deliberate tempering of the sublime and romantic terror by ideas of "agreeable surprise" and the comfortable assurance of social values.

These social considerations emerge more conspicuously when he turns his attention to the landscape that is seen or visited from the house, around which he grouped some formal features: a conservatory and a dairy, the latter a fine essay in the cottage style by his partner Nash (completed in 1802). Repton thinned trees to allow a view of a cottage (fig. 5.9) that would provide "an air of cheerfulness and inhabitancy to the scene which would without it be too sombre, because the castle tho' perfectly in character with the solemn dignity of the surrounding woods, increases rather than relieves the apparent solitude." He also planned the park so that its best features were accessible and reached by drives. By such means "frequent groups of carriages and company" would provide an "astonishing contrast to the solemn dignity" of the rest of the park:

5.9. View of the park from the house at Blaise Castle before Repton's landscaping, and the same view with the cottage revealed by clearing trees. Bristol City Museums.

> It is remarkable that no attempt should have been made to render objects of so much beauty and variety accessible in a carriage, for however interesting the walks in hilly countries may be, they can only be enjoyed by great labour and exertion; they require health of body and vigour of limbs to enjoy their romantic wonders, while the aged and the infirm have been excluded from the beauties of the place by the danger or difficulty of exploring them.

"One of the striking features" of Blaise, according to Repton, was its view toward the mouth of the River Severn (fig. 5.10). He deliberately eliminated its single perspective, a picturesque structure framed by trees, and provided instead a longer range of varied prospects of "water, of shipping, and distant mountains" that may be taken as the visitor *moves through* the park. It was an important early declaration by Repton that no landscape could properly and in practice be considered as a painting: "The spot from whence the view is taken, is in a fixed state to the painter; but the gardener surveys his scenery while in motion; and, from different windows in the same front, he sees objects in different situations."[47] As with the gardener, so with the regular inhabitants. Their daily involvement in a garden requires a variety of mental activities that no dedication to picturesque pleasure could provide. The "ideas of animation and movement," so crucial to his designs at Blaise and elsewhere, are not sufficiently clear in the conventionally picturesque sketches that he inserted in the Red Books. At Blaise itself he confessed that "I can show the effect of a new house instead of an old one, but I cannot describe those numberless beauties which may be brought before the eye in succession by the windings of a road, or the contrast of ascending and descending thro' a deep ravine of rich hanging woods." It is a paradox of Repton's work that even as he expresses his reservations about picturesque gardening he still presents clients with Red Books which contain seductive images that draw upon a full repertoire of picturesque idiom.[48] Moreover, his designs for finished landscapes like Sundridge Park were engraved for collections of picturesque views of country seats. But if his graphic work seems to make him as important a figure, say, as Gilpin in the picturesque vogue, his *written* commentaries constantly insist upon the different visual and psychological structures of gardens that are in use. It is almost as if he relies upon the different time sequences and modes of language to counteract the static qualities of any visual image. Pictures cannot convey movement, yet movement—either of deer or of boats on water[49]—

5.10. Views before and after removing the tunnel of trees along the drive which looks out over the River Severn at Blaise Castle. Bristol City Museums.

Repton thought a vital ingredient of landscape; and this his prose, unlike his sketches, *can* suggest. Occasionally his graphic work uses wider angles of vision than a painter would adopt, while some of his garden plans convey the sense of a passage through varieties of garden, obviously in an attempt to underline the psychological involvement of spectators with scenery. But he relies mostly upon his prose to remind us of movement in a landscape, either of objects in it or of the perceiving human spectator whose progress around a garden insures him many aspects and angles of vision.

Blaise Castle Red Book dates from 1795–1796. Though his trade card that appeared in it (see fig. 5.7) remained the same, with its richly wooded and romantic scene, dominated by the lonely tower from the Milton he loved to quote,[50] his practice increasingly emphasized the other element of its emblematic scene: Repton himself taking detailed measurements of a specific landscape in which human activity played a crucial part. Individual Red Books may indulge in picturesque "lapses," when the context allowed or required it, but the gradual temper of his designs, as the published compilations and commentaries insist, moved towards increased formality, especially around the house, and consequently a more frequent invocation of earlier garden styles and devices. Sensibility, in short, was carefully tutored by sense.

Repton's aesthetics may, indeed, be profitably compared with certain values that Jane Austen promotes in her novels. Though his name is, of course, invoked disparagingly in *Mansfield Park* ("any Mr. Repton")[51] when the question of Sotherton's improvement is being discussed, it is—in the light of that reference—surprising how many of her descriptions and discussions of landscaping parallel Repton's ideas. The education of Elizabeth Bennett, for instance, in *Pride and Prejudice* involves very Reptonian emphases. Her temperament favors inspiration, spontaneity, enthusiasm, and the personal touch; her sister's responds to regularity, propriety, and the comforts of discipline and precedent. Elizabeth learns to submit her personality to the claims upon it of rival modes of thought and conduct; her education is matched by Darcy's pride coming to appreciate Elizabeth's more spontaneous reactions. This process by which Elizabeth learns to "evaluate all that has happened to her in terms of the mean between the two extremes of the 'art' of human relationships and humans in their 'natural' association"[52] seems to me an exact parallel to the evolution of Repton's ideas during his career.

Her early exclamation—"What are men to rocks and mountains?"[53]—recalls Knight or Price. A large part of the process by which her judgment of human importance is altered is her experience of the very Reptonian landscape at Pemberley Woods:

> The park was very large, and contained great variety of ground. They entered it in one of its lowest points, and drove for some time through a beautiful wood, stretching over a wide extent.
>
> Elizabeth's mind was too full for conversation, but she saw and admired every remarkable spot and point of view. They gradually ascended for half a mile, and then found themselves at the top of a considerable eminence, where the wood ceased, and the eye was instantly caught by Pemberley House, situated on the opposite side of a valley, into which the road with some abruptness wound. It was a large, handsome, stone building, standing well on rising ground, and backed by a ridge of high woody hills;—and in front, a stream of some natural importance was swelled into greater, but without any artificial appearance. Its banks were neither formal, nor falsely adorned.[54]

Not only is it a typically Reptonian landscape—the richly wooded approach is curiously like Blaise Castle—with a careful adjudication between natural and formal elements around a house that stands upon rising ground (as he recommended at Blaise and at Welbeck) and from whose windows (in proper Repton fashion) Elizabeth sees the objects of the landscape "taking different positions";[55] but Elizabeth's approach takes her through the picturesque features toward the social world of the house and this movement coincides with her feeling that "to be mistress of Pemberley might be something." I think it is this landscape, carefully engineered for human participation, that forces us to register how far Elizabeth has come in educating her prejudices.

There is a similar use of a very Reptonian landscape in *Emma,* where Donwell Abbey is also the means by which readers are alerted to the heroine's new appreciation of her role in society:

> She felt all the honest pride and complacency which her alliance with the present and future proprietor could fairly warrant, as she viewed the respectable size and style of the building, its suitable, becoming, characteristic situation, low and sheltered—its ample gardens stretching down to meadows washed by a stream, of which the Abbey, with all the old neglect of prospect, had scarcely a sight—and its abundance of timber in rows and

> avenues, which neither fashion nor extravagence had rooted up. . . . It was just what it ought to be, and it looked what it was—and Emma felt an increasing respect for it, as the residence of a family of such true gentility, untainted in blood and understanding.[56]

The scene embodies many of Repton's principles—the propriety of the buildings, the avoidance of overly calculated picturesque vistas, the retention of old timber, and such formal features as avenues, together with the estate's exact appeal to the mind's judgment. Her phrase, "it looked what it was," even echoes Repton's advice on the cottage at Blaise Castle, that it "must partake of the wildness of the scenery without meanness; it must look like what it is, the habitation of a labourer who has the care of the adjoining woods, but its simplicity should be the effect of Art and not of accident; it must seem to belong to the proprietor of the mansion and the castle, without affecting to imitate the character of either."

Though Repton may seem to rely simply upon visual effects, his ultimate appeal is to the thinking as much as to the seeing visitor. His skepticism of Rosa-like romanticism is grounded on a conviction, frequently expressed, that there was no aspect of landscape gardening "so often mistaken or misunderstood, because mankind are apt to judge by the eye rather than by the understanding."[57] The eye, he thought, had excessively dominated the picturesque landscaping of a Knight or a Price. But the *mind* will only find a landscape interesting "when made habitable."[58] The habitations of men require not only considerations of their comfort and convenience, but a due regard for the ideas that their minds will be forced to entertain there.

Repton is determined to submit landscape ideas to what in *Sense and Sensibility* is called "the reasonable basis of common sense and observation";[59] "observation" nicely involves the seeing with the thinking response. Repton rebukes Knight and Price, as Tilney reproves Catherine Morland's Gothic and picturesque imagination, by invoking the "understanding" and a "sense of the probable."[60] Catherine's excessively visual preoccupations are satirized by Austen at one point with an echo of Price, who like the heroine of *Northanger Abbey,* found the "whole city of Bath . . . unworthy to make part of a landscape."[61] Jane Austen's criticism there of picturesque taste is the same as Repton continually makes; the positive and, indeed, logical outcome of his emphasis was his involvement in the urban planning of Cadogan and Russell Squares.[62]

Repton's demand of a landscape that it satisfy the mind's understanding of its schemes as well as the eyes' pleasure links him firmly, as it does Jane Austen, with certain eighteenth-century predecessors. Dr. Johnson, for example, never very warmly disposed toward landscape gardening, discovered upon his visit to Sir Rowland Hill's seat at Hawkstone that its calculated and impressive picturesqueness did not satisfy the mind. In his journal for 25 July 1774 he records that the

> ideas which it forces upon the mind, are the sublime, the dreadful, and the vast. Above, is inaccessible altitude, below, is horrible profundity. But it excels the garden of Ilam only in extent. Ilam has grandeur tempered with softness. The walker congratulates his own arrival at the place, and is grieved to think that he must ever leave it. As he looks up to the rocks his thoughts are elevated; as he turns his eyes on the valley, he is composed and soothed. He that mounts the precipices at Hawkestone, wonders how he came hither, and doubts how he shall return.

And just as Dr. Johnson recalled that the inhabitants of Hawkstone would not be "men of lawless courage and heroic violence," like actors from some Salvator Rosa melodrama, so Repton's understanding of a landscape commission paid specific attention to the people for whom he worked.

Both Repton and Jane Austen believed—and it is a notion that may be traced back through the eighteenth century to Shaftesbury—that fine aesthetic taste denotes excellence of moral character. It is implied in the remark from *Persuasion,* "the Musgraves, like their houses, were in a state of alteration, perhaps of improvement";[63] or, in Repton's words, "the same principles which direct taste in the polite arts, direct the judgement in morality."[64] He implies the equation of aesthetic and moral qualities, too, in the frequent appeal (more frequent as his career advances) to the role of understanding in judging landscape design. In his introduction to *Sketches and Hints* he makes what is a commonplace eighteenth-century remark, to the effect that "*true* taste in *landscape gardening,* as well as in all the other polite arts, is not an accidental effect, operating on the outward senses, but an appeal to the understanding";[65] he cites in support a similar remark from Burke's preface to the *Sublime and Beautiful.* Repton chooses, like Johnson at Hawkstone, to neglect the sublime in the interests of exactly those "social impulses" that Burke found more properly associated with the idea of the beautiful. And some pages after his quotation of Burke, Repton, discussing Tatton Park, proposes to make such improvements as will direct the mind to those situations where the sublime or "greatly extensive" is blended with the beautiful or "comfortable" and "interesting."[66]

Johnson's criteria are not only, like Repton's, ones of use, of who should inhabit a landscape, but also those of probability, appeals to what Repton in the *Fragments* calls a "taste founded on Reason."[67] What is reasonable, what the mind rather than the eye or fashion endorses, is Repton's basis for both principles and practice. Where his commentators have tended to see inconsistencies in his work I would prefer to identify the various results of a constant appeal to the understanding. Sometimes, for example, he allows Brown's habit of a ride in a belt of trees around an estate; at others, he argues that such a feature is ridiculous and lacks congruity in a park that is too small to need visiting in that way. He could oppose fences, especially when they obstructed the mental curiosity that he thought a proper human attribute; yet he argues against invisible fences that divide what the mind knows cannot be united anyhow—a park and a garden.[68] Often he may dislike Brown's shaven lawns stretching right up to a building, yet at Welbeck it seems reasonable to allow it because the house is thereby given an elevation that the mind requires for such a scale of building. The raised ground at Welbeck is a deceit, like the addition of the far piece of water at Tatton Park to imply a continuity with the body of water near the house; such deceits, Repton insists, must always satisfy "the mind, as well as the eye."[69]

Such appeals to the mental understanding endorsed, above all, Repton's return to formal gardening. Early in his career he recognized the necessary influence of architecture upon gardening design: "The perfection of landscape gardening depends on a concealment of those operations of *art* by which *nature* is embellished; but where buildings are introduced, *art* declares herself openly, and should, therefore, be very careful, lest she have cause to blush at her interference."[70] The logical extensions into a surrounding garden of a building's evident art dominate his thinking more and more, until he can write in *Fragments* of the need to "study the convenience of the mansion, to which the ground about it must be altered in the way most conducive to its uses and appearance, without fettering the plan by any fancied resemblance of nature. I am quite sure that the old magnificent taste for straight lines, and artificial shapes of ground, adjoining a palace, was more consonant to true taste and greatness of character, than the sweeping lines and undulating surface of modern gardening."[71] If one outcome of such thinking was his dedication to designs for London squares, another was his reintroduction into gardens of features from earlier styles: the imitation Tudor Lodge at Woburn Sands was provided with a garden and flowers copied from sixteenth-century paintings in the Duke of Bedford's collections. His designs for Cobham in Kent furnished, he thought, "a striking example of artificial arrangement for convenience, in the grounds immediately adjoining the house."[72] At Ashridge, Repton managed a fine modulation of formal elements, providing both the variety essential to the mental pleasures of a garden and the order required near architectural features. Ashridge, like Woburn Sands, testifies to his research among earlier gardening styles for such devices as the raised flower bed or the trellis-covered walk. While at Endsleigh, one of his most famous last designs, similar features accompany a terrace that is introduced to mark man's proper domain near the house and its separation from the landscape beyond. Such discriminations and their realization in actual designs declare Repton's vital contribution to the history of landscape gardening.

PART TWO

Pictures, Picturesque, Places

6 PICTURESQUE MIRRORS AND THE RUINS OF THE PAST

The eighteenth century is so specially a watershed between Renaissance and modernism that its artistic culture is susceptible to both atavistic and progressive interpretations. However, it is the latter that tend to predominate. For our debts to nineteenth-century liberalism and expansionism ("the ringing grooves of change"[1]) are still repaid by critical assumptions which are, at their most demure, evolutionary, at their most aggressive, revolutionary. Discussions of the English landscape garden—crucial, because it is a unique product of the eighteenth century—assume that it must be explained in teleological terms; thus Erwin Panofsky, under the engaging cover of discussing "The Ideological Antecedents of the Rolls-Royce Radiator,"[2] sees the "new English garden with its rolling lawns, its seemingly casual though artfully arranged clumps of trees, its ponds and brooks, and its serpentine footpaths" (p. 274) as "essentially modern" (p. 276). Panofsky reads the "informal" landscaping, "subjective and emotional," as "diametrically opposed" (p. 275) to Palladian classicism in contemporary architecture:

> In short, the English eighteenth century stands, at one and the same time, both far to the right and far to the left of contemporary developments on the Continent: a severely formal rationalism, tending to look for support to classical antiquity, contrasts but co-exists with a highly subjective emotionalism, drawing inspiration from fancy, nature and the mediaeval past, which, for want of a better expression, may be described as "Romantic." (p. 277)

It is a generally accepted account of the English landscape garden.

But the conduct and terminology of such arguments are very revealing. "Romantic" is invoked for want of a better label—it is chosen, in fact, because the landscape movement seems to have culminated in, at least contributed to, romanticism. But this teleological assumption has already effected Panofsky's description of the landscape garden as "subjective and emotional," which in its turn leads toward labeling it as "essentially modern." Further, he sees even *within* the landscape movement a similar progression, which also spreads its later color over the whole cycle; he writes of "the great English gardeners of the eighteenth century from Bridgeman, the original designer of Stowe . . . through William Kent, 'the true father of modern gardening' . . . to Lancelot ("Capability") Brown. . . ." (pp. 273–274). In that historical perspective, to borrow a phrase from Joyce's story, "The Dead," "Brown is everywhere." But the stylistic radicalism which we associate with Brown is *not* to be found in the work of the earliest of those landscape gardeners, Bridgeman, to whom Panofsky's lyrical passage on "rolling lawns" does not apply.[3]

The "new, English garden," in short, was never as new as historians like to think. When William Kent is termed by Panofsky "the most advanced among the contemporary garden designers" in the Palladian circle around Burlington (p. 276), he is being judged in the same teleological way; whereas his garden designs are just as crucially conservative, atavistic, translating into English some Italian Renaissance assumptions about classical gardens and villas.[4] In which case, of course, there would be no question of the strange alliance which Panofsky diagnosed at Chiswick between an "uncompromisingly 'classical' style of architecture with an essentially modern treatment of the surrounding grounds" (p. 276). For both allude nostalgically to Italy.

Panofsky's witty and agile essay furnishes one other methodological lesson. His title invites us to contemplate a historical inquiry into the *antecedents* of the Rolls-Royce radiator; these are traced backward to the eighteenth-century landscape garden, to thirteenth- and fourteenth-century illuminations and Gothic ornament, and to early Latin writing in England, in all of which he discovers the same "strikingly contrastive phenomena" as the Rolls-Royce displays: "it conceals an admirable piece of engineering behind a majestic Palladian temple front; but this Palladian temple front is surmounted by the windblown 'Silver Lady' in whom *art nouveau* appears infused with the spirit of unmitigated 'Romanticism'" (p. 288). But the basic assumption is not historicist so much as culminatory—the radiator "sums up, as it were, twelve centuries of Anglo-Saxon preoccupations and aptitudes," just as it is impossible to read the seventh-century rhapsody, *Hisperica Famina,* "without thinking of Ossian and William Turner" (p. 283). Were it not for the insistent impression I derive from Panofsky's essay that he may generally be satirizing Pevsner's *The Englishness of English Art,* to which one of his footnotes alludes, his argument might be offered as another example of history written in terms of a "mythology of prolepsis," whereby actions must await the future to achieve their meaning, which our retrospection provides.[5]

Another aspect of English eighteenth-century culture where analysis tends to offer prefigurative accounts is the picturesque. Modern criticism has been attracted to this phenomenon because it offers intimations of our contemporary aesthetics; there is, for example, the picturesque manipulation of purely formal effects, its separation of aesthetic from moral and religious categories.[6] This is evidently "modern," as are its celebration of instinct and accident, the dissociations and random juxtapositions "without copula of logical enunciation," and the witty complexity and playfulness of picturesque compositions.[7] This discovery of particulary modernist habits in picturesque aesthetics is most explicit in H. M. McLuhan's "Tennyson and Picturesque Poetry," an essay which traced the picturesque moment through Hallam's critique of Tennyson's early poetry to the *paysages intérieurs* of modern symbolism. But even Martin Price, in "The Picturesque Moment," is concerned to chart what he calls the movement "from the picturesque to the sublime, from the aesthetic to the moral or metaphysical"; it was a movement, he added, which had its "pivot in Wordsworth" (p. 287). His interest in this moment of eighteenth-century aesthetics certainly enlarges our view of the picturesque itself; but his overall strategy is to neglect the specific cultural contexts of what Northrop Frye has called the "age of sensibility"[8] and merge it imperceptibly with the romanticisms of Wordsworth and Keats, even though Frye had strenuously argued for a very different late-eighteenth-century climate of feeling and ideas in which the picturesque flourished.

As with the modern critical histories of the early English landscape garden, our interest in the picturesque tends to be proleptic, concerned more with what it produced, more with what romantic artists achieved by rejecting, absorbing or somehow going "beyond" it, than with why and how it became crucial in the first place. Even Christopher Hussey's full-scale treatment of the phenomenon defines it as an "interregnum between classic and romantic."[9] The dynamics of the picturesque for Hussey are revealed in each art's passage through its influence into a world where "the eye and the imagination had learnt to work for themselves" (p. 17). The tendency, therefore, of such criticism is to tolerate the picturesque or the early "formal" elements of a landscape garden, to register them as necessary stages on the route to a larger perfection.

The "interregnum" notion of Hussey or Panofsky's "contrastive" one may help us appreciate a peculiar doubleness in cultural ideas; but it does so at the expense of asking where the constituents of that intermediate territory came from in the first place. Picturesque critiques focus upon the theories of Gilpin, Price, Alison, or Knight, for example, which are themselves *post facto,* rather than upon the habits and procedures which supplied the materials of those aesthetics, upon how people behaved as amateurs of the picturesque and upon why its patterns answered some of their mental, psychological needs.[10] In the essay that follows these preliminary grumbles about our habitual methods of studying the past in terms of its subsequent dénouement, I want to penetrate behind not only modern theories of the picturesque, but late eighteenth-century and early nineteenth-century ones as well. I start by examining two practical aspects of the picturesque moment—its use of the mirror and its fascination with ruins. Then it may be possible to explain an essential but generally unremarked historical fact—that the picturesque had its most articulate and pervasive moment at a time when the traditions of *ut pictura poesis* were being challenged.[11] Not only Lessing's famous attack on the sister arts in his *Laocoön,* but French and English scepticism about the allegorical, hence readable, syntax of painting opened the way for the picturesque attention to formal beauties, leaving unresolved any fresh means of linking mental and emotional explanations to visual experience. The picturesque was an attempt, I suggest, to discover those means. This historical perspective will perhaps explain why William Gilpin, for instance, was hailed by a contemporary as the "*ne plus ultra* of the pen and pencil united."[12] For the picturesque moment was constituted of historical and aesthetic doubleness: looking backward to traditional Renaissance modes of formulating experience as well as forward to our own private and purely formal expressions; looking to both visual and verbal languages, in old and new conjunctions, for its proper dialect.

If there was a picturesque moment in practice, it occurred whenever a tourist looked into his "Claude glass," called after the French painter, Claude Lorrain, although it is fairly certain that he himself never used one.[13] The use of the glass is recorded in a pencil study by Gainsborough (fig. 6.1) and constantly recalled by the illustrations to Gilpin's picturesque *Tours* with their views held in oval frames (fig. 6.2). The glass was popularized and exemplified in Thomas Gray's notes on his Lake District walking tour, published in 1775:

> On the ascent of the hill above Appleby the thick hanging wood and the long reaches of the Eden . . . winding below with views of the castle and town gave much employment to the mirror. . . .
>
> From hence I got to the *Parsonage* a little before sunset, and saw in my glass a picture, that if I could transmit to you, and fix in all the softness of its living colours, would fairly sell for a thousand pounds. . . .[14]

As Gray makes clear, the "glass" was, for him, a mirror, which William Mason explained as "a Plano-convex Mirror of about four inches diameter on a black foil, and bound up like a pocket book."[15] The mirror used by the artist in Gainsborough's sketch is circular, but some being sold as late as 1883 in Philadelphia were rectangular. The glass, however, could also be what that name implied—a series of variously coloured glasses, framed and mounted like a pocket magnifying glass; by looking through different combinations of them, the user could tint the landscape he was viewing *au choix*. This was, in fact, the common denominator of glasses and mirror, for the latter could be backed—as was Gray's—with dark foil, but silver backing for overcast weather was a recommended alternative.[16]

The use of the mirror (I shall be less concerned, for reasons that will soon be clear, with the simple glasses) concentrated for its owner all picturesque possibilities. Here is Gray again, this time at Kirkstall Abbey: "The gloom of these ancient cells, the shade & verdure of the landscape, the glittering & murmur of the stream, the lofty towers & long perspectives of the church . . . detain'd me for many hours, & were the truest subjects for my glass I have yet met with."[17] The mirror captures the rough, intricate textures and chiaroscuro; Gray records this appeal both to his sense of aesthetic formalism and to his mental curiosity—the concern of the eye matched with a verbal exposition; the experience of real space among the ruins—his "long perspectives of the church"—is translated into the illusionist reflection in the tinted glass. There is, perhaps above all, the exquisite solitariness, the privacy of the

6.1. Thomas Gainsborough, artist using a Claude glass, drawing. Department of Prints and Drawings, British Museum, London (Oo.2–27).

6.2. "Furness-abbey," from William Gilpin, Observations, relative chiefly to Picturesque Beauty, made in the year 1772, on several parts of England; particularly the Mountains, and Lakes of Cumberland, and Westmoreland *(London, 1792). Dumbarton Oaks, Trustees for Harvard University.*

glass, into which a large scene was gathered by the slightly convex surface of the mirror, yet which only Gray's eyes could contemplate. This private occupation would have been further emphasized by the necessity for Gray to turn his back upon the scene to be viewed in his glass.

As well as these personal dimensions, the mirror had various traditional sanctions. It was the privileged metaphor of artistic representation, authorizing—according to one's emphasis—either accuracy of vision or the capture of the *belle nature.* To the picturesque tourist and amateur artist it reflected the real world, yet also collected carefully chosen images within the oval or rectangular frame and colored them with its one, coordinating tint. It was both an objective, cognitive activity and a private, creative one, as the mirror's user turned his back upon the scene and withdrew into his own reflections.

The reversed images in the glass, paralleling of course the upside-down images we receive upon our retinas, were a visible token of that joint world of optical and mental *reflections,* the latter being what Locke called "the notice which the mind takes of its own operations, and the manner of them." This doubleness of *reflection* is likewise announced in the relationship of *speculation* and *speculum,* the Latin for mirror. And the human, psychological activity is dramatized in the myth of Narcissus gazing at his reflected image in a clear spring, an extremely popular theme in post-Renaissance painting, especially Poussin's[18] and in eighteenth-century descriptive poetry. Many passages in Thomson's *Seasons,* for instance, explore the doubleness of *reflection,* none of them more suggestively than the description of the "sprightly youth" in *Summer,*

> *Gazing the inverted landscape, half afraid*
> *To meditate the blue profound below.*

The unusual transitive usage of both *gaze* and *meditate* contributes strongly to the poet's sense of the congruence of looking and thinking.[19]

Many of these implications are suggested in picturesque texts. Joseph Spence at Stourhead, visiting the Temple of Apollo, seems to intuit the double aspect of *reflection* when he writes: "When you sit deep within the Temple, you wou'd think it was built close by the Lake, & when you walk round the Latter below, you are almost continually entertained by the Reflection of it, in the water."[20] Similarly, in one of William Gilpin's accounts of using his mirror, not while stationary, but while riding in his chaise, we learn that its images "are like visions of the imagination; or the brilliant landscapes of a dream. Forms, and colours in brightest array, fleet before us; and if the transient glance of a good composition happen to unite with them, we should give any price to fix and appropriate the scene."[21] Cognitive and creative processes seem to unite there, exemplifying the sense, which Martin Price drew to our attention in the picturesque moment, of play between "the need for reasonable common truths" and the "imaginative power of arbitrary structures and accidental associations."[22] Because of their rapid passage across the glass in this instance, the forms and colors are both objective and dreamlike. And, as Gilpin says, they may be "appropriated" in sketch or watercolor, where factual record and creative enterprise are mutually supportive, where specificity, the desire to make memoranda on the spot, and the idealizing and generalizing instincts of traditional landscape painting also modify each other's endeavors.[23]

Ruins were a prime ingredient of any picturesque view. They satisfied, in the first place, a love for broken and rough surfaces, which was at the center of the picturesque practice: "in ruins, even of the most regular edifices, the lines are so softened by decay or interrupted by demolition; the stiffness of design is so relieved by the accidental intrusion of springing shrubs and pendant weeds."[24] Yet long before the picturesque aesthetic was formulated at the end of the eighteenth century, ruins had obviously called into play what would be the picturesque imagination later. Thus Vanbrugh's famous suggestion to the Duchess of Marlborough that she should send for a landscape painter to design the Blenheim landscape was perhaps prompted by his wish to preserve and make central in a new design the ruin of Woodstock Manor (see fig. 1.4).[25] And William Gilpin's first recorded use of the term *picturesque* in 1748 was in front of some simulated ruined arches in the gardens at Stowe (fig. 6.3).[26]

But equally essential in a ruin was that it should have been "of some grandeur and elegance" and "should refer to somewhat really interesting"[27] so that the associative faculty could be brought into play. For what attracts one to ruins is their incompleteness, their instant declaration of a loss which we can complete in our imaginations. From Thomas Burnet, enquiring into the causes of the broken world of mountains in *The Sacred Theory of the Earth,* to Turner or Byron, meditating upon the vacancies of Roman remains, ruins have invited the mind to complete their fragments. Thus at Stowe it was the con-

6.3. "An Artificial Peice of Rock-work," from Stow. The gardens . . . *(Buckingham: B. Seeley, 1750). Dumbarton Oaks, Trustees for Harvard University.*

trived fragments of a Temple of Modern Virtue juxtaposed to the completeness of the nearby parish church and Temple of Ancient Virtue that enabled Gilpin to work out and complete the meaning of the Elysian Fields.[28]

The formal and the associative aspect of ruins are often encountered together. The influential treatise, *Cours de peinture par principes,* of 1708 by Roger de Piles, translated into English in 1743, advised that "BUILDINGS in general are a great ornament in landscip, even when they are *Gothick,* or appear partly inhabited, and partly ruinous"; but in addition to that general visual appeal, "they raise the imagination by the use they are thought to be designed for."[29] And from painted *landskips* the transition to garden scenery was easily accomplished; Batty Langley suggested as termination points for garden walks "mishapen Rocks, strange Precipes, Mountains, old Ruins."[30] A series of gardenist theorists and practitioners from Pope, through Shenstone and Chambers, to Walpole and Whately found some of their most satisfying visual and mental experiences before ruins: Pope at Netley Abbey[31] or in the gardens of Lord Digby at Sherborne—"What should induce my Lord D. the rather to cultivate these ruins and do honour to them, is that they do no small honour to his Family; that Castle, which was very ancient, being demolished in the Civil wars after it was nobly defended by one of his Ancestors in the cause of the King."[32] For Shenstone "RUINATED structures" pleased for the irregularity of their structure as well as "the latitude they afford the imagination, to conceive an enlargement of their dimensions."[33] Such completion of ruined spaces, colonizing of their vacancies, becomes part of the absurd manipulation of visitors in William Chambers's Chinese projections: in his 1757 *Designs of Chinese Buildings etc.* ruined structures become simply one element in a repertoire of Gothic chinoiserie, apt if eccentric examples of Burke's sublime, adumbrated in his treatise the previous year; in 1772, perhaps because Chambers had meantime had the opportunity of realizing some Chinese gardenist ideas at Kew, the effects of ruins are explored in slightly more measured and explicable terms.[34]

But the cult of and response to ruins serve to document an important change in eighteenth-century habits of mind. To put it succinctly,[35] there is a movement from registering precise and detailed meanings of ruins, completing their vacancies with learned and specific knowledge, to responding simply to their impressionistic suggestions of decay and loss. The graph of representative responses might be drawn from Marvell's detailed extrapolation of personal (Fairfax's) and public (English) history from the nunnery ruins at Nun Appleton to Walpole's enthusiasm at Hagley: "There is a ruined castle, bult by Miller . . . it has the true rust of the Barons' Wars."[36] A similar pattern of responding to ruins has been traced in France: a movement from learned identification of specific classical remains to generalized evocations like those in Hubert Robert's paintings, which Diderot praised for their inducement of "la rêverie et . . . la mélancholie."[37]

The English antiquarians of the seventeenth century found their country particularly rich in post-Reformation ruins; their sense of the past itself, as in Aubrey's writings or more sustainedly in a work like Dugdale's *Monasticon,* was of ruined fragments needing reconstruction.[38] In much topographical painting during the later seventeenth and eighteenth century we may trace a similar attention to ruins in the English countryside.[39] And in the early English landscape garden, if not ruins, at least fragments of other or former worlds were designed to elicit careful and precise reactions from visitors; such were the intentions of items as different as the classical statues supposedly filched from Hadrian's villa, which adorned Lord Burlington's exedra at Chiswick, and the mineral specimens covering the walls of Pope's grotto.[40]

Yet as the taste for gardens, landscape paintings and scenery itself grew during the eighteenth century, as more people acquired the habit of responding to items in a landscape, yet brought to it less skill and learning than earlier amateurs, antiquarians, and virtuosi, the specificity of attention diminished. It depended, inevitably, upon the genre employed: Philip Yorke, visiting Fountains Abbey (fig. 6.4) in 1744, records approximate measurements of various parts of the former monastery in some attempt to *understand* the ruins, and he writes a private journal which accommodates such amateur archaeological interests; a poem on the same topic of the 1730s, however, is committed rather to mood and more general reminiscence:

Where Prayers were read, and pious Anthems sung,
Now Heaps of Rubbish the Apartments throng.
Up roofless Walls the clasping Ivy creeps,
Where many a Bird of Prey in Safety sleeps:
Or finds in dreary Caves a kind Retreat,
And broods on Rapine in her gloomy Seat.

William Gilpin's visit to Fountains is recorded in his *Northern Tour;* his interests are largely visual—dismay at Aislabie's tidying up of the site, concern to establish for his readers the precise disposition of a ruin and its relationship to the ground on which it stands; otherwise his only interest in the meaning or significance of the abbey is that it promotes "Solitude being therefore the reigning idea of the scene."[41]

The history of the taste for ruins, then, may be seen to exemplify or parallel Thomas Whately's account of a shift from emblematical to expressive images in gardens, which is discussed more fully in chapter 3 above. The shift relates to a change from a landscape where the premium is upon precise encoding of ideas, stories, themes to one where the visitor's decoding is privileged, even if this in its turn accentuates more personal, solipsist, and (what Whately's called) "transitory" ideas. However, at whatever point in this scale of public/private meaning we alight, the crucial aspect is always the languages—visual (painterly), verbal, or gardenist—invoked to articulate the ideas.

In *Polymetis* Joseph Spence expressed his mistrust of allegorical and emblematic devices and prefered to fall back upon the position that "the figures of things themselves speak . . . the clearest language."[42] This, depending upon your position and artistic practice, entailed either some difficulties or some exciting advantages. The clear language of things, unlike the by now largely arcane grammar of the emblem book, yielded

6.4. *Anthony Walker after Balthasar Nebot,* Fountains Abbey, Yorkshire, *from the park of Studley Royal, 1758. British Library.*

few generally shared ideas and promoted more personal and ad hoc interpretations. We may see the absence of a traditional readable syntax at work in Thomas Gainsborough's landscape paintings and studies, which eschew such conventional modes of meaning to concentrate upon the formal delights of represented shapes and pigment (fig. 6.5). Gainsborough is here at one with the picturesque movement. Thus William Gilpin in his essay on "Picturesque Beauty" celebrated the forms, texture and "outlines" of nature, the "bark of a tree . . . the rude summit, and craggy sides of a mountain"; similarly, he argued that the architect would "break the front of his pile with ornaments . . . to add variety" of texture.[43] This divorce of aesthetic, formalist qualities from the moral and religious meaning and values of a picture or scene was doubtless both cause and effect of the disaffection with allegorical and related imagery.

Now the consequences of this shift in the modes of reading and representing scenery, registerd so dramatically, as we have seen, in garden design and theory, also had repercussions on the picturesque. Indeed, the close connections of picturesque and landscape gardening, no less close for being often elusive,[44] would explain how it was that upon the picturesque movement (including reactions to it) devolved the attempt to recover fresh modes of linking mental, emotional, and verbal explanations to visual experience. Hence the tribute which the *Anti-Jacobin Review* paid to Gilpin in 1800 that he possessed "the eye of the Painter, the Poet, and the Moralist."[45]

Gardens were thought of, if not specifically designed on the model of, pictures (as Stourhead may have been[46]). Vanbrugh's classic advice to "send for a landscape-painter" has already been noticed. No less famous was Addison's recommendation to a man of taste "to make a pretty *Landskip* of his own possessions."[47] There were two consequences of this pictorial structuring of gardens: they shared, at least in the early part of the eighteenth century, the iconographical language of painterly traditions; they trained the eye to appreciate shape, form, and organization of landscape outside the garden. But the invocation of paintings also became a fairly loose language by which to record one's reaction to a scene either in or outside a garden. Thus Horace Walpole can describe to Richard Bentley the beauties and associations of Hagley Park by invoking Sadeler's prints and Poussin's painting: "There is a hermitage, so exactly like those in Sadeler's prints, on the brow of a shady mountain, stealing peeps into the glorious world below! and

6.5. Maria Catherina Prestel after Thomas Gainsborough, The Country Churchyard, *aquatint, 1790. The engraved inscription relates this quintessentially picturesque view—with its ruins and busy detailing of the shrubbery and trees—to Thomas Gray's famous "Elegy in a Country Churchyard," and thereby locates it within the verbal/visual traditions of the picturesque. Yet, without a caption (as in a related sketch by Gainsborough), the scene is largely a graphic play with forms and texture.*

there is such a pretty well under a wood, like the Samaritan woman's in a picture of Niccolo Poussin!"[48] From using pictures in that way, as a kind of shorthand between friends, it was a small step to neglecting painterly syntax altogether and expressing one's own feelings at any given point of a landscape as best one could. Capability Brown's gardens, of course, deliberately eliminated traditional iconographical imagery—though Spence refused to understand it even when it did survive. Amidst Brown's creations, in the proper sense *formal* gardening, the eye provided the mind with no precoded messages, no language of idea or feeling. What temples and statues survived must have been, as figures in landscapes for Gainsborough, just "some little business for the eye." Repton, in his picturesque phase after "succeeding" Brown, could offer Grecian or Gothic architecture to clients, not for any intellectual purpose, but simply for the aesthetic possibilities of their shapes among forms of tree.[49]

Yet the picturesque emphasis upon aesthetic effects, although the movement's major contribution and probably the aspect which most appeals to our modern sensibilities, was never separated entirely from those human concerns for which in the past iconographical language had spoken and for which a new one was evidently needed. A need for both verbal and visual responses to experience, in fact, seems a permanent constituent of the human brain.[50] A fresh syntax with which to describe landscape experience with due regard to verbal as well as visual was ensured in two ways—through reactions to the excessive or "mere" formalism by designers and philosophers nevertheless sympathetic to the picturesque; and through the very contingencies by which picturesque amateurs practised and proclaimed their enthusiasm.

The reactions to mere formalism are again most quickly illustrated from garden history. In face of Capability Brown's austere designs, which appealed for their marvelously consistent manipulation of natural shapes, lines and colours, other designers brought "meaning" back into the garden, however absurdly. William Chambers introduced Chinese imagery at Kew; but signficantly this solution was generally ridiculed because it directed the attention too categorically. Richard Payne Knight, who caricatured a typical Brownian park in his poem "The Landscape" as excessively bald and spare, sought to fill it with details which were derived from and visitors were supposed to relate to their experience of landscape paintings by Rosa and the Dutch school. This in its turn annoyed Humphry Repton, but throughout all his adjustments of some of the more absurd picturesque practices Repton upholds the idea that landscape architecture should appeal as well to the mind as to the eye. In this he came close to Knight, though the Knight who is author of *An Analytical Inquiry into the Principles of Taste* rather than the excesses of "The Landscape, A Didactic Poem." Knight wanted the mind to have opportunities for free association, without, as Chambers's Chinese items had done, dictating to it:

> To a mind richly stored, almost every object of nature or art, that presents itself to the senses, either excites fresh trains and combinations of ideas, or vivifies and strengthens those which existed before: so that recollection enhances enjoyment, and enjoyment brightens recollection. Every insect, plant, or fossil, which the peasant treads upon unheeded, is, to the naturalist and philosopher, a subject of curious inquiry and speculation, first, as to its structure, formation, or means of existence.[51]

It is obvious that such mental associations, whatever the mechanism by which you explain them, require words for their articulation. The role of the word in other aspects of picturesque theory and practice, if generally unremarked, is no less crucial. We have seen how the sight of ruins prompts the spectator to complete them. The mirror also authorizes both visual and mental worlds. It was therefore inevitable that the picturesque constituted itself as a fresh alliance of those old (and ugly) sister arts of poetry and painting.

There were various modes of combining word and image. The least interesting, but usually the more verbose, was the verbal commentary made upon the formal visual delights of texture, shapes, variety, chiaroscuro, etc. (fig. 6.6). Thus Gray, walking in Borrowdale in the Lake District, articulates his aesthetic pleasure in the landscape itself, while declaring less overtly how his eye seeks painterly structures from foreground to background:

> Our path here tends to the left, & the ground gently rising, & cover'd with a glade of scattering trees and bushes on the very margin of the water, opens both ways the most delicious view, that my eyes ever beheld, behind you are the magnificent heights of Walla-crag; opposite lie the thick hanging woods of Egremont & Newland-valley, with green & smiling fields embosom'd in the dark cliffs; to the left the jaws of Borrodale, with that turbulent Chaos of mountain behind mountain roll'd in confusion; beneath you, & stretching far away to the right, the shining

> purity of the Lake, just ruffled by the breeze enough to shew it is alive, reflecting rocks, woods, fields, & inverted tops of mountains, with the white buildings of Keswick, Crostwaitchurch, & Skiddaw for a background at a distance.[52]

Such a commentary seeks to translate what was notable in a visual experience into verbal discourse.

Another use of word with image was, as we have seen in Payne Knight, the articulation of associations—Gray's allusion to a capitalized "Chaos" in that passage above suggests the scope and purpose of this form of picturesque commentary.[53] The translation of mental associations often took the form—analogous perhaps to an eighteenth-century painter's use of allegorical images—of citing popular literary passages; Pope's "Eloisa to Abelard" provided frequent quotations for picturesque travelers, as did the poetry of William Mason and James Thomson. Thus, Mrs. Elizabeth Montagu, watching the Cordeliers at Spa, Germany, in 1763, uses whether consciously or not, Pope's "Eloisa":

> Their solemn step, lugubre habit, and the base voice of their chaunting deepen'd the murmur of the falling floods, and shed a browner horror on the woods. The dreary desart, the woods, the rocks, the cascades, and all the objects we look'd upon borrowed from, and lent solemnity to this religious ceremony.[54]

Other poets yielded travelers a public and established syntax for explaining their more than formal delight in natural phenomena. The influential "Description of the Lake at Keswick" by John Brown discourses graphically on the "broken" cliffs hanging over the lake, of "a variety of waterfalls," and of the sudden glimpses of distant mountainscapes and then caps this formal enthusiasm with the lines

> *Where active Fancy travels beyond Sense,*
> *And pictures things unseen.*[55]

Other tourists, less sensitive visually, simply invoked the fancies of James Thomson or William Mason, as William Hutchinson's *Excursion to the Lakes* (1776) did to treat of the famed Lodore Falls. Mason's phrase, "the lone majesty of untamed nature," served Mrs. Carter, friend of Mrs. Montagu, to categorize the scenery outside Tunbridge Wells.[56] This picturesque habit of, in Anna Seward's words of *Ossian,* "Poetical descriptions and pencilled resemblances,"[57] required a fairly agile literary memory. An alternative means of associating words with

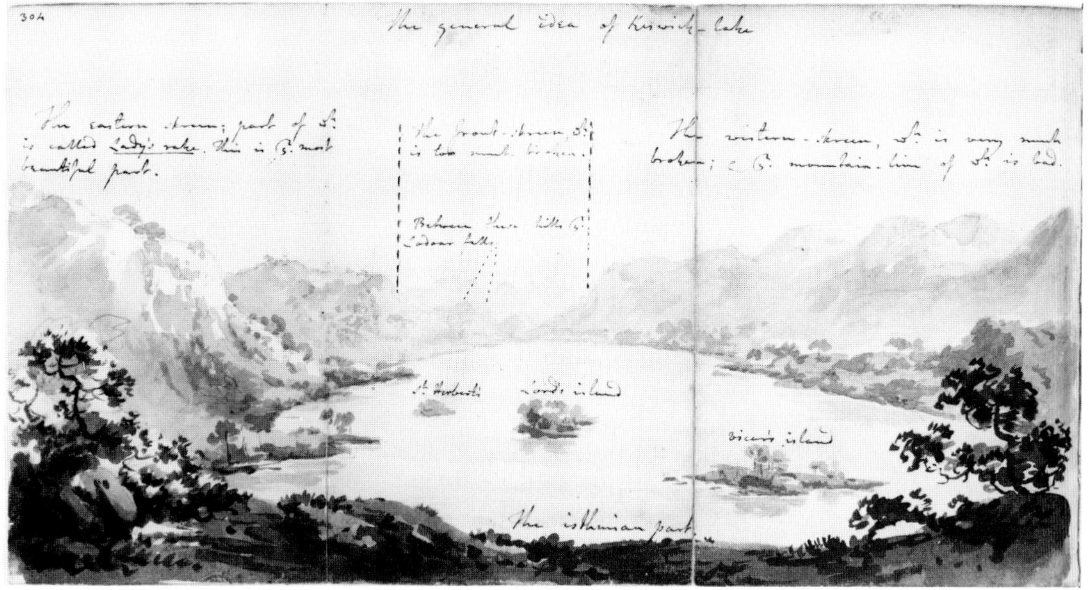

6.6. William Gilpin, "The general idea of Keswick-lake," from the manuscript of his Lakes Tour Notebook (1772). Bodleian Library, Oxford. Gilpin's memorandum glosses visual notations with words of identification and association.

visual experience was often achieved by the simple expedient of carrying on one's travels the published commentaries of other people—Hutchinson in Keswick had Brown's famous *Letter;* Hannah More in 1789, like the Wordsworths later, carried a copy of Gilpin down the Wye. "I had rather," said Mrs. Montagu, "wander in the woods with such an Author."[58]

One presumably inevitable feature of this literary element in the picturesque is that the verbal commentary announced or recalled the pictorial education that lay behind the cult; thus Brown explained that "the full perfection of Keswick"—namely "beauty, horror, and immensity united"—could only be indicated by the "united Powers of Claude, Salvator and Poussin":

> The first should throw his delicate sunshine over the cultivated vales, the scattered cots, the groves, the lakes and wooded islands. The second should dash out the horrors of the rugged cliffs, the steeps, the hanging rocks and foaming waterfalls, while the grand pencil of Poussin should crown the whole, with the majesty of an impending mountain.[59]

Such invocations, for amateurs of the picturesque, were an acceptable shorthand (Walpole's "Precipes, mountains, torrents, wolves, rumblings, Salvator Rosa"[60]) and, for the fashionable mob of picturesque travelers, easy because empty gestures; at Taymouth, another bluestocking, Mrs. Chapone, announces that "even a Milton's pen, or a Salvator Rosa's pencil would fail to give you a complete idea of it."[61] Yet it is significant that even its most trite formulation invokes both verbal and visual languages to constitute the picturesque response.

In the light of these unstrenuous reactions it is not surprising that the picturesque came under heavy fire in the early years of the nineteenth century. It is a commonplace that many major artistic figures in English romanticism—I am thinking in the first place of Wordsworth and Coleridge, Constable and Turner—found that they had to reject picturesque ideas and strategies. The taste, especially in its extreme emphasis upon formal rather than moral or metaphysical elements, was a way of refusing experience or of limiting it to selected visual items. Rowlandson's illustrations of Dr. Syntax in search of the picturesque simply and wittily underline that limitation by applying the visual values of variety, ruggedness, and surprise to the human figure rather than the scenery. And Jane Austen mocked those of her characters who preferred mountains to men or who were so sophisticated in their picturesque taste that they could not bear to look at the whole city of Bath because it did not lend itself to pictorial representation.[62]

Yet the rejection of the picturesque did not mean a radical break with its characteristic strategies. Just as the early English landscape garden continued to use iconographical language and to derive some of its essential ideas from Italian Renaissance gardens, just as the picturesque movement found fresh adjustments of old habits, so romanticism maintained distinctly picturesque modes of proceeding. This would require another essay to explore. But let me end with suggestions on the three items discussed here. The day of the ruin, especially artificial ruins and ruins in gardens, may have been over; but the instinct for the fragmentary, the indistinct or the suggestively incomplete, with which the cult of ruins had been imbued, survived, for example, in something like Constable's record of hidden, partial, or obscure items in a landscape and the related application of his paint in broad, diffuse ways, all of which require us to explore and even "explain" them. Similarly, Claude mirrors held in the hand went out of fashion, but they surrendered their primacy to reversed images in real water—Wordsworth's "bosom of the steady lake," Constable's Stour or Turner's Venetian lagoon—and to the mind's reflections.

A writer like Wordsworth may have tried to evade a primary dependence upon the visual in his elaboration of a new poetics, where visual sight and verbal insight attempted to colonize what Louis Marin has called the "empty place of fiction between figures and discourse."[63] The old "place" of collaboration had been evacuated by an emblematic and allegorical imagery—though Wordsworth, for example, and Turner both invoke it still—but the need to convey and extend the *meanings* of visual experience continued to evoke words. Even for painters. It is true that romantic painting sought and discovered excitingly new *visual* expressions of meaning. But it is worth emphasizing also that painters still found that they needed words in the picturesque tradition: Turner in catalogue notes and sometimes elaborate titles; Constable at the end of his career having recourse to letterpress in *The English Landscape* where words are brought in aid of the visual imagination.[64]

ed. The garden at the
tulips and lilac: (honeys
the riverside — an arbour
out quite to the water,
aped with beautiful trac
ber — it is used as a tim
most beautiful thing I
l moat round the whole
filled with the sweetest
dens — chiefly in flower w
ed deep red tulips — not
ed — bloomed with blue
le; the grey walls abo
, all their towers yet m
ness sketches. And
ppletrees — partly in blo
ve. Com my dearest Fath
m most affect. son
J Ruskin

7 JOHN RUSKIN AND THE PICTURESQUE

John Ruskin's earliest tastes for architecture and landscape were formed by the picturesque movement. He therefore provides a usefully specific instance of some of the more general ideas raised in the previous essay. His particular perspectives upon how we read or respond to buildings and scenery (treated most famously in *The Seven Lamps of Architecture, The Stones of Venice,* and *Modern Painters*), though at times complicated, even long-winded, and contradictory, should not be missed by students of landscape architecture, even if they have customarily neglected them. This essay and the two that follow are attempts to bring this prolific but important writer into the orbit of thinking about developments in attitudes to landscape.

Just because Ruskin argued in *Modern Painters*[1] that "all true opinions . . . show their life by being capable of nourishment: therefore of change," we should not be fooled into believing that some of his earliest ideas were abandoned, even decisively changed. This is especially true of his picturesque taste, though he also ruefully noted that "I am always blamed if I approach my subject on any but its picturesque side."[2] Sometimes he does not even declare his specific picturesque penchant, as when he argues in *Modern Painters* that "the greatest thing a human soul ever does in this world is to *see* something, and tell what it *saw* in a plain way." But that conjunction of image and word is wholly in the picturesque tradition, already traced in this series of studies; Ruskin continues in a fashion that shows how his own special attitude colors that tradition: "Hundreds of people can talk for one who can think, but thousands can think for one who can see. To see clearly is poetry, prophecy, and religion,—all in one" (V, 333).

That triad had its roots in his early established debt to eighteenth-century picturesque aesthetics and his long-held obligation to its ideas about experiencing landscape and reading landscape paintings, all of which can be recognized in *The Poetry of Architecture,* his first formal publication of any consequence, and continued to inform all his work at least until 1860, despite his public renunciations of picturesque taste.

When in *The Poetry of Architecture* he talks of our education by landscape—the "nobler scenery of that earth . . . has been appointed to be the school of . . . minds" (I, 132), he is rehearsing his own youth, which his poetry and sketches reveal as being a frequent exposure to the picturesque. Yet that claim for the intellectual and moral benefits of travel is (maybe deliberately) opposed to an assertion by the leading eighteenth-century popularizer, William Gilpin, that "picturesque travel" should not be brought "into competition with any of the more useful ends of travelling."[3] It is typical of Ruskin's mixture of debt and independence, which informs his later treaty with the picturesque, that he adjusts Gilpin's emphasis to suit his own convictions, even while writing a series of essays that draw upon much experience of viewing scenery in Gilpin's manner.

It is a commonplace that Ruskin's youth was a substantial education in the picturesque. In 1880 he recalled that one of Samuel Prout's drawings, bought by his grandfather, and which

> hung in the corner of our little dining parlour at Herne Hill as early as I can remember . . . had a most fateful and continual power over my childish mind. In the first place, it taught me generally to like ruggedness . . . the conditions of joints in moulding, and fitting of stones in walls which were most weather-worn. (XIV, 385)

His father's own modest artistic talents were distinctly picturesque,[4] and on his travels as a sherry merchant securing orders from customers all over Britain his letters home reported frequent picturesque encounters: "old oak trees . . . twisted and knotted in the most fantastic manner . . . the Ruins of Kennilworth a very interesting scene."[5] And the family's annual excursions, ostensibly in search of further sherry orders, were a progress from one picturesque site to another, with the young John watching landscape framed "through the panoramic opening of the four windows of a postchaise" (XXXV, 16). And in adult life these experiences continued, as he toured Europe to view its scenery as Prout and Turner had painted it. And I think that painting—Turner's certainly, but Carpaccio's and the Bellinis' also—largely determined his approach to Venetian art; while his study of illuminated manuscripts, as much as his researches among the churches of Venice, determined his ideas on the Gothic craftsman.

The three crucial ingredients of picturesque aesthetic and practice that Ruskin seems most to have adopted—though much also of a more peripheral nature was borrowed—were its fascination with ruins, its organization of some fresh alliance of word and image in the wake of the eighteenth-century rejection of the traditions of *ut pictura poesis,* and its use of mirrors. It cannot be denied that these adopted picturesque ideas, modes of experience and methods of analysis were, inevitably, adapted by Ruskin during his career. The famous reformulation of Turnerian or noble picturesque by the fourth volume of *Modern Painters* would be the most obvious example.[6] Yet the three picturesque ideas or strategies remained, even while undergoing revision, basic to his whole work. They are even, I'd want to suggest, the signature of Ruskin's imaginative world.

One of Ruskin's earliest surviving drawings is of the ruins of Dover Castle,[7] while his juvenile and generally tedious verses establish ruin as a central motif; at the age of eleven he apostrophized the "old walls" of Haddon Hall in a cheerful song, the refrain of which was "Hey, ruination and hey, desolation,— / But created to spoil the creation!" (II, 284). Three years later, traveling down the Rhine, this youthful connoisseur of dilapidation encountered only a "tiresome repetition of ruins, and ruins too which do not altogether agree with my idea of what ruins ought to be" (II, 349). The remark is loftily *un*explained; but from other remarks and reactions on this 1833 journey it is possible to deduce that Ruskin required ruins which he was able to complete with some specificity—thus at Andernacht they were "mighty . . . and majestic in their decay, *but* their Lords are departed and *forgotten*" (II, 355, my italics). But it was actually his geological interests that extended his early picturesque preoccupations: in the "ruined universe" (II, 373) of the Alps his highest standard of ruin was satisfied: "before me soared the needles of Mont Blanc, splintered and crashed and shivered, the marks of the tempest for three score centuries, yet they are here, shooting up red, bare, scarcely even lichened, entirely inaccessible, snowless . . ." (II, 382). His poem on "The Chrystal-Hunter" provided a fresh identity for the picturesque tourist. In the next family tour of 1835 there is an eloquent record of some hours spent beside the Glacier du Trien; a conventional picturesque experience ("a most beautiful ruin, a superb desolation, a most admired disorder") also involves his completion of the ruins of the "veteran crags" ("telling to every traveller a wonderful tale of ancient convulsions").[8]

In his only attempt to write a novel, which survives as the fragment "Velasquez, the Novice," one of the characters is given a speech that was later revised for inclusion in *The Poetry of Architecture:* "the cypress befits the landscape of Italy, because she is a land of tombs, the air is full of death—it is the past in which she lives, the past in which she is glorious—she is beautiful in death, and her people, her nation, are the dead; and the throne of her pride is the *hic jacet*" (I, 542). In *The Poetry of Architecture* this emphasis on ruin is intensified with more picturesque details like a "fallen column" (I, 19). Since *The Poetry of Architecture* is largely dedicated to exploring how the mind as well as the eye must be satisfied in both architecture and landscape (and therefore, by implication, in what we would call landscape architecture), a mental and hence verbal response to images of ruin or dilapidation is established as ruin's proper complement. When he talked in *Modern Painters* of his early years, which informed the essays contributed to Loudon's *Architectural Magazine,* he spoke of being "never independent of associated thought. Almost as soon as I could see or hear, I had got reading enough to give me associations with all kinds of scenery . . . and thus my pleasure in mountains or ruins was never, even in earliest childhood, free from a certain awe and melancholy, and general sense of the meaning of death" (V, 365–366).

By this third volume of *Modern Painters,* however, Ruskin had decided that the modern taste for ruin was excessive (V, 319); yet on the other hand ruin was by then established as the theme of all his writings. *Modern Painters* discovers its essential subjects equally in what is elsewhere called "the ruined mountain world" (IX, 294) of alpine geology and in the Hesperid dragon—"the worm of eternal decay" (VII, 420)—of Turner's *Garden of the Hesperides.* Inasmuch as his work does focus upon Turner, Ruskin's peroration singles out one all-important fact about his subject—that "through all the remainder of his life, wherever he looked, he saw ruin. Ruin, and twilight . . . And fading of sunset, note also, on ruin" (VII, 432). And in the midst of his long composition of *Modern Painters,* Ruskin did the research and wrote *The Stones of Venice,* which is constructed, as its first page declares, out of ruin. His Venetian letters, notes and sketches are constantly lamenting and annotating ruin, just as the text of his book is slowly reconstituting it.

Even when he collects materials that are not obviously ruined, Ruskin's memoranda (fig. 7.1) themselves choose to fragment Gothic buildings.

So that although picturesque ruin and its sentimental associations are specifically derided by the mid-1850s, the attraction to decay and incompleteness becomes the foundation of his whole work. The reason, I believe, is that his religious upbringing contrived to make ruin an essential feature of his spiritual landscape. His mother's evangelical training never ceased to insist upon the imperfections of human life and its achievements. The ruination of the Garden of Eden, encountered and adumbrated on each daily Bible reading, became a matter of conviction and accordingly a characteristic image of his adult vision. On the early tours to Switzerland of 1833 and 1835, the Alps from Schaffhausen and the Valley of Chamonix were both close to a "heaven-like dwelling place" (II, 392); but the former are described in *Praeterita* as having been "the seen walls of lost Eden" (XXXV, 115). And in *Modern Painters* the valley of the Trient between Valorsine and Martigny, which provides the type and specific location of "Mountain Gloom," is an extended, but by no means isolated, example of ruins discovered in pastoral enclaves:

> The other [i.e. Savoyard] cottage, in the midst of an inconceivable, inexpressible beauty, set on some sloping bank of golden sward, with clear fountains flowing beside it, and wild flowers, and noble trees, and goodly rocks gathered round into a perfection as of Paradise, is itself a dark and plague-like stain in the midst of the gentle landscape. Within a certain distance of its threshold the ground is foul and cattle-trampled; its timbers are black with smoke, its garden choken with weeds and nameless refuse, its chambers empty and joyless, the light and wind gleaming and filtering through the crannies of their stones. (VI, 389)

For such a temperament as Ruskin's, the idea of ruin had a vital fascination. It seems furthermore to have permeated his whole psychology long after Ruskin ceased to subscribe to his mother's religious teaching; consequently, we find that he is ready to identify and discuss ruin even in contexts that do not otherwise declare any strong evangelical attitudes. His account of "romantic association," for instance, is based upon its response to ruin:

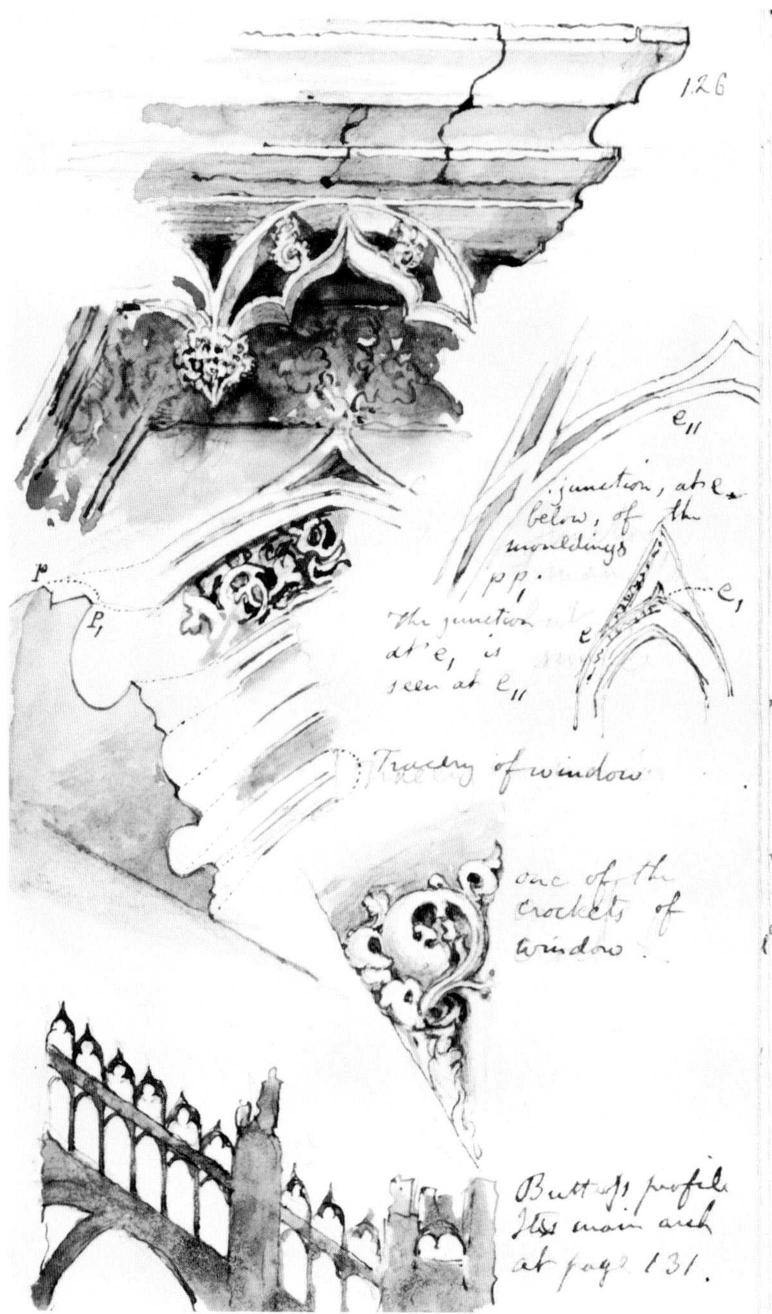

7.1. John Ruskin, page 126 from his "Architectural Sketchbook" (n.d.). Pierpont Morgan Library.

> It rises eminently out of the contrast of the beautiful past with the frightful and monotonous present; and it depends for its force on the existence of ruins and traditions, on the remains of architecture, the traces of battle-fields, and the precursorship of eventful history. The instinct to which it appeals can hardly be felt in America. (V, 369)[9]

Long before he maneuvered toward redefining the noble or Turnerian picturesque in *Modern Painters* IV, he defended Samuel Prout's picturesque sketches of buildings by insisting on Prout's "feeling which results from the influence, among the noble lines of architecture, of the rent and the rust, the fissure, the lichen, and the weed, and from the writing upon the pages of ancient walls of the confused hieroglyphics of human history." (III, 217) The idea there is characteristically picturesque, and Ruskin goes on rather nervously to defend it from any superficiality by arguing for the "deeper moral" of Prout's "ideal appreciation of the present active and vital being of the cities" which he depicts; that is to say, Prout successfully images what he sees in dilapidated cityscapes and what he can thence deduce of their past. Ruskin's own fascination with ruin, itself partly learnt from Prout, as we saw, has to be defended in similar ways. He is tempted into a brief, but eloquent description of the facade of San Michele at Lucca—

> the mosaics have fallen out of half the columns, and lie in weedy ruin beneath; in many, the frost has torn large masses of the entire coating away, leaving a scarred unsightly surface. Two of the shafts of the upper star window are eaten entirely away by the sea-wind, the rest have lost their proportions; the edges of the arches are hacked into deep hollows, and cast indented shadows on the weed-grown wall. The process has gone too far, and yet I doubt not but that this building is seen to greater advantage now than when first built. . . . (III, 206)

—yet he goes on immediately and severely, as if suddenly aware of his own indulgence, that this "is no pursuit of mere picturesqueness; it is true following out of the ideal character of the building."

The ideal building would exist, then, simply in the imagination.

> Let the reader, with such scraps of evidence as may still be gleaned from under the stucco and paint of the Italian committees of taste, and from under the drawing-room innovations of English and German residents, restore Venice in his imagination to some resemblance of what she must have been before her fall. (III, 213)

His obsessional need to "preserve" ruin was probably at the root of his lifelong hostility to the restoration of ancient buildings: "I have never yet seen any restoration or cleaned portion of a building whose effect was not inferior to the weathered parts, even to those of which the design had in some parts almost disappeared" (III, 205). So that if architectural restoration was anathema and the fall of Venice could never be redeemed by recovering its buildings (nor, with stucco, re-covering them), their vacancies must be completed while still leaving them ineluctably fragmentary—completed, therefore, in the imagination. This version of the picturesque required verbal elaboration of the visual image.

For these reasons Ruskin insisted upon the necessity of an alliance between image and word. His belief that a human soul does best by telling what it saw has already been quoted and undoubtedly lies behind his use of "the words painter and poet quite indifferently" (V, 221).[10] The example of Turner's own use of elaborate titles and catalogue entries for his pictures was one that Ruskin inevitably took seriously; Constable's recourse to letterpress in the 1830s for *The English Landscape* he chose to ignore, for reasons that presumably have to do with his preferential defence of Turner. But he was convinced that modern artists should attach written statements to their work to complete their meanings and in the Pre-Raphaelites he saw a new union of the sister arts (VI, 32 and V, 127 respectively).

Yet Ruskin was also often at pains to remind his readers that "words are not accurate enough, not delicate enough, to express or trace the constant, all pervading influence of the finer and vaguer shadows throughout" Turner's works (III, 308). Such admissions, however, are almost inevitably the prelude to one of Ruskin's more strenuous and rhetorical analyses, as he rises to the challenge of translating visual into verbal discourse. But he was not tutored in the picturesque for nothing, and one of its legacies to him was an addiction to formal effects in nature or paint, before which words seem especially inefficacious. Thus he is unusually mute—merely listing the relevant subjects—before Turner's late Swiss watercolors (III, 551). He certainly never faces the problem of painting's formal language very steadily in *Modern Painters,* yet there is much scattered attention of a high order dedicated to it. Specifically, the discussion of color, growing in confidence and scope throughout *Modern Painters*—and fueled by its central role in his appreciation of Venetian architecture—is never brought together into a coherent section, except for the panic admission in a note to volume five that he hasn't got around to doing so (VII, 414). Yet his random discussions of color reveal some real feeling for formal elements in visual art, which language may point toward but cannot translate into its own terms. The analysis of scarlet in volume four (VI, 69ff.) is especially good.

These hesitations about the primacy of the visual over either the joint endeavors of visual and verbal or the verbal *tout simple* obviously derive in part from his own competence with both. Though his parents only encouraged his drawing and painting to the level of gentlemanly accomplishment, he expressed himself fluently with both image and word. As a child he devised his own books where both forms collaborated (fig. 7.2), a dual enterprise that was given added stimulus after the discovery in 1832 of Rogers's *Italy* with its vignettes after Turner. His adult letters will often switch from sentence to sketch and back again to complete his meaning (fig. 7.3). But God, as we are reminded in the first volume of *Modern Painters* (III, 345), was in the still small voice rather than the forms of earthquake, wind and fire. Elsewhere we are told that God is served better with few words than many pictures (V, 86), though that is a by-product of Ruskin's endless doubts as to the moral efficacy of landscape painting.

Such inconsistencies largely stem from Ruskin's ambivalent feelings toward the picturesque, a movement which contrived as well as inherited certain difficulties which have to do with the relations of word to image. Ruskin points indirectly to some of them when he notes how Turner broke away from the iconographical traditions of pictorial allegory and mythological subjects and learnt to use instead the landscape of natural forms:

> it is one of the most interesting things connected with the study of his art, to watch the way in which his own strength of English instinct breaks gradually through fetter and formalism; how from Egerian wells he steals away to Yorkshire streamlets; how from Homeric rocks, with laurels at the top and caves in the bottom, he climbs, at last, to Alpine precipices fringed with pine, and fortified with the slopes of their own ruins; and how from Temples of Jupiter and Gardens of the Hesperides, a spirit in his feet guides him, at last, to the lonely arches of Whitby, and the bleak sands of Holy Isle. (V, 329)

Ruskin isolates a vital truth there, even while characteristically ignoring other relevant evidence (it is one of the startling omissions from *Modern*

And vineyards clothe the bending brow
'Stead of the clinging copsewood now

How lightly the waves of the broad Meuse
crisped with the first breath of the mor
ning as we swept over the long bridge
that crosses the river from Namur, and
looked back on the rich dome of its small
but beautiful cathedral, as it began to
smile to the first glance of the joyous
sun that was drinking up the delicate.

7.2. John Ruskin, a page from one of his childhood journals (poetry notebook IX), showing his debts to the Gilpinesque traditions of verbal and visual narration and of the visual organization of views. Beinecke Rare Book and Manuscript Library, Yale University.

7.3. John Ruskin, sheet from a letter in which he invokes both verbal and visual descriptions of gardens, buildings, and scenery. Pierpont Morgan Library.

Painters that he never treats Turner's early picturesque years). Turner's gradual (though not at all consistent) abandonment of mythical and iconographical imagery through his career—Constable, of course, rarely if ever invoked it—declares the late eighteenth-century loss of confidence in one of the main components of *ut pictura poesis*—namely, imagery that could readily be translated into verbal discourse.

Ruskin's skepticisms with the extreme manifestations of the picturesque appear early, in *The Poetry of Architecture,* and they center precisely around the largely eighteenth-century emphasis upon the clear language of things, discussed in chapter 4. He shared, as we've seen, the picturesque propensity to treat simply of forms and shapes, as in the variety and roughness of ruins or in geological samples. There things speak for themselves to our eye. But he also shared the rather old-fashioned idea that landscape and architecture should address themselves to our minds as well as to our sight, though what had now been lost from that tradition was any generally available language in which it could be done.

Both in his conservatism and his loss of conventional language Ruskin seems close to the later ideas of Humphry Repton on landscape design. Repton's writings were collected for publication in 1840 by J. C. Loudon, Ruskin's mentor in the late 1830s and the man who accepted the essays on *The Poetry of Architecture* for his *Architectural Magazine* during 1837 and 1838; Loudon even included a piece of Ruskin's ("On the Proper Shapes of Pictures and Engravings") in the volume of Repton's works.[11] It seems likely, then, that Ruskin would have heard much of Repton's ideas; certain parts of *The Poetry of Architecture* declare this influence quite strongly—notably Ruskin's praise of the formality of terracing introduced around Italian villas as a necessary "link between nature and art" (I, 86). But in their general emphasis upon a landscape's appeal to the intellect, especially to the mind's adjudication of proper connections between buildings and surrounding scenery and between that location and the building's ornamentation, Ruskin and Repton have much in common. Thus Ruskin makes fun of what he calls "edificatorial fancies" of contemporary picturesque architects, which he parodies in the style of *Pickwick Papers* that he was just then reading:

> the humour prevailing at the present day among many of our peacable old gentlemen, who never smelt powder in their lives, to eat their morning muffins in a savage-looking tower, and

> admit quiet old ladies to a tea-party under the range of twenty-six cannon, which, it is lucky for the china, are all wooden ones, as they are, in all probability, accurately and awfully pointed into the drawing-room windows. (I, 153)

This is comparable to Repton's query whether the picturesque vocabulary of "Salvator Rosa, and our English Mortimer" is fitly copied "for the residence of man in a polished and civilized state."[12] The appeal to the mind, which is neglected in both examples, involves a lack of consideration for the propriety and reasonableness of association: "the spirit of the English landscape is simple, pastoral and mild, devoid, also, of high associations," which the Scottish Highlands by contrast would possess (I, 169).

The problem for both Ruskin and Repton was that "meaning" in a building or landscape could no longer depend upon a clear iconographical language, in which objects were readily "translated" according to established allegorical syntax, which Ruskin had already seen Turner abandon. Yet in order to avoid the mindless absorption in either merely formal effects or random fancifulness, Ruskin thought that landscape needed to be seen as having meanings—he uses variously the terms, "character," "soul," "animation"—which the spectator could understand. His essays are at times rather confused as to whether these meanings come "ready-made" in the different landscapes he treats of or whether a properly educated sensibility registers as elements of a scene what are in fact constituents of that person's consciousness.[13] But in either case the visual experience has mental repercussions, which it is the business of verbal discourse to identify and explain. In this Ruskin shows, what is never mentioned by his critics, an obvious debt not just to picturesque paintings but to contemporary landscape gardens, many examples of which he saw during the family's annual excursions around Britain; witness his remark, "Nature . . . is a good landscape gardener."[14]

Ruskin would continue to use the term "picturesque" in a perjorative fashion, to indicate his disapproval of a "narrow enjoyment of outward forms" (VI, 23) and the mere display of the "skill of the artist, and his powers of composition" (VII, 255), even while he was relying upon other aspects of the picturesque aesthetic. He adopted one of the most blatent of picturesque visual enthusiasms, for example, upon which to base his lifelong attention to architectural ornament, yet at the same time made it the premise for his own reshaping of the picturesque alliance between words and visual images.

William Gilpin had described how, to "satisfy the eye" before picturesque objects, there must be a textured surface:

> various surfaces of objects, sometimes turning to the light one way, and sometimes in another, . . . give the painter his choice of opportunities in massing, and graduating both his lights, and shades.—The *richness* also of the light depends on the breaks, and little recesses, which it finds on the surface of bodies.

As an example, Gilpin adduced the architect who "break[s] the front of his pile with ornaments."[15] Now it is these decorations by an architect of his basic structure that Ruskin, in *The Poetry of Architecture,* argues will obtain "character" for a building (I, 136). And "character," in the terminology of picturesque aesthetics, means what initiates and guides our associations, which language in its turn articulates. Ruskin engages, I think, in some circular thinking at this point: decorations promote "character," which in its turn promotes associations; associations involve the mind not just the eye; decoration is what distinguishes human architecture from animal building.

> The mere preparation of convenience, therefore, is not architecture in which man can take pride, or ought to take delight; but the high and ennobling art of architecture is, that of giving to buildings, whose parts are determined by necessity, such forms and colours as shall delight the mind, by preparing it for the operations to which it is to be subjected in the building. (I, 105)

Hence the insistence, appearing early in *The Poetry of Architecture,* that "the proper designing of ornament" (I, 135) must be an architect's prime concern.

It is, of course, the premise of much of *The Seven Lamps of Architecture* and *The Stones of Venice,* where Gothic ornament becomes the whole object of his discourse—"fair fronts of variegated mosaic, charged with wild fancies and dark hosts of imagery" (VIII, 53)—*and* at the same time provides the language for Ruskin's text—"not a leaflet [in northern Gothic ornament] but speaks, and speaks far off too" (VII, 28). In *The Poetry of Architecture* is first heard the characteristic Ruskinian formulation of a landscape or a building *speaking* to us through its details: a cottage is "a quiet life-giving voice" (I, 12) or a very old forest tree has its age "written on every spray" and is "always telling us about the past" (I, 68). In later works this emphasis on the mute language of visible things coordinates three picturesque strategies—the search for textured roughness, for ornament in Venice or a geological formation in the Alps is generally ruined, or seen fragmentarily by Ruskin; the picturesque alliance of word with image; and the address via that fresh language to the mind.

The rich ornamentations of Venetian building, like the "sculptured and coloured surfaces" of Nature's crags and crystals (VIII, 145), are formal delights beyond the imagination of any picturesque traveler. They are also "hieroglyphs," and the stones of Venice, as of Chamonix, require translation. The Gothic building, Ruskin argues in "The Lamp of Memory,"

> admits of a richness of record altogether unlimited. Its minute and multitudinous sculptural decorations afford means of expressing either symbolically or literally, all that need be known of national feeling or achievement. More decoration will, indeed, be usually required than can take so elevated a character; and much, even in the most thoughtful periods, has been left to the freedom of fancy, or suffered to consist of mere repetitions of some national bearing or symbol. It is, however, generally unwise, even in mere surface ornament, to surrender the power and privilege of variety which the spirit of Gothic architecture admits; much more in important features—capitals of columns or bosses, and string-courses, as of course in all confessed bas-reliefs. Better the rudest work that tells a story or records a fact than the richest without meaning. (VIII, 229–230)

And in discussions of mountain scenery, which he connected to his architectural studies by emphasizing the community of cathedral and Alp, he was equally alert to visible fact and translatable meaning:

> For a stone, when it is examined, will be found a mountain in miniature. The fineness of Nature's work is so great, that into a single block, a foot or two in diameter, she can compress as many changes of form and structure, on a small scale, as she needs for her mountains on a large one; and, taking moss for forests, and grains of crystal for crags, the surface of a stone, in by far the plurality of instances, is more interesting than the surface of an ordinary hill; more fantastic in form, and incomparably richer in colour,—the last quality being, in fact, so noble in most stones of good birth (that is to say, fallen from the crystalline mountain-ranges), that I shall be less able to illustrate this part of my subject satisfactorily by means of engraving than perhaps any other, except the colour of skies.

And in that significant admission of the uselessness of visual illustration, Ruskin prepares for his necessary act of literary translation of those facts and meanings. Such interpretation provides the occasion for most of Ruskin's famous set pieces, the purple passages so dear to those who select gobbets from his works for us to peruse. Yet without their context of a criticism which constantly stresses our obligation to interpret the mute poesy of ornament or mountain structure, those fine periods are themselves merely picturesque, evidence of *our* "narrow enjoyment" of Ruskin's "merely outward delightfulness" (VI, 15).

The last of the three picturesque procedures which seem central to the functioning of Ruskin's imagination concerns the use of the mirror or Claude glass. Ruskin did not, as far as I know, ever use a Claude glass, though some of his juvenile verse is composed as if he did.[16] But he nonetheless found that the picturesque obsession with mirrors and reflections answered many of his own beliefs and even coincided with imagery derived at an early age from his study of the Bible. Ruskin frequently invokes the traditional artistic metaphor of art holding a mirror up to nature—not of course a specifically picturesque idea—and, as we might expect, places contradictory constructions upon it. Sometimes it is simply the image for unsatisfactory and incomplete imagination:

> And then, lastly, it is another infinite advantage possessed by the picture, that in these various differences from reality it becomes the expression of the power and intelligence of a companionable human soul. In all this choice, arrangement, penetrative sight, and kindly guidance, we recognize a supernatural operation, and perceive, not merely the landscape or incident as in a mirror. . . . (V, 186–187)

On other occasions the mirror represents the narcissistic arrogance which is disclaimed on the title pages of *Modern Painters* via some lines of Wordsworth's, who does not want to be counted among those who only prize

> *This soul, and the transcendent universe,*
> *No more than as a mirror that reflects*
> *To proud Self-love her own intelligence.*

Yet the mirror equally sanctioned Ruskin's requirement of an artist that he carefully delineate the natural world, that he look—at any rate as a preliminary stage of his education—not at what his predecessors have done but at the details of the natural world caught in the glass of his careful private scrutiny. If Alberti saw the Narcissus myth as a translation of three into two dimensions, Ruskin invoked the mirror as the artist's guide back into a proper apprehension and renewed contact with three dimensions: "Every object, however near the eye, has something about it which you cannot see, and which brings the mystery of distance even into every part and portion of what we suppose ourselves to see most distinctly. . . ." (III, 337)

This paradoxical reversal of the mirror's loss of depth is first explored in his—this time specifically picturesque—astonishingly perceptive discussion of the lake as mirror in *The Poetry of Architecture:*[17]

> When a small piece of quiet water reposes in a valley, or lies embosomed among crags, its chief beauty is derived from our perception of crystalline depth, united with excessive slumber. In its limited surface we cannot get the sublimity of extent, but we may have the beauty of peace, and the majesty of depth. The object must therefore be, to get the eye off its surface, and to draw it down, to beguile it into that fairy land underneath, which is more beautiful than what it repeats, because it is all full of dreams unattainable and illimitable. This can only be done by keeping its edge out of sight, and guiding the eye off the land into the reflection, as if it were passing into a mist, until it finds itself swimming into the blue sky, with a thrill of unfathomable falling. (I, 90)

The lake's mirror, better far than any picturesque equipment, because God-given, invites and accommodates the imagination's inward reflections. And because the "surface of water is not a mockery, but a new view of what is above it," as he says in *Modern Painters* (III, 542), reflections can be used as the emblem of the highest imagination. For Ruskin this is Turner's, which mirrors the natural world accurately as well as provides a "new view of what is above it." Ruskin defends Turner from hostile contemporary criticism by applying to his work the basic truth of what watery reflections teach. The whole of *Modern Painters* is an effort to answer the question that is posed by our fascination and puzzlement with mirrors, expressed by another visitor to Italy in 1821:

> Why is the reflection in that canal far more beautiful than the objects it reflects? The colours more vivid yet blended with more harmony; the openings from within into the soft and tender colours of the distant wood and the intersection of the mountain lines surpass and misrepresent truth.[18]

In "misrepresenting" and surpassing truth, Ruskin shows that Turner, who was himself obsessed with reflections in water, especially in his Swiss and Venetian subjects, not only combines all traditional sanctions of the mirror, but becomes in his turn "a mere instrument or mirror, used by a higher power for a reflection to others of a truth which no effort of his could ever have ascertained" (VI, 44).

The picturesque mirror and the biblical mirror eventually coincide in the chapter called "The Dark Mirror" in the final volume of *Modern Painters.* In this Ruskin is most exercised about whether "it might seem a waste of time to draw landscape at all." He pulls together by way of response many threads from the previous nine interconnected volumes of his work—*The Poetry of Architecture, The Seven Lamps,* three volumes of *The Stones of Venice,* and the first four of *Modern Painters* itself—and he passes in review most of the concerns that I have tried to elucidate here.

He notes that the picturesque at its lowest is a degradation of the contemplative or reflective faculty. He reaffirms, however, the great artist's attention to the "historical association connected with landscape" and with cities like Venice. He reminds his readers that "in these books of mine, their distinctive character, as essays on art, is their bringing everything to a root in human passion or human hope." He traces "every principle of painting" to "some vital or spiritual fact," which he has used his own verbal skills to translate even when "connections between art and human emotion" were sometimes "slight or local." He then justifies that emphasis upon man's inward rather than outward concerns, even in visual art, by saying that it is in his soul that man resembles the Deity: "the soul of man is still a mirror, wherein may be seen, darkly, the image of the mind of God."

He apologizes at once for these "daring words." Part of the boldness at this point in Ruskin's long endeavor to bring *Modern Painters* and its satellites to completion is perhaps that he finds he still must use an imagery which he encountered first in the picturesque movement, aspects of which he now rejects, and a picturesque imagery that forged strong bonds with religious ideas that he has also found insufficient (he is writing at most twelve months after his famous "unconversion" in 1858 before Veronese's *Solomon and the Queen of Sheba* in Turin). Continuity and contradiction are the twin hallmarks of Ruskin's mind. So the reliance upon ideas still drawn from modes of thought now rejected must be no surprise, except to those who need to make Ruskin into a systematic thinker. The "soul of man is a mirror of the mind of God" is quickly restated, after a brief defence of the original bold words, and in ways that are even more revealing of Ruskin's debts: "A mirror, dark, distorted, broken, use what blameful words you please of its state; yet in the main, a true mirror, out of which alone, and by which alone, we can know anything of God at all" (VII, 260). The human ruin, blemished and rough like any picturesque object—has in its turn to be interpreted and articulated as the hieroglyph of spiritual and divine history.

Ruskin's early schooling in the picturesque joined his mother's constant instruction of him in the Bible to shape his most characteristic ideas. At times he needed to insist that he had grown out of both disciplines; while it is certainly true that he remodeled them, I do not think that they ever ceased to determine the ways of his imagination and even the odd fashion in which his oeuvre (at least until 1860) was built up.

The love of ruin, of fragments, gave Ruskin, as it had given Thomas Gray, the "truest subjects for his glass." They offered him opportunities for exact delineation, a loving response to shape, form, color, and light. But they also provided occasions for interpretation. For even in what Ruskin calls "lovely nature," though there is "an excellent degree of simple beauty, addressed to the eye alone, yet often what impresses us most will form but a very small portion of that visible beauty" (V, 355–356). The key word there is *impress;* elsewhere in the first volume of *Modern Painters* (p. 201) the picturesque is specifically contrasted with the "impressive." I suspect what we have here is some fossilized jargon from the Lockean and associational traditions; it serves, however, to distinguish the merely visual from the visible's address to the mind. The impression upon that mind of beauty or truth in visual objects, however, needed fresh languages for its interpretation. Picturesque skill at recording formal delights was not a sufficient syntax; old allegorical and emblematic languages were in disrepute as being both too arcane and too public and general, not tailored for the individual sensibility. Fresh alliances of word and image must be forged to treat of truths which "may be stated by any signs or symbols which have a definite signification in the minds of those to whom they are addressed, although such signs be themselves no image nor likeness of anything" (III, 104). What he strove, therefore, to do was to honor in the same object both truths that he saw and truths that he deduced, for which a language traditionally existed in his own evangelical background: that of typology.[19] "I have throughout the examination of Typical beauty, asserted our instinctive sense of it; the moral meaning of it being only discoverable by reflection" (IV, 211). Reflection is thought *and,* as he claimed for Turner, our readiness to act as God's mirror.

The attention to fragments, which could be found to speak volumes, may also, we would be not uncharitable in thinking, serve as an analogy for Ruskin's own work. He talks frequently of its "warped and broken" text (VII, 257). But in it he could reveal by many images and even more words how ruin was of the essence of God's universe as we find it in the Alps and of man's world as we find it in Venetian ornament. He could catalogue and itemize their phenomenal as well as their noumenal significance. In his mirror he could keep, perhaps, the whole image steady for himself; it is not always so coherent when we try to peer over his shoulder. We can from time to time feel confident that we see him steadily and see him whole; but it would be just as fair to those other moments of our bewilderment to end by quoting his father's panic in face of the son's frenetic quest among the ruins of Venice on 25 May 1846, an activity that the old man seems to intuit, for he was no fool, as a strange revision of the picturesque:

> He is cultivating art at present, searching for real knowledge, but to you [W. H. Harrison, an old friend] and me this is at present a sealed book. It will neither take the shape of picture nor poetry. It is gathered in scraps hardly wrought, for he is drawing perpetually, but no drawing such as in former days you or I might compliment in the usual way by saying it deserved a frame; but fragments of everything from a Cupola to a Cartwheel, but in such bits that it is to the common eye a mass of Hieroglyphics—all true—truth itself, but Truth in mosaic. (VIII, xxiii)

8 RUSKIN, "TURNERIAN TOPOGRAPHY," AND *GENIUS LOCI*

This essay is about how we read Turner's landscape paintings, especially those which picture country estates. I use "read" about Turner's landscape paintings for a variety of reasons. First, because his paint upon the canvas is in two respects like words upon the page—it is a symbolic language whose relationship to the real is a matter of either convention or negotiation; and what we see, whether as colors and forms or as printed or written letters, requires *translation*. That we may be reduced by custom or familiarity not to notice these things does not diminish their significance: we do "read" them as transcriptions of actual scenes. And then, secondly, Turner's first great critic, John Ruskin, was emphatic that Turner's paintings were to be read, like classic literature. Now Ruskin can often be silly, willful, or downright wrong, but he seems always to ask the right questions, to direct attention to central problems; so that when he considers how a Turner landscape is to be approached or interpreted and he insists upon reading it, it is worth understanding why.

That Turner's work responds aptly to that approach makes my third point: both he and Ruskin were familiar with traditions of landscape experience for the full understanding of which both words and images were necessary. Earlier essays here have set out some aspects of these constructions of meaning in landscape. These can be taken further by a consideration of one of the greatest of English landscape painters and one of the most stimulating writers about landscape experience. Furthermore, both Turner and Ruskin depended upon traditions of landscape gardening, even though the latter at least did little to acknowledge this dependence; Turner, however, painted frequently on the country estates of his patrons.

Most critics and commentators dodge the issue of how we read landscape paintings, because, in contrast to pictures which deploy traditional iconographical imagery, landscapists do not seem to establish the same kinds of *meaning* or invoke the same kinds of vocabulary and syntax. Yet surely the genre requires attention to content as well as form. When we consider, for example, one of Turner's later topographical views (see, for example, fig. 8.11), to what precisely do we react? Do we judge the painted view for its accuracy, for whether or not we recognize the scenery? Is the criterion of a good landscape picture its excellence as (so to speak) a good map of the terrain?

In Turner's case, even if we do not know the subject, we are surely aware at once of what Andrew Wilton has called his "visionary modification of . . . topography."[1] An exhibition catalogue of *Turner in Yorkshire*[2] remarked that a drawing of Knaresborough "has been distorted somewhat from fact," while his view of Rievaulx (which can be compared closely with the site in its present state) narrows the valley, enlarges the stream (the River Rye), heightens the surrounding hills, and gives the valley head more character than in fact it possesses. Yet does knowledge of Turner's "inaccuracies" diminish an appreciation of these watercolors? The answer can only be that of course it does not.

But to say that is to commit ourselves to other criteria for successful landscape paintings: a landscape, we would now have to argue, is only the art of its brushstrokes, the occasion for formal excitements of shape and color that we have no obligation to refer back to their originals. This is easier to argue when Turner's landscape sketches are unidentified; then its subject can only be itself—or as John Russell's aphorism has it: "there is a sense in which landscapes do not exist until they have been painted."[3]

The truth, as often in such matters, probably lies between the formalist and the topographical approaches. But nobody, to my knowledge, has asked what is the relationship between our aesthetic principles and our criteria of scenic representation; nobody, that is, except John Ruskin. And his *Modern Painters* is in every way typical of that extraordinary man's erratic stumbling upon crucial problems, posing of apt questions, and somehow leaving us with less than satisfactory answers. He is, nevertheless, inevitably the place to begin.

Ruskin started *Modern Painters* in the early 1840s with the assumption that Turner's paintings were superior to other artists' precisely because they observed and recorded more accurately the phenomenal aspects of the natural world. But by his tour of Italy in 1845, when he visited the sites of some of Turner's subjects, and by his resumption of *Modern Painters* in the mid-1850s he was forced to acknowledge that Turner did not always practice topographical precision—that it would be impossible, for example, to match Turner's *Rievaulx* with a daguerrotype view. So in *Modern Painters* Ruskin set himself to explain and justify what he called "Turnerian Topography" (VI, chap. 2).[4]

Ruskin's central problem was that since great art is inventive, the work of imagination, "great landscape art cannot be a mere copy of any given scene" (VI, 27). Yet *Modern Painters* was elaborately constructed upon a documentation of Turner's superior accuracy, arguments which, two years later, in August 1845 were awkwardly called in question when Ruskin visited Faido on the St. Gothard in search of Turnerian subjects. He wrote to his parents:

> I have found his subject, *or the materials of it,* here; and I shall devote tomorrow to examining them and seeing how he has put them together. The Stones, road, and bridge are all true, but the mountains, compared with Turner's colossal conception, look pigmy & poor. Nevertheless Turner has given their actual, not their apparent size.

The next day he was reporting that of several roads and bridges, some ruined and three new, Turner had simply eliminated the latter; Ruskin made his own memoranda upon the scene and discovered that "it is beautiful to see the way Turner has arranged & cut out." He was now "convinced," he wrote his father on 21 August 1845, "that nothing is to be done in landscape without continual alteration and adaptation."[5]

But there was all the difference between registering Turner's imaginative adjustments in a letter home and theorizing about them nearly a decade later in the resumed *Modern Painters*. He tackles the problem characteristically by focusing as a preliminary upon another topic, that of picturesque scenery. The vital connection between picturesque scenery and Turnerian topography is that both manipulate actual scenery, in the case of the picturesque altering and adapting it in the interests of rough surfaces and busy texture. What Ruskin was reluctant to admit was that such rather tired picturesque adaptations of scenery could be as vital or as important as Turner's.

Ruskin's discussion of picturesque is focused upon two images of windmills by Clarkson Stanfield and Turner (VI, 16–17). Ruskin contrasts Stanfield's "surface-picturesque," a "merely outward delightfulness [of] . . . variety of colour and form" (fig. 8.1), with the

8.1. Stanfield's (left) and Turner's (right) windmills, from Ruskin's Modern Painters, *1898 edition.*

"expressiveness" of Turner's "noble picturesque." This superior form attends to something in its motifs for which Ruskin labors to find suitable, largely metaphorical language; it is variously "the record of its years written so visibly," the "epitome" of its kind, "expressing [a] spirit" which may be allowed "mental or human expression." These qualities are inherent not "parasitical," for they derive from the very essence of a scene or building. Turner bypasses a superficial interest in outward formal effects to penetrate to that essence of the windmill. Ruskin calls it the "inner character of the object" or, more awkwardly, "this great fact of windmill nature."

To appreciate Ruskin's point we might want to think of borrowing terms—*quidditas* or *haecceitas*—from Aquinas (via James Joyce's Stephen Daedalus) and Duns Scotus (via Gerard Manley Hopkins) respectively.[6] But he himself relies, in his stress upon an object's telling of itself, upon a fundamental strategy of the picturesque tradition—the use of verbal as well as visual description. He then proceeds to gloss this windmillness (gloss, etymologically, means to give a tongue to), and he concludes by claiming that in Turner's windmills, unlike Stanfield's, there is a "dim type of all melancholy human labour." "Type" is yet another verbal term, imported this time from biblical exegesis, that Ruskin seeks to employ in pinning down Turner's achievement.

At this stage of his discussion Ruskin turns to larger questions of topography. He distinguishes between the average artist who records those most precious things, "pure history and pure topography," and the artist who is "prophet." The average artist will not attempt to alter the facts of natural history or scenery; indeed, there is a duty to attend to interesting motifs. Ruskin obviously enjoins the example of his master, Turner, upon artists who do not possess Turner's imaginative energies, when he states that their duty is "to take subjects of which the portraiture will be precious in after times; views of our abbeys and cathedrals; distant views of cities, if possible chosen from some spot in itself notable by association" (VI, 31); this is, of course, only part of Turner's strategy, but it is the part which Ruskin had begun *Modern Painters* by proclaiming. Ruskin even urges such painters to accompany their pictures with written statements, which would detail the circumstances and reasons for choosing topographical material as well as note omissions which are forced upon them by the imperatives of accurate history painting: "the beauty of the whole town of Lucerne, as seen from the lake, is destroyed by the large new hotel for the English, which ought . . . to be ignored, and the houses behind it drawn as if it were transparent" (VI, 32). This concession, even for the average artist who is supposed to alter nothing, signals Ruskin's maneuver toward "Turnerian topography."

The painter with "inventive power," however, will not give the "actual facts" of a scene, but a painterly account of "the impression it *made on his mind*" (ibid., my italics). To illustrate this creativity which he identifies above all with Turner, Ruskin returned to the materials which he had gathered in the summer of 1845 on the St. Gothard; he contrasted his own sketch of the scene (fig. 8.2)—"a topographical outline of . . . the actual blocks of rock which happened to be lying in the bed of the Ticino at the spot from which I chose to draw it"—with a rendition of Turner's watercolor of 1843 (fig. 8.3). Since there "is nothing in this scene, taken by itself, particularly interesting or impressive," "any topographical delineation of the facts" is equally ordinary. But Turner gave "the far higher and deeper truth" of the scene; he offered a representation "totally useless to engineers or geographers, and, when tried by rule and measure, totally unlike the place." Yet it was a visual impression of the scene that accommodated the whole

8.2. Ruskin's sketch of the Faido Pass, from Modern Painters.

8.3. Ruskin's redrawing of Turner's version of the scene in figure 8.2.

experience of journeying through "the narrowest and most sublime ravines in the alps" and among the "highest peaks of the Mont St. Gothard" until Turner reached the spot where Ruskin later sketched. Here the artist read, for example, in the "confused stones, which by themselves would be almost without any claim upon his thoughts, . . . exponents of the fury of the river by which he has journeyed all day long." Turner's watercolor, in short, is "an entirely imperative dream" in which are gathered ideas and sensations which express what Ruskin calls "the full essence and soul of the scene" (VI, 33–43).

Now that is a remarkably persuasive account, which the Turner scholar Andrew Wilton has acknowledged is "very closely in sympathy with the artist and with his intentions in the late finished watercolors."[7] Yet Ruskin's analysis has several remarkable, even unsatisfactory, features. One is his reliance upon the language of religion or biblical hermeneutics to describe the "essence and soul" of a scene or the "spirit" and "type" of windmills; this is, of course, the legacy of his own evangelical upbringing, not to be thrown off (if at all) until his famous "unconversion" at Turin in 1858. But it is not perhaps as apt a language for Turner, despite the moral thrust of his later oil paintings, as another which Ruskin notices but does not pursue or use at all. I refer to the ideas and language of *genius loci* or spirit of the place, available to and indeed readily used (as will be shown) by Turner and by much of the poetry admired by Turner and by Ruskin himself.

Briefly, the tradition of *genius loci,* to which Ruskin himself only alludes obliquely in "Of Classical Landscape" in *Modern Painters* (V, chap. 13), derived from classical culture and its elaboration in Renaissance commentaries.[8] Polydore Vergil in *De inventoribus* of 1499 discussed the genii of places and buildings; Natale Conti in *Mythologiae* (1551) argued that Genius was the son of Jove and Terra, a pedigree which nicely united the divine with the landscapes of earth. By the time of Spenser and Milton the use of "genius" to designate a spirit or god of place was common.

Pictorial iconography followed literary usage, so that, for example, Virgil's Father Tiber, who greets Aeneas's arrival on Italian soil in the *Aeneid* (VIII), was equated with the antique statues of river gods unearthed during the Renaissance (fig. 8.4), and modern copies of the image became a familiar device in both gardens and paintings to signify what is specially numinous about a locality. River gods, reclining on their urns, inhabit the landscapes of Claude's *Landscape with Apollo, the*

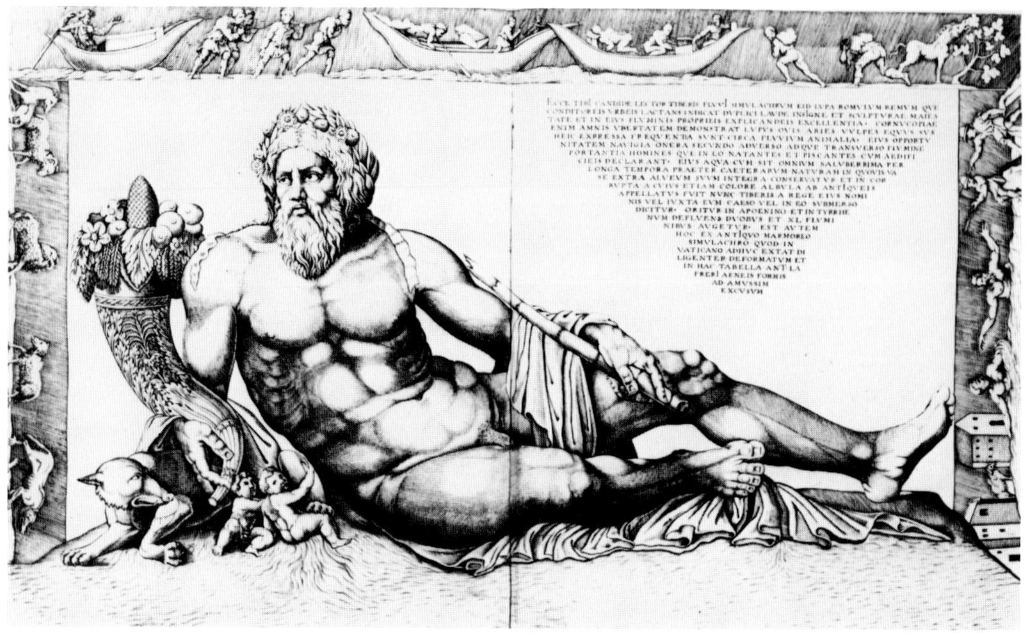

8.4. Engraving of an antique statue of a river god found in Rome, from Bernard de Montfaucon, L'antiquité expliquée et représentée en figures *(Paris, 1722). Dumbarton Oaks, Trustees for Harvard University.*

Muses, and River God (see fig. 4.7), Alexander Pope's poem, *Windsor Forest,* and his friend William Kent's landscape designs (fig. 8.5). In Thomas Gray's "Ode on a Distant Prospect of Eton College" Father Thames is addressed ("Say, Father Thames . . ."), but his brief and undescribed appearance suggests, among other things, that the poet is relying upon his readers' familiarity with the image and its code. It is not without significance for my argument that Gray's river god and his "Ode" were invoked by a reviewer in 1808 of Turner's *Thames at Eton* (now at Petworth House); what is also significant is that neither that oil nor a watercolor of the same subject in the late 1820s used a river god.[9]

Part of the reason for the absence of the Thames River god from Turner's view and for the faintness, the lack of authenticity we may detect in Gray's invocation of him is to be sought in the mistrust of such figures by the second half of the eighteenth century, a subject already explored in previous essays. William Blake in *The Marriage of Heaven and Hell* told how the "ancient Poets animated all sensible objects with Gods or Geniuses, calling them by the names and adorning them with the properties of woods, rivers, mountains, lakes, cities, nations." But he went on to denounce the vapidity of such rhetorical tropes.[10] His was but one variation on a major theme of intellectual and artistic concern in the late eighteenth and early nineteenth centuries: S. T. Coleridge told a correspondent that "it must occur to every Reader that the Greeks in their religious poems address always the Numina Loci, the Genii, the Dryads, the Naiads, &c, &c—All natural Objects were *dead*—mere hollow Statues—but there was a Godkin or Goddessling *included* in each."[11] Ruskin's own attack on the pathetic fallacy was a late manifestation of this romantic skepticism with a traditional vocabulary for describing place, for in his chapter "Of Classical Landscape" he traces the pathetic fallacy to a modern failure to grasp the essential Greek idea of a spirit inhabiting the body of a natural phenomena. *Genius loci,* according to Ruskin, degenerated into "a witty allegory, or a graceful lie, of which the entire upshot and consummation was a pretty statue in the middle of the court, or at the end of the garden" (V, 223).

Ruskin's association of the pathetic fallacy with defunct traditions of *genius loci* surely explains his failure to invoke and rely upon the latter when he came to celebrate Turnerian topography. He could not associate the landscape paintings of the greatest modern painter with a

8.5. William Kent, design for the Chatsworth hillside, with river gods beside the two temples. Trustees of the Chatsworth Settlement (26A, item 4).

habit he had previously denounced.[12] Yet his avoidance of the connections between Turner's landscape paintings and the traditions of *genius loci* should not prevent us from invoking them.

The idea of the genius of place, as it had developed by the late eighteenth century when Turner first began to paint, has some distinctive features.[13] The literary mode of *genius loci* was most usually the inscription poem, words telling of the numinous spirit of the place where they are supposedly discovered. Two special attributes of the inscription—used often by Turner[14]—are its articulation of some hidden, retired, or anonymous life in nature, which is perceived only with difficulty, and the effect of its call from some scene or building in a landscape which (in Hartman's words) "deepens the consciousness of the poet [or beholder] and makes him feel he is on significant ground." It is a moment of extraspecial sympathy between a subject and an object.[15]

These roles for the inscription were kept alive during the eighteenth century largely by the landscape garden, first using classical sources and then making the English garden speak its own language. These gardenist inscriptions were one of Turner's main sources, I suggest, for his own development of *genius loci,* and I want to look at two paintings which reveal the extent of his debts to this inscriptional mode in landscape gardens. These are the 1808 *Pope's Villa at Twickenham* (reproduced here in its engraved version: fig. 8.6) and *Thomson's Æolian Harp* (fig. 8.7) of the following year. Both hung together in the Morrison Collection from the 1820s until the 1970s, for they are closely related by having one particular place as their central subject and by their exploration of forms which a visual artist may invoke to communicate it.[16]

Both pictures directly or indirectly celebrate Alexander Pope's villa, pulled down in 1807;[17] the elegiac mode of the first consists in depicting the destroyed villa at a distance across the Thames, its sacred spot separated from the continuing human activities of the boatmen; but also supporting the mood of the pictorial elegy are the rather wan figures in the foreground and the recumbent sheep. In some verses Turner composed on the destruction of Pope's villa he invokes quite explicitly the inscriptional form by which *genius loci* addresses its visitor:[18]

8.6. John Pye and Charles Heath after Turner, Pope's Villa, engraving, 1811. The Tate Gallery.

8.7. J. M. W. Turner, Thomson's Æolian Harp, *1809, oil. Manchester City Art Gallery.*

Dear Sister Isis tis thy Thames that calls
See desolation hovers o'er those walls
The scatter'd timbers on my margin lays
Where glimmering Evening's ray yet lingering plays.

His painting performs the visual equivalent of inscription: it identifies sacred ground, a locality that is instinct with some quality not simply available in its outward forms; in this case the genius of the place involves also the genius of a poet and gardener who had given to his Twickenham home its special meaning. As Thomas Love Peacock wrote two years later in his poem, *The Genius of the Thames,*

Now open Twitnam's classic shores,
Where yet the moral muse deplores
Her Pope's unrivalled lay

Though tasteless folly's impious hand
Has wrecked the scenes his genius planned;—
Though low his fairy grot is laid . . .[19]

The Thomson picture alludes to the same theme visually in its distant prospect of villas along the Thames—in fact, distorting topography to include Pope's villa which otherwise would not be visible[20]—and in its ruined classical temple in the foreground, as well as indirectly and verbally in the opening two lines of the verses with which the painting was exhibited:

On Thomson's tomb the dewy drops distil,
Soft tears of Pity shed for Pope's lost fane.

The inscriptional device of the lines is echoed by the more simple inscription, THOMSON, on the pedestal of the tomb in the painting. Peacock's poem on *The Genius of the Thames* would also celebrate the connection of Thomson, the poet of *The Seasons,* with Richmond and affirm its due sense of place:

The Seasons there, in fixed return,
Around their minstrel's holy urn
Perennial chaplets twine . . .

Peacock may perhaps have been stimulated by Turner's picture; but I quote him rather to stress how prevalent was the whole notion of *genius loci,* above all when identified with landscapes which had been associated with earlier writers. Turner's fondness for Thomson is well known and in his frequent explorations of the Thames during the first decade of the century he must have appreciated Thomson's own acknowledgment of its genius in lines from *Seasons* ("Summer") which describe how "On every hand / Thy villas shine":

> *Slow let us trace the matchless vale of Thames;*
> *Fair-winding up to where the muses haunt*
> *In Twit'nam's bowers, and for their Pope implore*
> *The healing god; to royal Hampton's pile,*
> *To Clermont's terraced height, and Esher's groves,*
> *Where in the sweetest solitude, embraced*
> *By the soft windings of the silent Mole,*
> *From courts and senates Pelham finds repose.*[21]

Turner's two paintings of 1808 and 1809 contrive their sense of *genius loci* in various forms: by visual representations of famous villas, each of which (as Thomson's lines allow) evinced its own special sense of place; by choosing as motif Pope's villa which had by Turner's day already taken its place in Thames mythology, since dozens of views of it were painted (perhaps more than of any other house at any period). All these images of Pope's villa were in their turn sustained by Pope's own careful literary promotion of his Twickenham villa, grotto, and garden.

A similarly literary motivation lies behind Turner's Thomson picture: his lines allude to Thomson's poem *The Seasons,* which had made the seasons and the weather rather than pagan gods the presiding deities of the natural cycle; his title alludes to Thomson's own "Ode on Æolus's Harp"; while the event depicted refers to Collins's "Ode Occasion'd by the Death of Mr. Thomson," which describes how the poet's sylvan grave is decorated by nymphs. This literary recension of poetic genius and the places associated with it was carried on by Wordsworth's "Remembrance of Collins," published in 1798, which alludes both to Collins and to Thomson in its semi-inscriptional verses "Composed upon the Thames near Richmond." Turner's dependence upon inscription is clear from the named tomb in the Thomson painting, and from his own verses which provide both inscriptions for the painting and at the same time rehearse the *genius loci* of the scenes represented. In addition, there is his own implied recreation in visual terms of such literary forms: the painting becomes visual inscription.

Finally, there is the motif of the aeolian harp itself:[22] as Turner's verses imply and as Coleridge's poem on the same theme, published in 1796, makes even clearer, the aeolian harp stands for or emblemizes the poet's responsiveness to the slightest influences of nature. Placed in the grove of Turner's painting it signals both the special spirit of place associated with Thomson and the especially responsive genius of the poet whom a sympathetic painter in his turn commemorates.

What is striking about these two pictures is Turner's combination of explicit, emblematic imagery, and of expressive naturalist scenery to communicate meaning. For, as we have seen,[23] both kinds marked the gardens which these two pictures directly or indirectly commemorate and, more importantly, the landscaped gardens where Turner spent so much of his early painting life. Nowhere would Turner have encountered such strong and precise forms of *genius loci* than at the country seats of patrons like Walter Fawkes, William Beckford, Sir John Leicester, or Lord Egremont. Their parklands were the latest manifestations of the English landscape movement, whose guiding principle had been formulated by Pope himself:

> *Consult the Genius of the Place in all*
> *That tells the waters or to rise, or fall,*
> *Or helps th'ambitious hill the Heav'ns to scale,*
> *Or scoops in circling theatres the vale,*
> *Calls in the country, catches opening glades,*
> *Joins willing woods, and varies Shades from Shades . . .*

Pope's "genius of the place" is subtly poised between, on the one hand, an actual presiding local divinity who inspires the landscaper to bring her best features to light ("But treat the goddess like a modest fair, / Nor over-dress, nor leave her wholly bare") and, on the other, a more naturalistic appreciation of the terrain to be improved on the part of the landscaper. In the gardens which Pope visited and often helped in shaping these two elements of his own metaphor were variously present: the emblematic, which included both iconographical representations like river gods or nymphs of the grot as well as inscriptions (Pope's own for his grotto was a particularly famous one, and see also fig. 8.8), at the same time as expressive or natural features, where art had tactfully brought out the best aspects of the particular spot. We may see this double imagery of allegory and description invoked by William Kent, the landscape designer whose art so skillfully combined both, in frontispieces for *The Seasons* (fig. 8.9), that long poem by Thomson which Turner admired.

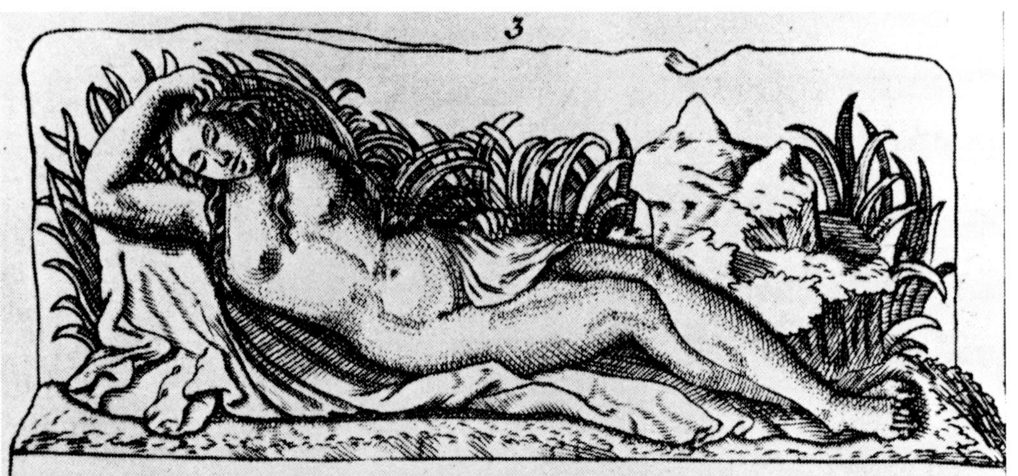

8.8. The nymph of the grot, from Bernard de Montfaucon, L'antiquité expliquée.

8.9. William Kent, engraved frontispiece for Thomson's "Spring," 1730. Author's collection.

During the last quarter of the eighteenth century this double imagery came increasingly under attack. What was happening in garden design, the erosion of emblematic in favour of expressionist imagery, is reflected also in Turner's landscapes, from which therefore we may learn to look afresh at designed park scenery. John Gage has discussed two Scottish views of Turner in this connection:[24] the watercolor of *The Falls of the Clyde* of 1802 (fig. 8.10) actually depicts the nymphs or naiads, what Akenside in Turner's source calls "allegorical deities, or powers of nature," in order to suggest the interaction of sun and running water which given "motion to the air" and excites the "summer breezes." By the oil painting of the late 1830s (fig. 8.11) these representatives of *genius loci* (or at least of a natural phenomenon that marks a particular place) have been subdued if not virtually eliminated—for, as Akenside himself recognized, "ancient divinities" are a rather atavistic device and one not particularly calculated to be "interesting to a modern reader."

Turner's paintings and related romantic poems, however, suggest that *genius loci* was not such a lost or despised cause, and that it survived and continued to matter, even if traditional modes of articulating it wore rather thin.[25] By the early years of the nineteenth century romantic poetry had found ways of letting landscape speak directly—usually through a version of inscriptional composition—without any intervention of allegorical devices which even Akenside, let alone Wordsworth and Coleridge, had thought old-fashioned and ineffective. In landscape gardening inscriptions themselves seemed awkward and obtrusive: "frivolous attempts," Thomas Whately said, to produce character in a place.[26] Yet a note to Peacock's *The Genius of the Thames* on the visibility of "genius loci" and even a competition in the *Gentleman's Magazine* of 1808 for the best translation of an inscription supposedly found on a hermitage suggest that the older modes survived and were still popular.

Turner's paintings of places deploy all these vocabularies with an amazing eclecticism, which perhaps derives from the particular needs and emphases of a given painting. There are inscriptions in paintings; inscriptions composed or selected for exhibition with paintings; inscriptions, like that for Pope's destroyed villa, composed solely for the artist's private imagination; allegorical or mythological machinery; but also the expressive naturalism of scenery itself. But it seems to me that the decisive influences on Turner's renditions of *genius loci* must have been, in the first place, those picturesque subjects already, as Ruskin put it, "notable by association." For part of the picturesque fascination

8.10. J. M. W. Turner, The Falls of the Clyde, *1802, watercolor. Walker Art Gallery, Liverpool.*

8.11. J. M. W. Turner, The Falls of the Clyde, *late 1830s, oil on canvas. Lady Lever Collection, Port Sunlight, Cheshire.*

with associations is that, verbalized, they serve the same function as inscriptions which announce *genius loci.*

Nowhere would this picturesque strategy be more apparent and, at the same time, more private than in all the landscape parks of Turner's patrons. What is crucial about these motifs is that country estates required of the landscape artist both a visual naturalism and an instinct for their special sense of place: on the one hand, optical and visual accuracy, and on the other celebration of something more elusive than simple topography; what the visiting eye would see as well as the special rapport that its owners and residents would have for an estate. We need much more research on precisely what associations, both public and private, were available to Turner and on how he translated these into visual form; available, that is to say, in the proliferating guidebooks to picturesque abbeys. castles, and country seats as well as available within family and estate traditions.[27] Places with historical associations—Stonehenge, Old Sarum, Fountains Abbey, etc.—were presumably more accessible both as places to visit and as having some shared, public meaning than the estates of private landowners.

When Turner paints scenes on Fawkes's Yorkshire estate at Farnley (fig. 8.12) he must be actively exploring meanings, associations, special apprehensions of *genius loci,* that are doubtless lost to us today except (if at all) by laborious research; the recovery of such historical nuance will be especially tricky, I imagine, even to those still in the family.

For example, Turner's view down the Avenue is toward the eighteenth-century part of Farnley Hall—what role did that play in Walter Fawkes's conscious cultivation and promotion of historical associations?[28] Did another view, from Thornberry Hill towards Almscliff Crag, with on the right the wood with its rustic walk, have particular associations, associations that in earlier management of landscape garden prospects might well have been decorated with statue or inscription to control the visitor's response? Yet another view, of Lake Tiny, seems to give this local Yorkshire view a distinctly alpine flavor, with conifers and goats, details that may allude to another Turner watercolor, this time of Chamonix, already in Farnley at the time the lake view was done about 1818—does this different (alpine) sense of place now contrived for the Farnley estate derive from some special local and family associations which Turner tried to involve in his picture?

Such questions must wait upon a deeper (perhaps impenetrable) familiarity with historical materials and attitudes. But Turner's special

8.12. J. M. W. Turner, The Woodwalk, Farnley Hall, *1818. Watercolor. Fitzwilliam Museum, Cambridge.*

sense of place, which we may document variously throughout his oeuvre, as I have tried to do with the views of Pope's villa and Thomson's tomb, is surely not likely to have deserted him while painting in the country estates of patrons who inherited through traditions of landscape gardening—at Stourhead and at Fonthill, for instance—both special attitudes toward *genius loci* and special means of establishing and communicating them. And these approaches to spirit of place within enclaves where meanings were so concentrated must have sustained Turner's work outside landscape parks. I have argued elsewhere[29] that habits learned in landscape gardens were carried into the larger landscape of the British Isles by travelers and writers during the later years of the eighteenth century; it would seem surprising if Turner also did not do the same.

His notebooks especially reveal how careful he was to record landscape subjects from different points of view or in different weathers, times of day, or even the moods in which he painted, for only in this way does a particular place yield its fullest genius. But this effort places considerable onus on the artist's stamina and imagination, so we are back with Ruskin's emphasis upon the artist's superiority and inventive energy in "Turnerian Topography." But we are also in touch with other important aspects of eighteenth- and nineteenth-century traditions of "genius loci"—notably the need to make classical *topoi* speak good English[30] and the role, not now of the place itself, but of the genius of the responding artist. The two are related.

If the whole idea of presiding spirits of place was classical in its origins, the continuing invocation of this machinery of *genius loci* posed problems for British artists who were increasingly drawn to native scenery for their subjects. The "progress of poetry" motif—the traditions descending from Greece and Rome through Italy and France to British shores—had its less articulate and somewhat differently timed counterpart in a progress of painting, including Turner's dedication to British subjects, the accidents of patronage perhaps, nevertheless coinciding with his own imaginative bent. Some of his preferred poetic sources—Thomson, Gray, Akenside—had all contributed to a naturalizing of classical material. As Thomson wrote in "Rule, Britannia!"

The Muses, still with freedom found
Shall to thy happy coast repair.

The juxtaposition of ruined classical vault and the sweep of riverside villas in Turner's *Thomson's Æolian Harp* implies a similar progress in both landscape architecture and in painting.

Poetry's most characteristic strategy, then, was to project a fusion of the native, British *genius loci* with the poet's genius. As many inscriptional verses explained, it was the spirit of place which guided the artist, initiating him into the mysteries of his native land; the poet acknowledges this with such recurrent syntax as "lead me," "teach me," "let me be thine." Inscriptions were here of paramount importance for they addressed themselves to sensibilities alert enough to appreciate the special message of the place where they were found. A similar strategy became available in the landscape garden: first via explicit emblems, including inscriptions, then by more expressive, less coercive scenery in which the visitor's own moods were capable of being merged with the special meaning of the landscape, itself being increasingly registered as British. No longer was the local topography explicit and definitive in its declaration of meaning, but the visitor was given more responsibility to create his own sense of landscape—what Wordsworth at Tintern Abbey, echoing an earlier poem of Akenside's, identified as

> *all the mighty world*
> *Of eye, and ear,—both what they half create,*
> *And what perceive.*[31]

Half creating, half perceiving is Wordsworth's version of what Ruskin called "Turnerian Topography" and is closer, too, to inscriptional traditions of *genius loci.*

What the poet acknowledges above all is the ultimately inseparable and imaginative liaison between *genius loci* and an artistic genius encountering it. Coleridge made this fusion of subject and object in a new awareness of both an essential element in his definition of the imagination.[32] Ruskin was heir to such romantic strategies when he analyzed how the windmill reacted with Turner's genius, the object fusing with the artist's subjective "largeness of sympathy," to produce a distinctive moment of Turnerian topography. "The dignity of the picturesque," he wrote, "increases from higher to lower, in exact proportion to the sympathy of the artist [with his materials in their fullness]" (VI, 23). In this encounter and creative transformation the artist must be capable of the fullest involvement whereby neither wilderness nor artist remains the same afterward.

For romantic poetry which takes these encounters as its theme the narrative of that encounter and fusion is as much the actual subject matter as the original landscape. No longer is a scene simply described, but "the very process of inscribing or interpreting it" is also incorporated. Hence the romantic lyric's affirmation of spontaneity and the nineteenth century's discovery of similar attitudes in earlier poets like Warton, whose "Inscription in a Hermitage at Ansley-Hall, in Warwickshire" was said to be composed "upon the spot, with all the objects around him, and on the spur of the moment."[33]

As almost all these inscriptional poems, by their very nature, make clear, a landscape is given voice at the same time as we learn how it possesses meaning. It is also clear that landscape gardens featured as prime sites for actual inscriptions or for implied inscriptional experience. Like reading poetry, moving through a landscape garden encourages a sense of meaning as process and product.

Painting, on the other hand, cannot easily rehearse its own composition. Though done in time, it does not easily if at all preserve that sequence in its final form. Nor, by its very nature, can a painting distinguish, as can a lyric poem, between its subject (artist) and object (landscape). But for reasons that I think are closely connected with his paintings' approaches to *genius loci* Turner seems to counteract these apparently ineluctably formal obstacles, and perhaps this was a lesson learned above all by his moving through landscape. Ruskin, for example, was able to distinguish between artist and landscape subject in the drawing of Faido; and we may see both of them whenever we recognize "visionary modification" of some topography. And in absorbing within his vision of Faido the active memory and experience of the day's journey before he reached the spot actually depicted, Turner is also in some crucial way introducing an element of time within a nontemporal medium. His fascination with sudden effects of weather is also strongly suggestive of temporal succession, while his constant recording of locations within close distance of each other also suggests the necessary route from one to another. And finally, when we see side by side two views of the same subject,[34] it is surely apt to view one as a painting that honors its motif or landscape subject over its handling and the other as one where Turner explores his medium and its imaginative excitements rather than a landscape subject.

PART THREE

Picturesque, Impressionism, Modernism

9 FRENCH IMPRESSIONIST GARDENS AND THE ECOLOGICAL PICTURESQUE

And he is really too foolish who so concentrates on a picture's colors that he is unaware of the things that are depicted.

—Pope Gregory I, late sixth century

For Alexis De Boeck

Gardens were a favorite subject of impressionist painters. Their rich and fecund images of a blooming, apparently natural world, often engulfing the human figures enclosed within it (fig. 9.1), have in their turn become a source of delight today. The huge modern popularity of impressionist renderings of gardens and other landscapes both derives from and fuels a taste for the picturesque as well as strong ecological zeal. We love these paintings because their imagery revitalized the long traditions of seeing nature through art (indeed, impressionism put the picture back into picturesque). At the same time they seem to lead us unresisting into a perfect environment of uncontaminated nature, all the more persuasive because we know that some of the same artists who ensconce us in unspoiled gardens also imaged the destruction of the countryside outside their protective fences—suburban trains rushing through the fields, the smear of factories along the Seine at Argenteuil. Yet there is a fundamental paradox in celebrating at the same time both the picturesque and the ecological efficacy of impressionist gardens.

Modern criticism of French impressionism lends considerable authority to the idea of gardens as loci of tranquility and unmediated nature. Yet for all their powerful reputation for peace and quiet, repose and contemplation, gardens have also always been battlegrounds, or at least proving grounds, where the rivalries of art and nature, of town and country, of social classes and of sexes, of past and present are acted out. Impressionist painters were more alert than is generally admitted

9.1. Pierre-Auguste Renoir, Garden in the Rue Cortot, 1876. *Carnegie Museum of Art, Pittsburgh.*

to the privileged role of gardens in these matters, and their pictures of this subject tell us a great deal about the part that late nineteenth-century garden art played in traditional and longstanding debates.

By no means all critics even acknowledge the centrality of garden subjects in impressionist work; but even for those who do, the meaning and significance of those garden depictions receive no special attention.[1] Perhaps that is just because impressionist experts are not concerned to approach the paintings as garden historians. Nor, in their necessary insistence upon the fashion in which impressionism dedicated itself to representing modern life, do they acknowledge the place which these late nineteenth-century garden pictures occupy in a long tradition of garden representations. But gardens and images of them never come into being *ex vacuo;* they are created in conscious or unconscious response to a whole congeries of facts, events, and ideas in the physical, social, and intellectual world of their makers.

This essay, then, will explore the modern moment of garden art that is revealed to us in impressionist paintings, the dialogue of that modern moment with the past, and its site as proving ground, especially for the paradoxical encounter of the picturesque and ecological holism.[2] As a thread into this labyrinth we may follow the novelist Emile Zola, who placed Claude Monet among painters whom he termed "Les Actualistes": these are the people who "interpret their epoch as men who live in it." For Zola, Monet had "sucked the milk of our age," loving "with particular affection nature that man makes modern."[3] Given the impressionists' dedication, then, to modern subjects, we must consider to what extent and how one of their most frequent subjects—the garden—was modern; whether (in Zola's terms) man made garden nature modern, or whether—as most current critical wisdom has it—gardens represented simply a welcome escape from all that modernist effort.

I

It is usual, following such stimulating art historians as T. J. Clark[4] and Robert L. Herbert, to relate impressionist interest in the landscape to the larger context of topographical, demographic, and social change during the Second Empire. Impressionist painters were, of course, attracted by Paris's new spaces and its public life, but they also followed the crowds of day-trippers and pleasure seekers out into its rural environs on their leisure days. Thus landscape became one of their abiding concerns. Included in those landscapes were either the gardens of the new developments or subdivisions that sprang up around the expanding city or, less frequently, more long established gardens. But gardens were not by any means—either in reality or on canvas—simple extensions of the countryside that served as pleasure ground for new classes of people. Gardens offered different experiences, which drew their strength from being opposed to both the new city life and the new rural entertainments and from discovering fresh associations with picturesque traditions apparently lost in the city and along the banks of the Seine. So we must look first at those sites.

Several objectives determined Baron Haussmann's wholesale reorganization of the city under the Second Empire. One was to contain riots by making new boulevards too wide for barricades; another, to allow quick access from the railway stations into the center for troops if necessary as well as citizens on business or pleasure; another was to improve sanitation by eliminating the labyrinthine alleyways.[5] Demolition and reconstruction destroyed the intimacies of the old city in the interests of wide public spaces; its center was linked to the suburbs with a network of new streets ("les grandes percées").

Yet Haussmann did not give up the city to an asphalt jungle. The boulevards were lined with trees (fig. 9.2), often large specimens transplanted during the night: instant greening.[6] Public gardens were added—Montsouris in the south and the Buttes-Chaumont in the north, both conversions of abandoned and derelict areas. As a result of Louis Napoléon's admiration for London squares and parks, Paris also acquired similar landscaping—though significantly Parisian squares were enlarged streets set amid the noise and dust of the traffic.[7]

All this was an admirable creation of social, civic, democratic space. The Irishman and garden writer William Robinson praised the "freshness, perfect keeping, and the number of people who are seated . . . reading, working, or playing" in Parisian open spaces and he compared this equality with the "few privileged persons" given access to London squares.[8] Pierre Zandomenghi's view of the *Square d'Anvers,* eleven years after Robinson's remarks, seems to endorse this democratic occupancy (fig. 9.3). Robinson (among others) also noticed how even the vigorous planting contributed to this egalitarian revivification of Parisian space, contrasting it with the "costly green toys" typical of London gardening.[9]

But what was eliminated or preempted in Paris was any sense of private garden space along with its appropriate planting.[10] At risk of

9.2. Engraving of Boulevard Richard-Lenoir, early 1860s, planned by Baron Haussmann to cover an old canal.

9.3. Pierre Zandomenghi, Square d'Anvers, *1880. Galleria d'Arte Moderna, Piacenza.*

oversimplification, what was lost was the experience of gardens for which Robinson would become famous in the years immediately after he published in 1869 his laudatory discussion of *The Parks, Promenades, and Gardens of Paris*. Indeed, it was in the very next year, 1870, that his celebrated book *The Wild Garden* gave a wholly fresh impetus to garden design. The striking difference between the two books may be merely the result of Robinson's journalistic opportunism;[11] yet at the same time this author and his two works identify and straddle a cultural fissure in late nineteenth-century gardening theory and practice. It was a divide which Robinson himself associated, as we shall see, with picturesque traditions in landscape architecture.

In Paris the impressive reconstitution of city spaces for a new, obedient, and healthy public necessarily neglected any opportunities for intimacy, small scale, and appropriate planting. What had been private domains, like the ex-Jardin (now Parc) Monceau, are seen—by Claude Monet in 1878 (Metropolitan Museum)—as haunts of Parisian crowds; Stanislaus-Victor Lépine confirms that the Tuileries (National Gallery, London), too, were a public playground. It was a rare moment for Monet to paint the Parc Monceau in 1876 (Metropolitan Museum), two years before that other canvas, as a virtually empty clearing in the encircling city. Yet even here, if we attend carefully, the new buildings peer through the protective greenery and at the far end of his vista are hints of the ubiquitous crowds, the "promenade publique" into which "le plus adorable jardin de France" had been turned.[12] Given Monet's other imagery of gardens, even this view of the Parc Monceau may share the distaste that Victor Fournel voiced when he described it as "le plus désastreux, le plus navrant échantillon du système suivi dans les restaurations des jardins publics" (the most disastrous, the most appalling example of the system applied to the restoration of public gardens). And within the green spaces of these new parks and gardens, benches and other social items recognized and determined public interests; grillwork,[13] fences, and flowerbeds directed visitors just as much as Haussmann's grid of avenues did the traffic within the larger city. The newly remodeled parks at the Bois de Boulogne (1853–1858) and the Bois de Vincennes (1857–1864) also invoked a version or notion of English landscape gardening where vistas, massed planting, and spacious areas were engineered for large social use.

If we look for representations of small, intimate private garden worlds within the city, we must go to Montmartre in areas that eluded the Baron's ruthless remaking of the city. It is here that Armand Guillaumin in 1865 found a small garden space rarely documented in this period. Alfred Sisley four years before still showed Montmartre as an urban jumble on the edge of un-Haussmannized open ground.[14]

The Paris more regularly recorded by the impressionists, because it so intrigued them as the stage of modern life, is, of course, the world of the tree-lined *grands boulevards,* the open public spaces of the Quai du Louvre or the Jardin d'Enfant (fig. 9.4), or the new gardens which constituted the grounds of the Exposition Universelle of 1867 seen from the viewing platform on the Trocadéro—a brand-new public garden which Manet in 1867 shows with its instant flowers carefully protected from trampling feet by statutory wire hoops (fig. 9.5). Another prime image of Manet and his impressionist followers was the public gardens of the city in their guise as entertainment grounds, theaters of leisure—Manet's *Music in the Tuileries* of 1860–1861 shows a site that twenty years later, painted by Jean Berand,[15] was even more decorous and refined and as a consequence less "rural." In contrast, the open-air cafes of Montmartre still preserved a country ambience.[16] But along the tree-lined boulevards, the urban verdure signaled how all real distinctions between city and country had been lost. "Boulevards" had once been walks along fortifications and ramparts—decisive zones between urban and rural; Haussmann's instant greening of his new boulevards blurred these boundaries, as his device of bringing avenues, an essentially rural feature, into the city also effectively announced the confusion of city and country.[17] And immediately off most of the *grands boulevards* were streets with no trees at all, which quickly negated the illusion of country.

II

There were many voices raised in anger at what Haussmann and his lieutenants did to the gardens of Paris.[18] The impressionist delight in small, intimate garden spaces of private houses is a similar, though oblique, admonition. But perhaps the most pervasive mode of protest came from those Parisians who did not want the ambiguous moments of *rus in urbe;* indeed, even before Haussmann there were those who, lamenting the lost public gardens like Marboeuf, Beaujon, or Tivoli, placed their confidence in the "entrepreneurs de plaisirs champêtres" beyond the suburbs.[19] Taking advantage of the new railways, Parisians in ever-increasing numbers escaped to the nearby countryside, the "real

9.4. Claude Monet, Le Jardin d'Enfant, *1867. Allen Memorial Art Museum, Oberlin College.*

9.5. Edouard Manet, The Universal Exposition of 1867, *1867. National Gallery, Oslo.*

9.6. Berthe Morisot, View of Paris from the Trocadéro, *1872. Santa Barbara Museum of Art.*

thing" (or so they thought). There people of all classes could entertain the illusion that their free time and private lives were not manipulated, restructured, by the new topography and commercial interests of Haussmann's Paris; they could escape the "city of straight lines and unreadable facades" and discover what passed for picturesque scenery.[20] The city could seem intolerably new and raw, as in Manet's view from the newly established Buttes de Chaillot, which Berthe Morisot, one of the finest garden painters, also saw as a bare urban vista (fig. 9.6). But outside the city and its suburbs was the seemingly ancient world of nature, a world of picturesque scenery; here were no *pélouses interdites*.

The impressionist painters were quick to follow the crowds, eager to track modern life in its outreach to the leisure grounds of the Grande Jatte, the river banks at Argenteuil, or the bathing place called La Grenouillère. As T. J. Clark has documented, these country retreats contained many signs of the commercial exploitation of the new leisure, not least of which were the omnipresent railway line and the industries which serviced the growing metropolis.

Clark draws our attention to two paintings of Monet which addressed this erosion of the countryside in the year 1875, views on the Boulevard Saint-Denis at Argenteuil which show the vista from his house and how it looked, with its green shutters, from beside the railway embankment. The new villa and boulevard had come into existence precisely because the railway gave easy access in and out of Paris.[21] The view from the house (fig. 9.7) shows the messy detritus of this new commercial development—railway sheds, wicker fences, the square in front of the station with its grid of plane trees, factories beyond. In short, Monet saw the town eroding and tarnishing its rural setting, just as the pedestrians dirty the snow in their hurry to and from the railway station. "It stood," writes Clark, "for everything painting was supposed to ignore." And Clark opposes it to the private garden, in the one passage of his book that touches upon this motif; the private garden, unseen behind the green palings of Monet's first view—a garden where the

> painter would make his own landscape . . . a place filled with intimate things, hoops, hats, coffee, children, wives, maids. It would be an interior, a fiction, a hortus conclusus. There would be people in it, brought on to emphasise its artificiality . . . and finally the garden [would be] brought into the house— a watery, vegetable, uterine stillness, all polished floors and potted plants.

9.7. Claude Monet, View of Argenteuil (from the Artist's Rented House), *1875. Nelson-Atkins Museum of Art, Kansas City.*

We may all recognize impressionism's garden motifs in that summary of its garden world; indeed we shall see many of them in my later images. But while it is a response that perhaps grows logically out of Clark's analysis of the same painter's treatment of leisure and pleasure in the countryside, as a consideration of the impressionist garden it seems inadequate.[22]

Impressionist gardens have largely been ignored as part of their artists' confrontation with modern life; doubtless this is due to the relative paucity of strikingly modern or modernist interventions in landscape architecture.[23] For whatever reason, however, criticism has written gardens out of the record of modern landscape, which is admitted as being "one of the great subjects of impressionist painting";[24] they survive as private fictions, artificial and timeless zones totally unimportant compared with the worlds of either Haussmann's Paris or the tourists' countryside; or they are elided with the countryside and lose their own identity.[25] Yet gardens were a unique element in that new landscape beyond the urban grid—look for example at the lines of raw new villas which Monet painted at Petit Gennevilliers[26]—and therefore they were necessarily part of impressionism's response to the modern. The modern world cannot, in fact, be represented (as it is by most writers on impressionism) only in terms of factories along the Seine, ubiquitous railway lines and smoking trains, and a mixed bag of day-trippers out from the city with all their uneasy fascination with this new thing, leisure. Gardens, too, could be deliberate, if less obvious or aggressive, representations and accommodations of the modern world.

III

What is immediately striking about most impressionist gardens is that they are emphatically not the nasty new creations with which Parisians newly establishing themselves in the suburbs were satirically credited. They were emphatically not the "odious turf of . . . villas *extra muros,* these lawns brought over from England on the Dover or Southampton boat . . . a globe of silvered glass [see fig. 9.8] round the corner, and a little fountain pissing its monotonous song."[27] Nor again were impressionist gardens "stylish[ly] surrounded by walls and closed off on their facades by iron gates," nor "sloping gardens separated by new walls, iron gates, lawns, greenhouses, and vases of geraniums."[28] It is as if, despite the incidence of garden benches[29] exactly like those in the Parisian public gardens (fig. 9.9), Manet, Monet, Morisot, Caillebotte, Bazille, and Renoir eschewed any comparison with the city, and, despite geraniums and greenhouses (to which we shall return), they also avoided any semblance of these new subdivisions, old aristocratic land cut up into "a thousand parcels" or vineyards redeveloped with "cardboard chateaux" into a "rural *argentea mediocritas*."[30]

Furthermore, neither was the impressionists' garden world the neat patches of ground shown in Monet's *Houses at the Edge of the Field* (fig. 9.10). Their diminutive gardens seem rebuked by the expansive and mobile sky and the rich colors—mustard yellow, strong poppy reds—of the flowery fields. Jejune and even raw, these Argenteuil plots are planted with young trees that provide no shelter along the strips of lawn; the absurdly serpentine path, prominent down the garden of the central dwelling, meanders through no growth of shrubbery.[31]

All impressionist gardens look, by contrast, like well-wooded, heavily planted, dense, long-established territories (fig. 9.11). Some of the gardens painted were indeed old enough to have achieved this growth; some, however, like that of Monet's second house at Argenteuil were brand-new. Yet part of the double retreat from Paris in the first place and then from the spoiled countryside of its environs in the second entailed the illusion—on canvas if not on the ground—that the house in the country was surrounded by ancient gardens. The suburban villa, no less than Haussmann's Paris, could engage in the instant greening and coloration of its property.

Yet such fictions of longevity did not mean perpetuating old garden styles and design. Impressionist gardens, even those belonging to family homes like Caillebotte's, represented themselves as modern: modern in form and decoration, in planting and in use.[32] Consequently, they took their place as part of the well-known impressionist rivalry with the past: just as Manet's *Olympia* competes with and updates Titian's Venuses, or some of Monet's rural scenes vie with and replace Dutch seventeenth-century landscape with contemporary French ones, so gardens were also involved in a complex dialogue with earlier traditions of painting, landscape architecture, and horticulture.

The painterly tradition that was "made new"[33] was largely the French eighteenth-century of Watteau, Hubert Robert, Fragonard, Pater (fig. 9.12); yet behind those was a considerable Italian and especially Dutch repertoire of garden scene painting. The horticultural and garden traditions against which the new gardens of late nineteenth-century France (and indeed of England) defined themselves were a mixture of both old geometric layouts (André Le Nôtre's, par excellence) and a peculiar French version of the English picturesque (what may be called "drawing-board curvilinear").

9.8. Camille Pissarro, The Garden of Les Mathurins at Pontoise, *1876. Nelson-Atkins Museum of Art, Kansas City.*

9.9. Bench in Monet's garden at Giverny. Lilla Cabot Perry Papers. Archives of American Art, Smithsonian Institution, Washington, D.C.

9.10. Claude Monet, Houses at the Edge of a Field, *1873. Nationalgalerie, Staatliche Museen Preussischer Kulturbesitz, Berlin.*

9.11. Claude Monet, The Garden at Vétheuil, *1881. (Photograph courtesy Christie's, New York.)*

9.12. Jean-Baptiste Joseph Pater, On the Terrace, *1730s. National Gallery of Art, Washington, D.C.*

IV

Gardens encourage and accommodate a broad range of activities; in substance these have changed little through the centuries and are recorded in garden paintings from late medieval French manuscripts to Fragonard and Pater. Gardens are territories of play—both play as alternative to work or business and play as theater, make-believe, the whole gamut of role playing that is human life. Though this last is not obviously confined to gardens, it flourished there because gardens are special sites of artifice pretending to be nature; though if you were convinced a garden was wholly natural, you were tempted to think you could dispense with role playing.[34]

Gardens have been the locations for solitary meditation, which may run the gamut from reading books to dreaming, and to fantasizing. They have also been especially apt for love making, where the intensity of passion or seduction is mirrored in the garden's concentrated reorganization and embellishment of nature. Equally, they may serve as locations for group activity where some specific interest—be it close family, gender solidarity, or some other "clubbishness"—can feel confident that it is paramount and cherished; these moments of community may be symbolized in feastings or listening to the harmony of music or assisting at some other entertainment—all activities which, like gardens, meld art and nature.

In all these painted representations the garden displays usually two supreme qualities: firstly, it is private, or at least you get in because you know a club member or there is a limited "open house"; and secondly, it functions to materialize escape, giving the sense of a physical, felt, absolutely tangible place for floating free from the contingencies and obligations of the "real" world outside the garden; or, alternatively, if that outside life does enter the garden, it there obtains a new and sharper zest. Another dimension of this reification is the realization in gardens (and therefore in images of them) of the power and status of those able to bring all of these other things into being.

Now all of these traditional motifs in European garden painting can be paralleled in impressionism. The similarities are often striking, but that probably speaks simply of a garden's enduring control of human behavior. The contrasts, however, are more instructive, and given the impressionist sense of rivalry with the past probably more or less conscious (Monet, we know, admired Watteau).

One obvious contrast is that impressionist gardens witness the arrival of the French bourgeois;[35] in contrast to the aristocratic dramatis personae of Watteau or Fragonard, they present themselves, perhaps rather self-consciously, as ordinary, modern folk (fig. 9.13). Not, they are concerned to assure us, the likes of the day-trippers along the banks of the Seine: for one thing, their leisure is more leisurely, less snatched from the working week; their children play undisturbed or watched over by nursemaids (fig. 9.14); meals can be abandoned (and perhaps returned to) while ladies stroll off round the garden without bonnet or parasol (fig. 9.15). It is all less insouciant than in Watteau or Fragonard, but more deliberate and less boisterous than the picnicking along the Seine, more determined to show off the private, leisured garden world, even perhaps to try out what leisure is all about.[36] And privacy was the bourgeois' almost obsessive theme: not only were their gardens behind villa walls—you could not see the gardens from the front of Monet's house on the Boulevard Saint-Denis at Argenteuil—but they were compulsively represented as complete enclosures;[37] dense growth of shrubs or flowers block virtually every vista, especially of any length; trees eliminate even the sky that habitually tells of a world beyond the garden. Yet impressionist paintings, sold to the public through dealers and salerooms, paradoxically admit us to what Louis Blairet called the "mysteries of the private and pastoral life" of Argenteuil.[38]

Indeed the impressionists reverse the traditional emphasis on privacy of garden paintings—representations of princely or aristocratic power aside[39]—which always stressed the private and were in their turn largely for private scrutiny. Impressionists contrariwise painted their garden privacy for public display and for sale by their Parisian dealers and thereafter for viewing by purchasers among the nouveaux riches.[40] If work or business had always been left outside gardens, now the very business of painting was itself a garden activity, implied in all those canvases of garden subjects or even figured explicitly as a theme (fig. 9.16). Furthermore, the business of domestic chores now spills out into the gardens (as they never could in city apartments); the bourgeois pride in housekeeping becomes a leitmotif of their garden paintings (fig. 9.17), with doubtless a debt here to Dutch painting.

Commentators have recently made much of the boredom or even frustrations of these images of country living, finding easy parallels with writings by Flaubert or the Goncourts.[41] These modern ennuis may be represented in impressionist paintings; but then they were present too in earlier pictures—simply doing nothing can be boring as well as hugely enjoyable when outside the garden life has been busy

9.13. Claude Monet, Women in a Garden, *1867. Musée d'Orsay, Paris.*

9.14. Claude Monet, Monet's Garden at Argenteuil, *1872. The Art Institute of Chicago; Mr. and Mrs. Martin A. Ryerson Collection.*

9.15. Claude Monet, The Luncheon, *c. 1875. Musée d'Orsay, Paris.*

9.16. Pierre-Auguste Renoir, Monet Painting in His Garden, *1873. Wadsworth Atheneum, Hartford, Connecticut.*

9.17. Claude Monet, Camille Monet and Child in a Garden, *1875. Museum of Fine Arts, Boston.*

and fraught. What is, however, new, striking, and arguably more important is the frequent disclosure of social unease or even fracture. The long tradition of conversation pictures, often set in gardens, drew upon the root meaning of conversation: living in society with people, what used to be called intercourse.[42] The impressionist conversation painting (fig. 9.18) is more likely to offer interrupted conversations; or people walk too far away for us to "overhear" their exchanges; backs are turned from the viewer,[43] parasols mask faces; alternatively, the viewer is confronted suddenly and uneasily as if he or she were an intruder, with conversations inside the picture even broken off at that moment of interruption (compare this with the easy aristocratic acceptance of our "presence" in Pater or Fragonard).[44]

Another modern development of these bourgeois conversation pieces is the total disappearance of the garden as a site for love making. The lower classes, implies one Renoir picture now in the Getty Museum, do that in the countryside behind bushes. There are some moments of conjugal serenity, but far fewer than in Dutch and Flemish predecessors especially. On the rare occasions when love seems to be admitted, it is what the English poem by George Meredith of 1862 called "modern love"—difficult, anxious, fraught, as perhaps with Monet's portrait of his wife Camille on a park bench with a strange gentleman.[45]

V

These modern declensions of the genre of the conversation piece could not exist independently of the kind of gardens we are shown: a world of closed, elusive, unstable, ambiguous spaces. Backs are turned upon us, faces blocked in but vacant of expression; views rarely extend outside the garden, but often we cannot see very far within it either. Both painted figures in gardens and ourselves as "visitors" to them are suspended in uncertain space; where we are, where the paths lead or where they have come from, how we negotiate a passage from where we are to another part of the garden, all are enigmas. In older paintings, there were vistas, or some local item of sculpture that gave topographical meaning and point to the scene; in even the wildest rococo park, a clearing announced itself. In impressionist gardens there are virtually no statues[46]—these are the sign of public gardens—and all seems as if we are left somewhere unspecified except for the general notion of garden, in a dream of nature that is prolix, profuse, all-embracing, dizzy with color, and with the other senses seeming to bombard us

9.18. Berthe Morisot, In a Garden (Gathering Flowers), *1879. National Museum, Stockholm.*

also. Monet's garden at Giverny is an extreme case of this, the logical terminus of much impressionist concern with gardens in both its profusion and densities and in the garden as picturesque site. In short, the garden is a fictive rather than an actual place, made for and on the canvas.

Impressionist gardens characterized themselves as unlike either Paris gardens and parks or the raw artifice which the satirists and the scornful, as we have seen, identified with new suburban villas. The impressionist gardens were distinctly not Parisian; they were abundantly "country," yet without the industrial smudges on the actual countryside beyond their walls. They were something of a construction. At Vétheuil (in the period between Argenteuil and his final removal to Giverny) Monet wrote that he was becoming "more and more peasantlike,"[47] but his gardens were typical of all impressionist gardens in not being at all peasantlike (as we may see by comparing a few subjects of genuinely rural dwellers). Above all, work had a limited and special place in them.[48]

There were no straight lines, as in the classical French garden of the seventeenth century or in Haussmann's boulevards: possible exceptions, the famous straight line of Monet's Giverny (fig. 9.19) and its rectangular flower beds, are always shown as eroded, even threatened, by an explosion of plants from either side; significantly, one of the first things Monet did was to remove the clipped box down the orchard walk which articulated a geometry too precisely.[49] Otherwise, I cannot think of any impressionist path the end of which is shown. All is hidden, concealed; the visitor's onward glance always thwarted.

These curves and bends, however, are not those of the new parks like the Bois de Boulogne (figs. 9.20–21). There the urbane whirl of parabolas—almost wholly a creation of the drawing board (they are most unnatural)—signify a French rendition of the so-called informality of the English landscape park.[50] The extravagent curvilinear landscape style of the new Bois is apparently totally at odds with the straight lines of Haussmann's new city avenues, which, if anything, could be said to revive the imperialist geometry of Louis XIV and for analogous political purposes.[51] In fact, as such a hostile contemporary writer as Victor Fournel shrewdly perceived, Bois ("tout est factice") and boulevard displayed the same artifice. He rightly insisted that the apparently natural forms of earth and the trees had all been regulated: the curves were simply "un pendant à la rue de Rivoli."[52] Here Paris becomes a

9.19. Claude Monet, Garden Path at Giverny, *1902. Kunsthistorisches Museum, Vienna.*

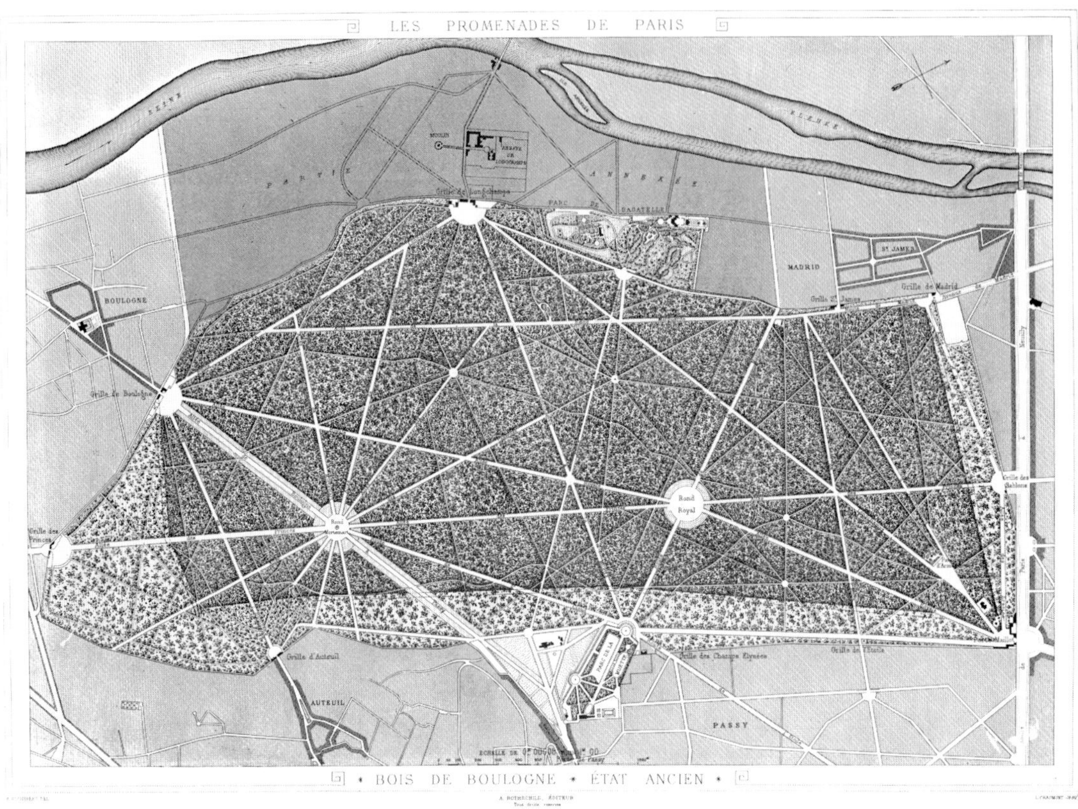

9.20. *The old Bois de Boulogne, from Adolphe Alphand,* Les Promenades de Paris *(Paris, 1867–1873). Dumbarton Oaks, Trustees for Harvard University.*

9.21. *The new Bois de Boulogne, from William Robinson,* The Parks, Promenades and Gardens of Paris *(London, 1869). Dumbarton Oaks, Trustees for Harvard University.*

BOIS DE BOULOGNE.

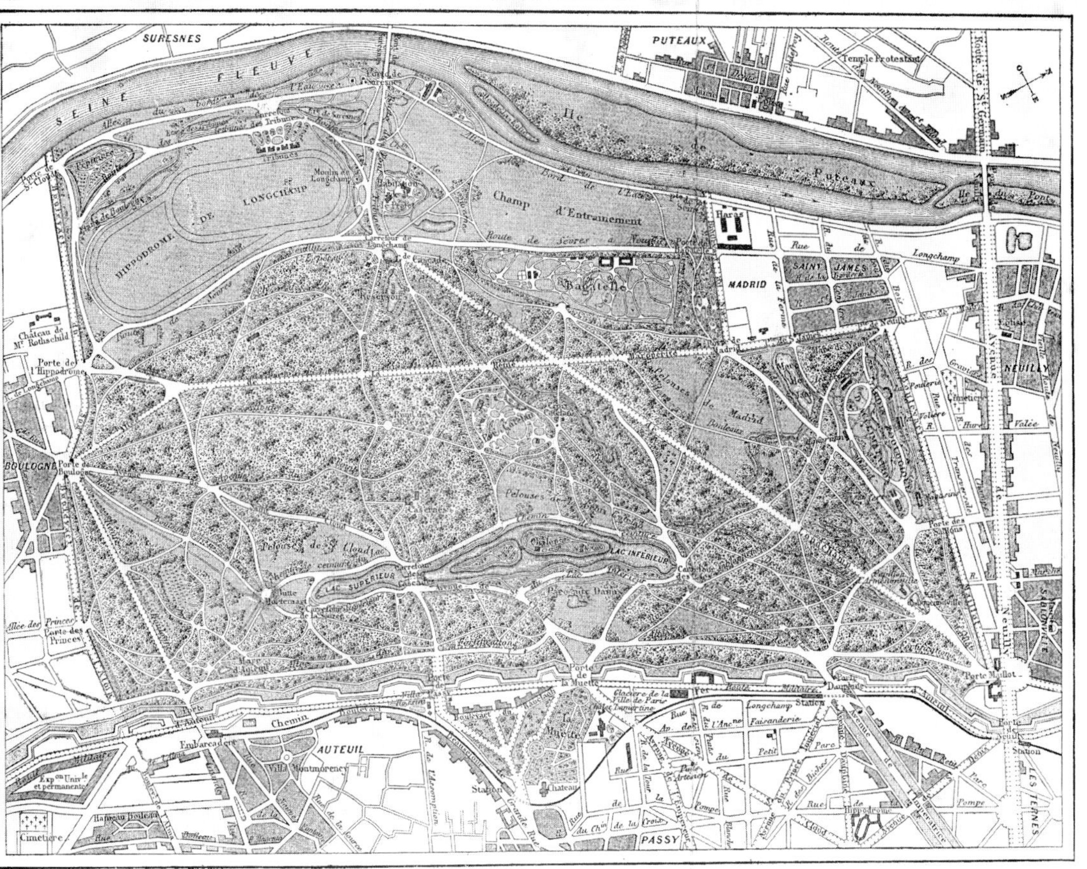

bureaucratically organized "nature" created by an architect and an engineer: "fabriqué en entier par le main de l'homme, où tout est faux . . . cet ingénieux jardin, travaillé bien mieux que nature [où] on a supprimé le parfum des fleurs" (fabricated in its entirety by the hand of man, where everything is false . . . this ingenious garden, organized much better than nature could, where the perfume of the flowers has been eliminated).[53] The planting, says Fournel, is correct, elegant, disciplined, "en harmonie avec les splendeurs égalitaires du nouveau Paris." And, as Berthe Morisot's paintings of the Bois reveal, their wide social spaces became as favorite a haunt of the new leisured classes as did the *grands boulevards* that Renoir painted.

The impressionist garden, then, has nothing to do with either the spatial arrangement of this newly renovated Bois or the planting there and in other public gardens under Haussmann's engineer turned gardenist, Adolphe Alphand. William Robinson was strangely enthusiastic about the style of this planting, which consisted mainly of large-leaved, half-hardy plants, the success of which was the bold statements they made in large spaces (figs. 9.22–23). Even if we discount their mode of depiction in Alphand's book *Les Promenades de Paris,* these gross musa, colocasia, dracaena, begonia, or coleus are totally alien to the impressionist treatment of plant material. Indeed, if Parisian plants were treated in the dense, clustered way of impressionism they'd be likely to yield the plantscapes of Douanier Rousseau!

Rousseau's works are a useful foil in trying to understand the slightly earlier impressionist garden world. His landscapes are wild and savage, the domain of beasts and buccaneers; their nature is old, primordial, with dense and heavy foliage, preternatural. Impressionism tries for the same sense of natural profusion, sharing therefore with Rousseau an opposition to "la cité neutre des peuples civilisés";[54] but it is purged of frissons or mystery. Where Rousseau gives each plant its shape and line (we know he studied in the greenhouses of the Jardin des Plantes), the impressionists render textures, colors, and shapes in order to represent the eye's spontaneous adventures in the light and shade.

But if we start to look closely at all those geraniums, begonias, dahlias, standard roses, we realize that this "natural" profusion is the result of careful attention and excessive care. The gardens which impressionists image necessarily depended upon a considerable industry of nurseries:[55] we may recall that 1860 saw the production of the double geranium; gladioli (fig. 9.24) were introduced also at this time.[56] Their horticultural technology is exactly like that of the Parisian groundsman,

9.22. P. Lambotte, "Colocasia Bataviensis," from Alphand, Les Promenades de Paris.

PLATE XV.

FINE-LEAVED PLANTS IN THE PARC MONCEAU.

Caladium. Aralia. Phœnix. Musa Ensete. Yucca.

9.23. William Robinson, "Fine-Leaved Plants in the Parc Monceau," pl. XV from The Parks, Promenades and Gardens of Paris.

9.24. Claude Monet, Gladioli, *1876.*
Detroit Institute of Arts.

as the presence of greenhouses in some of their paintings testifies. Yet the readiness to acknowledge the greenhouse, its produce, or its labor-intensive work—despite Renoir's splendid painting of the products of the greenhouse (Oskar Reinhart collection, Winterthur, Switzerland)—is not always forthcoming. Giverny in the end had five gardeners, but they are never shown. Occasionally, we see Monet himself at work (he like Caillebotte was an avid gardener), but this is garden work as hobby, pastime.[57] With the exception of some fine Caillebotte images of gardeners and of the vegetable gardens painted by the only working-class impressionist, Renoir,[58] garden maintenance is not generally part of the impressionists' visual message, though it had to be an integral part of their garden world.[59]

VI

The kind of garden represented by impressionism has become so much and so popular a part of twentieth-century garden culture[60] that we fail to recognize it for what it is. Above all we fail to situate it in a period of energetic horticultural activity (1867, for instance, saw the creation of the Ecole Municipale d'Horticulture et d'Arboriculture, moved to the Bois de Vincennes in 1936). Distinguished critics of impressionism such as John Rewald seem innocent of the ironies of, say, Giverny's construction; persisting with quotations like Lamartine's "Mais la nature est la / Qui t'invite et qui t'aime," they miss the rival emphases of contemporaries' accounts:

> Their [Monet's gardeners'] whole art consisted of caring for the garden seemingly effortlessly, giving Monet the impression of semi-abandon, of total freedom, under his rigorous surveillance. He was very strict, and I saw him flush with anger when an order was not carried out.[61]

Yet this garden artist who arranges and controls, in short makes art, has in his paintings marginalized his visible intervention in favor of the fecund hand of spontaneous nature.

It is, of course, an age-old debate and confusion: art that conceals art.[62] But it is at the same time and perhaps more importantly a sign of modern gardening's unease in the crosscurrents of twentieth-century garden design and taste.

In 1869 Robinson admired the brave new planting of Haussmann's Parisian gardens; yet the very next year he published *The Wild Garden,* with which he took possession of a substantial segment of the gardening public by opposing above all the system of carpet bedding in parks and gardens, "a species of extensive coloured cotton handkerchief," the absence of which he had welcomed in the Parc des Batignolles.[63] Robinson's wild garden "school" came to include Gertrude Jekyll, then Vita Sackville-West, Lanning Roper, Penelope Hobhouse, and many other luminaries of the twentieth-century garden.[64] The rival tradition stemmed from Reginald Blomfield's *The Formal Garden in England,* an arts and crafts revival style, which, though it in fact gave ample scope to similar kinds of planting as its rival, emphasized architectural layouts. One school seems artificial and contrived, the other natural (the terms are par for the course in any garden discussion of the twentieth century).

In hindsight the impressionists seemed to belong wholly to the Robinsonian line of development and seem to lend credence both to its antiquity and to its endemic naturalness (fig. 9.25)—their art, so the argument goes, shows "bloom upon bloom in an enduring variety of colours and shapes."[65] But as we gaze upon the painted surfaces of impressionist canvases, upon what has been called "the dance of likenesses, guessed at or half-glimpsed,"[66] we should recognize that their gardens were a novel confection: constructed in a special, specifically suburban, social context, with some dependence upon a new taste for half-hardy plants developed in Paris and some considerable painterly license in creating the illusion of old, rich natural profusions when the reality was either less prolix or was supported by greenhouses, gardeners, and something of the same technology that Haussmann's teams brought to bear upon the instant greening of the French capital.

The impressionist garden can, then, be called, paradoxically, the new ecological picturesque. It makes pictures of a world where art has been suppressed and nature allowed to thrive, yet seems at the same time to celebrate "dreams of a seasonless exotic world."[67] Unlike the earlier, hugely popular eighteenth-century picturesque which observed landscape in terms of painterly compositions and with which Robinson did not wish to associate his new garden style,[68] the modern version is the painterly imposition upon a garden world of its own delight not only in intricate patterns of colors in light and shade but in a natural world where human intervention appears to be negligible. It is a commonplace that figures disappear from Monet's gardens by the 1880s, even in much of the photography of them (fig. 9.26 and see, for instance, also fig. 9.19). That is just his strict pursuit of a logic always present in his and his colleagues' garden views.

9.25. Frontispiece by Alfred Parsons from William Robinson, The Wild Garden *(1881). Dumbarton Oaks, Trustees for Harvard University.*

So it is no wonder that the impressionist garden, endlessly popular, yet largely (if I am right) misread, continues to lend its authority to a contemporary ecological passion whose fanaticism and extremism often gets completely out of hand, displacing humans entirely from the earth.[69] So we should harken to that intricate and intelligent decadent, J. K. Huysmans, who knew that "decidedly, in these times of ours, horticulturists are the only and true artists."[70]

9.26. Monet's garden at Giverny. Lilla Cabot Perry Papers, Archives of American Art, Smithsonian Institution, Washington, D.C.

10 THE PICTURESQUE LEGACY TO MODERNIST LANDSCAPE ARCHITECTURE

The crucial moment of modernism occurred not circa 1900 but rather one hundred years earlier. This is when Yve-Alain Bois in a provocative article on the picturesque dates "the rupture of modernity."[1] The years around 1800 were also crucial in the history of landscape architecture theory and practice; indeed, it is largely to English design of that period that the rest of Europe as well as a new generation of landscape architects like A. J. Downing in the United States would look back. That moment constituted the watershed in landscape architecture for a variety of nonartistic reasons. Since then there has really been no comparably fundamental change in social, political, aesthetic, and psychological attitudes: we still exist in a world that was determined by what happened around 1800.

The failure to identify and understand that watershed contributed substantially to the historical and theoretical inadequacies of those who prompted modernist landscape architecture. Christopher Tunnard's *Gardens in the Modern Landscape,* published in 1938, is typical of this cavalier treatment of history; he included an ambiguous and absurdly eclectic account of the English landscape garden, highlighting eccentric though doubtless interesting moments like the Painshill grotto in a photo essay and laying out the portraits of the century's main gardeners—Kent, Brown, Repton—in unchronological order. His account of what he fondly calls "romanticism" was even more sloppy and useless.

This ignorance or cavalier disregard of history is part and parcel of a larger poverty of discourse; as Steven R. Krog has written, landscape architecture is "a discipline in intellectual disarray" and with a "deficiency of theoretical discourse."[2] Of all the modern arts none has displayed such a meager command of analytical, including rudimentary philosophical, language as landscape studies; this can be examined in some of the central English-language texts of landscape modernism—

Fletcher Steele, Percy S. Cane, Christopher Tunnard, and others discussed here. For example what was, despite its date, one of the first attempts to codify landscape architecture modernism, Elizabeth B. Kassler's *Modern Gardens and the Landscape,* evinced little historical discrimination.[3] And where else but in landscape architecture theory would an appeal to "the 'back to nature' philosophy of Rousseau" have seemed adequate intellectual history?[4]

But before we discuss some of these historical and theoretical failings, it will be worth considering, somewhat schematically, seven simple truths about the late eighteenth century that have been wholly neglected by modernist writings.

First, after 1800 garden design became available to a suddenly increased section of the population; there had always been small gardens, vernacular plots, but now there was the chance for far more landowners than before to invoke fine-art treatment of their property; landscape architecture invaded the suburbs and their villas, the public park, the burial ground. And as a consequence not only did the amount of landscape design increase but now more kinds of design were called for also (though not necessarily delivered). Further, with the work of Humphry Repton, John Claudius, and Jane Loudon, the art of garden design with all its new modes and styles was codified and broadcast through printed texts and journals (by contrast, their two foremost predecessors, William Kent and Capability Brown, had issued no theoretical or practical texts).

Second, this considerable growth in the gardening public coincided with a breakdown of the public claims for the fine arts (to which landscape gardening at that time aspired). This breakdown as it concerns painting has been set out by John Barrell,[5] and his admirable and cogent account should be studied by everyone interested in seeing why, quite suddenly toward the end of the eighteenth century, many arts surrendered the idea of service to some general, collective public will and fragmented into instances of personal expression.

Third, what Barrell explains in political, ideological ways may be tracked also in terms of psychology. The legacy of John Locke throughout the eighteenth century[6] culminated in the romantic privileging of the individual: each man or woman could enjoy—nay, could only have—his or her own perspective, mental set, sensibility, and, by extension, response to everything around them including gardens, parks, and the wilderness. The wilderness became fashionable precisely because it occasioned highly personal experiences of sublime frissons in opposition to the old socially engineered and sanctioned attitudes available within landscape parks and gardens.

Fourth, it was at the moment of the social expansion of landscape architecture, freed of its public art functions and now appealing to and encouraging the taste of whomever chose to invoke it, that style became available as if in some mail-order catalogue. Style for the generation of early landscape gardenists—those who designed Castle Howard, Stowe, and Stourhead among others—had been a matter of ideology; the medium was the message.[7] When William Kent featured Gothick and/or classical buildings, he was able to assume that at the very least for a small circle of cognoscenti their codes were readable; forty years on, Humphry Repton not only did not encode his architectural styles, but he offered his clients straightforward visual options (see fig. 5.3). By then style could be simply a formal choice, and if, say, *Gothick* had meanings—or more likely something as vague as associations—they were local, personal, and not obviously encoded in the visible style.

The picturesque fashion coincided, as has already been argued in this volume, with the diversity of views touched upon in the third and fourth points above. Though there was a considerable and weighty literature on the picturesque and though its afficionados proposed various rules and regulations for regarding the world picturesquely, in practice it endorsed, indeed it released, a plethora of personal responses to the environment. So the fifth point concerns a consequence of this diversity of styles—Chinese, Turkish, classical, Gothic—in landscape architecture; within the picturesque camp you could also opt for models in the pictorial styles of Claude, Dughet, Poussin, Teniers, Hobbema, and so on.[8] Given the surrender of any viable public role by the arts, taste became a term which each person constructed for him or herself; whereas in the early eighteenth century the invocation of "taste" largely still meant the taste of a small elite, confident and secure about its values (political, social, and aesthetic), now it was a notion up for grabs. Journalists vied to convince readers that their aesthetics and taste were right, but a community of right judgment in these matters had become a matter of opinion and fashion. Eclecticism of styles—the Victorian garden was a splendid exhibition ground of this—joined with an eclecticism of taste, visual values, and notions of what was beautiful in landscape architecture. We still inhabit this world of relative taste.

Sixth, the landscape architect could no longer count upon any normative value for *nature*. Everybody now had their version of nature, like the formal eclecticism just discussed. From the Renaissance to, say, Alexander Pope, though the term "nature" had a congeries of meanings, there was some coherence about their interpretation; within a given rhetorical context there would be a large consensus about meaning. So when garden design sought to represent nature there was some unanimity as to what was being represented and how. By 1800 the word *nature,* always a portmanteau term, was invoked by different individuals or social groups for varied purposes. Even in the limited meaning of the physical world of earth, water, vegetation, and so on, there were different natures depending, perhaps chiefly, upon the cultural, rhetorical, and topographical situation of the speaker. Nature had always taken its meaning in some structural relationship with other concepts; hence, I think, that tripartite arrangement of sixteenth- and seventeenth-century gardens where three distinct areas presented different ratios of control to wilderness.[9] But by 1800 its possible meanings had enlarged precisely according to the alternative structures opened to human experience; if somebody had traveled, say, through the Swiss Alps, they had a standard of "nature" quite different from somebody who had never left the English Home Counties.[10] We can explain the different emphases of Uvedale Price and Richard Payne Knight in the picturesque controversy at the end of the eighteenth century precisely by the relative wildness of their estates, Foxley and Downton. We still live with this structuralist determination of nature: to understand exactly what a person means when he or she craves the wilderness depends very much where on the scale of urban-rural-primeval that person is habitually situated.

In its heyday around 1800 the picturesque was one way of coping with this various and fluid natural world "out there." Whatever the small print of its seemingly interminable debates—precisely those journalistic skirmishes to win public support for one particular point of view noticed above—the main concern of the picturesque was how to process the unmediated wild world, how to control it or make it palatable for consumption by sanitizing it with art.[11] Given different needs, the picturesque could invoke different styles of picture to format the raw materials of the natural scene. For the more timorous, Claude or a homely Dutch style would serve; stronger spirits could mediate via Ruisdael or Salvator Rosa; but whatever you did, nature out there was recycled for civilized use and consumption.

One further aspect of the picturesque concerns us. It became programmatically opposed to other styles: to the so-called formal or regular styles of garden design, most obviously; but also even to the most refined vision of the landscape garden under Capability Brown, the representation of natural materials in their ideal, perfected forms. These were deemed too bare, too boring, largely because their aesthetic purpose was lost to sight. In their place was promoted the fuzzy, busy, colorful, endlessly textured picturesque. Long since denuded of the older assumption that picture meant human story, a strenuous version of the picturesque in which the likes of Alexander Pope and William Kent had still believed,[12] the picturesque from around 1800 to this very day has become the style to fill anything perceived as a landscape vacuum. Just as picturesque taste had been popularized by invoking the busy texture of engravings, where lines and scratches must fill all the surface of the plate, so the picturesque in garden design has crammed space with materials, determined to keep the eye endlessly busy.[13]

Few who have pronounced on the relation of modern design to its historical predecessors have appreciated that those radical alterations in theory and practice took place at all, let alone been able to date them to somewhere around 1800, or seen that they were significant and were orchestrated by nonartistic or at least broadly cultural factors. In other words, it was not just a matter of garden aesthetics.

From the late eighteenth century an obsession with one kind of garden—basically the English landscape or sometimes (significantly) the picturesque garden of the upper and middling landed gentry—seems to have prevented theory from addressing the many other types of site that the modern world has called for since that watershed of 1800. The grounds of a typical English country estate provided the model for all nineteenth-century developments: the cemetery, the public park, the golf course. And the fixation on that one hypothetical type doubtless explains some of the great missed opportunities of the twentieth century: airports, the highways (some American parkways aside),[14] the railroad (the failure to undertake interesting railroad landscaping everywhere is one of the appalling failures of the profession).[15] Garrett Eckbo, Dan Kiley, and James Rose did discuss the new possibilities of school and other community landscaping, urban spaces, and wilderness parks in a series of articles in the *Architectural Record* of 1939, and in so doing they were effectively aiming to recover the lost ground of art's dedication to politics which John Barrell has shown was abandoned by the early nineteenth century. But writers like Cane and Tunnard were still locked into thinking of landscape design as a question of private house + garden + (almost certainly) a larger terrain. It never occurred to them to ask whether all modern clients or projects can be treated like English Georgian squirearchy; indeed, there is a telling rebuke to Tunnard by Fletcher Steele in 1942 when the expatriate Englishman is urged to get to know the vernacular American way of life better before he sounds off on ideal design.[16] One of the few modernist voices to speak out against the model of the English landscape garden was, unsurprisingly, French—André Vera, who wrote that as a modernist he was not against the park but only "le Jardin paysager."[17]

Perhaps the more astonishing aspect of modernist landscape architecture has been its failure to respond to the essential privatization of art experience. Whether that is traced, as John Barrell does, to the breakdown of a public, political role for the arts, or to psychological and epistemological causes, the 1800 watershed meant, at its simplest, that no imagery—whether medium or message—could be counted upon to have a wide, shared, public appeal. There were many causes of this, many effects, none of which seems to have registered.

One effect, as early even as 1800, was that designers abandoned meaning for medium, in this wholly in line with the picturesque vogue. Individual clients during the nineteenth century could prescribe some local, private, and often quite eccentric content or iconography; public park authorities in northern British cities were also concerned about what popular imagery was apt.[18] But design largely retreated to matters of style. And because it did not address the question of what meanings were possible within garden space, modern landscape architecture got sidetracked into coveting the formal effects of other arts rather than considering what its own medium could achieve.[19] Only in its own specifically graphic communications—namely, the fashion in which projects are presented in drawing—has landscape architecture sometimes shown itself modernist; the exploitation of cubist, *pointilliste,* or *Jugendstil* visual language has sometimes been offered or been seen as an accommodation to modernist content.[20]

Another professional bias toward medium at the expense of message is an obsession with materials, especially modern ones; this was most notable in the frequent expressions of irritation with the lack of cooperation received from plant materials! These biases, together with merely formal obsessions—debates for and against axes, for and against "picturesque"—ensured that designers circled without daring to grasp the whole business of meaning in gardens. Fletcher Steele was perhaps typical in his refusal of what he oddly called "literary content" in design.[21] However, it is only fair to say that reading his contemporary adversaries among the antimodernists—one of whom directed the search for meaning to "the small cottage gardens of Renaissance Europe"[22]—one can sympathize with the modernist frustrations.

The problems of meaning in modern gardens are not negligible. Not least the very meaning of "meaning": this deserves an essay in itself, but the full thrust of the term includes not just sensual pleasure from colors and forms but experiences that are susceptible to a discourse also available in other zones of human culture, what the modern landscape artist Mary Miss has called "content."[23]

From 1800 each person notionally, even ideologically, felt free to register his or her own meaning, to do his or her own thing, and indeed probably did want something unique after the manner of the really brave spirits of romanticism. Yet what prevented a marvelous flourishing of ad hoc, idiosyncratic, or vernacular gardens was the nervous bourgeois temperament that wanted to do the right thing, that wanted to know whether the gardening periodicals authorized this or that. Gardening had entered the consumer society. An immediate consequence was the pervasiveness of bland uniformity of design: keeping up with the Joneses meant having your garden look like the Joneses' and sharing their values and meanings. Exceptions, predictably, were the occasional, independent-minded Victorian—perhaps some new, northern industrialist who had the guts to go the whole hog and have what he wanted and damn taste or public opinion.[24] Nor has this fundamentally changed since Victorian times: uniformity of mass-produced design with its rare corollary, the bizarre but infinitely more refreshing juxtaposition of divergent individual tastes, is everywhere apparent. And we should note here that, while beauty continues to be a source of appeal, there is little consensus on aesthetics—if you find yourselves in agreement with somebody about a beautiful design in landscape architecture, this happy accident can be explained in more cases than not by a shared class background or education rather than by any examinable philosophical criteria. Maybe if there was a more determined attempt to study and debate aesthetic questions, modern landscape architecture would benefit.[25]

Modern designs, perhaps to escape this solipsism, have insisted both upon design as problem solving and specifically upon designing for groups or the community.[26] Fletcher Steele in 1941 wrote that "From kindergarten to old man's home, we join the crowd."[27] Eckbo, Kiley, and Rose in their 1939 articles were wholly concerned with community spaces; Tunnard in an article two years later turned toward this too, though not enough for the American zeal of Fletcher Steele.

It is in the nature of modern governments and societies, whatever their political color, to conglomerate or to urge conglomeration in the name of national identity: it reassures citizens of their equality to live in rows of identical housing; it suited Romania's hard-line imposition of communism to resite rural inhabitants in high-rise agro-industrial towns where they could not express individuality by cultivating their backyards;[28] British Rail's uniform imposition of a standard station furniture and decoration throughout the country attempts to promote the identity and celebrate the efficacy of a nationalized network. Yet these attempts at imposing a sense of community neglect any sense of regional differences, the human will to diversity, and the fact that modern society is more fractured than some people like to admit. Furthermore, sociologists are beginning to think that too much faith is being put in the idea of community,[29] and there are signs among some landscape architects that bland community design needs replacing by strong examples that cannot please all or that could not be implemented anywhere except some specific locality. The difficulty is always to avoid—at the level of content, meaning, or significance, if that issue is addressed at all—appealing only to the lowest common denominator of comprehension.

Modern designers have not perhaps sufficiently bothered to find out what people really want of private or public gardens.[30] Granted that meanings (significances, cultural topics) which pleased and enthralled late eighteenth-century garden users have lost relevance, it cannot be beyond the wit of man to establish a new agenda of meanings for the garden, an agenda that offers plurality, variety and not simply formal maneuvers.

Some of these meanings, I realize, will be long established, archetypal. As far as I know, none of the modernist writing about garden design in the 1930s and 1940s bothered to confront this aspect of their subject and some even tried to eliminate long-standing gardenist experience. Sometimes blending with, sometimes striking out independently of archetypal experience, other meanings will be local—either geographical or political. Some of the most intriguing recent designs exploit locality—whether Warren T. Byrd's Virginia tidewater, Terrance Harkness's Midwestern plains, or the wild horses of Mustang Square, Las Colinas, Texas (fig. 10.1).[31]

In discovering the appeal of locality, we can take lessons from the past. The old-fashioned Embankment Gardens near Charing Cross Station in London is a precious green area between the Strand and the River Thames, alongside which the traffic rushes. This long, thin space (fig. 10.2) has been laid out with a slightly meandering walk—as if to say that business need not for this brief space shunt you straight from A to B—and along this walk are a miscellaneous collection of monuments: the old water gate of seventeenth-century York House, a statue of Robert Burns, monuments to the Camel Corps (Cleopatra's Needle is on the Thames Embankment nearby), another statue of Mr. D'Oyly Carte who built the Savoy Hotel which looms over part of the gardens and who also founded the famous D'Oyly Carte Company that performs Gilbert and Sullivan; Sullivan himself is there too, plus a few more seemingly random and odd tokens of London's pride. This eclectic, palimpsestic imagery would never pass muster with modernist designers. But it is noticeable how people stop and look, they read inscriptions, they somehow and maybe only fleetingly involve themselves in these garden messages. Not one of the messages is endemic to gardens; but that is where they are located and they give pause for thought in a green and flowered city space.

As far as modern private gardens are concerned, there seems little escape from the sterility of homogenized, packaged "good taste." It takes a bold spirit to strike out. The theorists of the 1930s and 1940s never dreamed either that public and private forms and imagery might be radically different from each other or that one feasible modernist strategy was to let every private person really do their own thing. Fletcher Steele invoked the American vernacular to admonish the immigrant Tunnard, but he himself never took up that radical challenge.[32] Even Tunnard actually allowed that "gardening, after all, is one of the oldest of the folk arts,"[33] but he seemed unable to do anything with that strikingly modernist perception.

Yet some of the liveliest twentieth-century gardens are indeed genuinely vernacular, whether the immigrant gardens that Frances Butler has published, the backyards of rural Georgia blacks which Richard Westmacott is studying, or those creations of the Parisian banlieue about which Bernard Lassus wrote in *Les Jardins Imaginaires*.[34] This contem-

10.1. SWA Group, Mustang Square, Las Colinas, City of Irving, Texas (photograph: Marc Treib).

10.2. Embankment Gardens, London (photograph: author).

porary folk art, even when it draws upon widespread popular imagery like Walt Disney or girlie magazines, is essentially personal; yet equally paradoxically, it has an energy and invention that are more than private and that clearly fulfill many desiderata of garden creation (fig. 10.3). Of course, it is likely to offend against "good taste," one of our other inheritances from that 1800 watershed (think of Jane Austen's gardens). And its other problem, inasmuch as we are seeking fresh ideas for private or indeed community gardens, is how we may (if at all) translate its achievements into nonvernacular modes. Bernard Lassus was led by that early research into proposing landscape schemes characterized by a deal of bold and inventive imagination, since he is determined to put back into garden and landscape experience a wide range of meanings and experience (fig. 10.4); but too few have been realized for us to test their ultimate success.[35]

The grappling with content and meaning in garden art that is represented by another isolated garden artist, Ian Hamilton Finlay, and his garden at Little Sparta in Scotland[36] has been resolutely eschewed by most modern designers, who rely instead upon the discussion of formal or stylistic effects. A special feature of this, though it gives the illusion of a quest for meaning, is the call to designers to discover the "innermost idea" of plant materials,[37] a romantic obsession with individuality, which we may track botanically to Linnaeus among others[38] and which sustained much aesthetics, such as Clive Bell's quest for significant form that Fletcher Steele triumphantly cites.[39] But in practice this dedication to inherent and distinctive qualities slides quickly into a concentration once again upon formal elements, perhaps the most striking and depressing feature of modernist landscape architecture writing.[40]

This is of course a direct legacy of post-1800 emphases, but ignores a whole chapter of previous garden history in which style was informed by content or meaning. In the first edition of *Gardens in the Modern Landscape* Tunnard could rightly attack the "medley of styles" in the nineteenth century without registering how it had come about or what the plethora of styles represented (what, if you like, they encoded). In the preface to his second edition he even pleaded for eclecticism of styles, still without pausing to ask about their cultural basis or determination, even though he has somewhat enhanced his treatment of Victorian design. In the same year as Tunnard's first edition, 1938, Rose found abstract art his best inspiration in landscape design simply because it addressed matters of style that were devoid of content.[41] We might

10.3. Snow White gazes at the horizon in Monsieur Charles Pecqueur's garden, from Bernard Lassus, Les Jardins Imaginaires *(Paris, 1977).*

10.4. Bernard Lassus, facades at Uckange, Lorraine, 1980s (photograph: Bernard Lassus).

note, however, that in other modernist arts formal preoccupations did not neglect content: cubism or Pound's *Cantos,* for example, need a subject matter in order to explore new formal means. Perhaps the vitality of those arts is that medium and message once again were melded after some inert alliances or separations of the late nineteenth century.

The combination of Tunnard's somewhat improved invocation of the nineteenth century in the 1948 edition with his unrevised absurdities about the eighteenth effectively cut him off from considering the strategies of periods before what T. S. Eliot called the "dissociation of sensibility."[42] This disjunction separated not only form and content but thought and feeling, also beauty and use. It is, indeed, striking, how that third form of the dissociation of sensibility was accepted uncritically by landscape architects: Fletcher Steele seems ignorant of the bonding of *utile* and *dolce* in Renaissance aesthetics.[43]

The stress upon formal matters has been widespread, the rage against axes[44] and symmetry particularly vociferous. It occurs to none of these modernist writers to ask why axes and symmetry were invoked and on what occasions, what they articulated of human concerns and views (the notion, for example, that symmetry holds a deep appeal to the human mind is never raised, even by Fletcher Steele who objected strongly to Tunnard's rejection of the axis by invoking its native American precedents; he might have considered how its order suited a people struggling against a wild continent).[45] Such, indeed, is the fear of geometry and formality in any of their historical manifestations (and a short-sighted association of them simply with the Beaux-Arts tradition) that modernists have rather pinned their faith upon some version of picturesque, even though they should rather have spurned its messy and sentimental lures. Christopher Tunnard was perhaps the shrewdest, rejecting both "picturesque or romantic effect" and "formal" or axial planning; except that left him naked after discarding both suits of imperial clothes and ensured his retreat to town planning and problem solving.

Essentially what a concentration upon formal matters has done is to bypass the whole matter of garden experience in the fullest sensual-emotional-imaginative-intellectual range. The authors of the recent book *The Poetics of Gardens* are to be congratulated for their double insistence upon garden art involving "the emotions and mind of the spectator" in its creative process and upon gardens as memory theaters, exercise grounds for the "adventures of the imagination."[46] Otherwise, while we still hear much of design structure and design vocabulary, the structure and syntax of garden experiences and significances are missing. Again, this is a dismal legacy of 1800: eclecticism of styles marginalizes any consideration of how gardens appeal to their users and how creators/users express themselves or represent much of their total experience in and through gardens.

Landscape architecture needs to recover a desire and a capability of addressing experience. It need not be a question of iconography, though that is an obvious way forward. More subtly, we need to recover a sense of gardens as expressions or representations[47] of a culture's position vis-à-vis nature. This was not lost after 1800, though it always tended to get submerged beneath stylistic concerns. Even if what has been called the "born-again language of fundamentalist ecology"[48] is not to everybody's taste, it is nevertheless a dominant aspect of our culture and its expression in garden art may come to be judged as *the* mark of this phase of contemporary gardening. And part and parcel of that ecological commitment is a fresh attention to plant materials as content, meaning: this clearly explains the enthusiasm for the work of Roberto Burle Marx;[49] or the one successful moment in the otherwise silly Parc de La Villette in Paris, where Alexandre Chemetoff's bamboo grove (fig. 10.5), despite its concrete and pseudo-high-tech setting, contributes to a new agenda of garden meanings for a society for whom ecology, including the resources and materials of the natural world, matters as never before.[50]

Yet one of the serious disabilities of the ecological tradition from William Robinson's *The Wild Garden* of 1870 to Ian McHarg's *Design with Nature* of 1969 and beyond is that it failed to acknowledge a fallacy it inherited from 1800: the fallacy consists in seeing only a conflict between art and nature, between which we must supposedly choose. Yet these are not at loggerheads; as Renaissance commentators on the garden realized, they are always engaged in a creative collaboration.[51] Nature is not a stable, objective norm against which art is pitted; rather each derives local and historical meaning from their relative places on a scale, where their meanings are determined in terms of each other, in structural collaboration as well as tension, which differ at every period and in different countries. Since 1800 this essential dialogue has been obscured, with unhappy consequences that range from aesthetic crudity to ecological zeal.

10.5. In Alexandre Chemetoff's bamboo garden, Parc de La Villette, Paris (photograph: author).

It is into that empty space of discourse between culture and nature that landscape architecture needs to insert itself again.[52] Someone who has done precisely that is Ian Hamilton Finlay, one of the most perceptive of contemporary theorists and practitioners. His designs constantly identify the garden as a theater where the treaty between nature and culture is continuously and changefully played out. His contribution (now, alas, languishing in storage) to the Glasgow Garden Festival in 1988 is an illustration of how exciting can be the results of addressing public and simultaneously releasing private meanings in landscape design, of refusing to submit either to the lure of the picturesque and other mere formalisms or to the banalities of common-denominator values.

Down what appeared to be a curving country lane one encountered a series of stiles (a rural item that is quintessentially British) which were presented in various styles, each complete with a different Latin motto (figs. 10.6–7). The design was in itself elegant and witty, its verbal/visual pun alerting us to the possible meanings of this overfamiliar rural object, which were further problematized by its relocation in a festival site created out of derelict industrial land. Were we in the countryside where garden experience (seats and inscriptions) was invoked to structure our stroll? Or were we in a garden (park?) where the "real" countryside had been represented? Did the Latin recall a historical, Roman history of British landscape that challenged or melded with an indigenous Anglo-Saxon one that the stiles reified? And did that enactment of historical experience not recall the eighteenth-century landscape garden where similar historical perceptions were available?[53] However one chose to respond to this design, Finlay had focused our minds squarely upon the fashion in which the world of nature and the world of culture were intricately related; he had created a zone where representation, metaphor, and meaning had taken root and where the public role of landscape architecture as an art might be recovered without necessarily inhibiting a personally nuanced response. And like the high moment of English landscape design in the eighteenth century, what one learned in the circumscribed and artificial zone of a "country lane" or a "wilderness walk" extended and enhanced one's experience in the cultural landscape beyond.

It was no accident, I think, that Finlay's lane and stiles were part of an urban garden festival. Gardens in the city have not, until recently, exercised the imaginations of landscape architects; yet this particular

10.6. Ian Hamilton Finlay, Country Lane with Stiles, Glasgow Garden Festival, 1988 (photograph: Marina Adams).

10.7. Ian Hamilton Finlay, Country Lane with Stiles, Glasgow Garden Festival, 1988 (photograph: Marina Adams).

type brings into sharp focus many of the issues canvassed here—the relativity of terms, of spatial needs; the different demands upon space and "nature" of public and private existence. The needs of urban inhabitants have changed over the last two hundred years, as have the views of the authorities who preside over what is permitted in both private and public spaces. Perhaps parks and gardens have always offered themselves as urban interludes (the ludic pun is deliberate).[54] But they become different experiences, even within cities, when density of population forces apartment blocks skyward and shrinks garden space to roof terrace or window box. They are different, too, and therefore occupy another point on the nature-culture scale, when more and more of urban populations have access, by road or television, to (let us call it) the wilderness.[55] Man-made settings then seem negligible, or they can come to display, in a new structural tension with nature, either more artifice or more ambiguity. Perhaps where the modernists went wrong is that they tricked themselves into thinking it was a battle of past/art versus present/nature. In fact, it was a replay of a long-standing, never-ending dialogue or *paragone*.

POSTSCRIPT

GARDENS IN *UTOPIA*: UTOPIA IN THE GARDEN

Singe die Gärten, mein Herz, die du nicht kennst . . .

Speakers' Corner is aptly located in Hyde Park, which is historically the extended garden of Kensington Palace (fig. 11.1). This privileged place of utopian discourse, where proposals to right the wrongs of this world are formulated and entertained, would be unthinkable outside the green world of the landscaped park. For utopias have frequently invoked the special and resonant spaces of gardens, just as gardens have often been utopian in impulse, design, and meaning. It is this exchange of symbolic meanings that I want to explore; I shall be concerned somewhat less with the place of gardens in utopian literature, though that will be my starting point, than with the strongly utopian dimension of some Renaissance and post-Renaissance gardens.

The first garden we come across in Thomas More's *Utopia* is the one in Antwerp where the discussions that form the book take place. We are told little about it, except for one feature to which I shall return. But in the actual description of the Utopian cities in Part Two, gardens are more prominent: behind the houses are "broad gardens," of which the inhabitants are proud and in which they take great pleasure:

> In them they have vines, fruits, herbs, flowers, so well kept and flourishing that I never saw anything more fruitful and more tasteful anywhere. Their zest in keeping them is increased not merely by the pleasure afforded them but by the keen competition between [city] blocks as to which will have the best kept garden.[1]

So not only do gardens feature centrally in the utopian cityscape, but they are the occasion for some good citizenly rivalry. And just as More

11.1. Speakers' Corner, Hyde Park, London.

and his companions retire to a garden for their discussions, so the inhabitants of the utopian cities resort to their gardens in summertime for "recreation."

More had perhaps personal and certainly literary reasons for this emphasis upon gardens. His own at Chelsea was famous, cherished in its owner's lifetime and mythologized after his death. The oil painting in the Victoria and Albert Museum attributed to Rowland Lockey depicts More, his family and descendants sixty-five years after his execution in a domestic space which conspicuously includes a garden (fig. 11.2). This is a simple area, walled but with a gateway that either gives access to less carefully plotted grounds beyond or permits direct access to the garden without passing through the house; the beds are laid out in a simple geometric pattern (a maze shape that is readily traced); at one corner of the garden is a pavilion, a summer house or study. By 1600 when this picture was painted More's garden had passed into the possession of Sir Robert Cecil, but he was so busy completing Hatfield that it is doubtful whether he had much time for this garden in Chelsea. Therefore we may see here something very like the garden of More's time, though the corner pavilion looks to me of later construction. But the point is that the artist felt it was part of the Morean myth to invoke a garden. More had himself been proud of his garden's natural and emblematic richness: "As for Rosemarine I lett it run alle over my garden walls, not onlie because my bees love it, but because 'tis a herb sacred to remembrance, and therefore to friendship." And one of his friends, Thomas Heywood, has left us an equally resonant description:

> After the meal they went to walk in a garden that was about two stone's throws from the house. On a small meadow (in the middle of the garden and at the crest of a little hill), they stopped to look around. The spot pleased them greatly, both for its comfort and for its beauty. On one side stood the noble City of London; on the other, the beautiful Thames with green gardens and wooded hills all around. The meadow, beautiful in itself, was almost completely covered with green and flowers in bloom, and tender branches of fruit trees were interwoven in such beautiful order that they seemed, to the guests, to resemble an animated tapestry made by Nature herself. And yet this garden was more noble than any tapestry, which leaves more desirous than content the soul of him who beholds the images painted on cloth.[2]

11.2. Attributed to Rowland Lockey, Sir Thomas More and His Family, *1600. Victoria and Albert Museum, London.*

Unfortunately we know little else about More's garden. It has been suggested by Craig R. Thompson that Eusebius's garden in Erasmus's colloquy *The Godly Feast* may have as one of its models that of More at Chelsea.[3] Dates, however, suggest the reverse: *The Godly Feast* appeared in 1522 and it was only in the following year that More purchased the land at Chelsea; Erasmus might well have been thinking of More's other gardens at Bucklersbury. But over and above the matter of models and who influenced whom is the kind of vision of gardens that More and his friends like Erasmus would have shared. We can already detect in his own remarks, just quoted, and especially in Heywood's description that gardens were not simply, God wot, lovesome things. Herbs like rosemary were emblematic, and they served the bees which Virgil's *Georgics* had celebrated; nature was so contrived by the gardener as to imitate the craft of tapestry, yet "Nature herself" was the artist; the garden's verdure was "almost perpetual," the closest that Chelsea could come (even then) to an eternal spring. Such rhetoric recalls the traditions of garden imagery from which no garden description of the sixteenth and seventeenth centuries, nor probably any contemporary garden either, could manage to free itself.

The one Erasmus describes is no exception. It is divided into five sections: a flower garden to the front, a herb garden in the courtyard, and beyond a combined kitchen and medicinal garden, then a grassy meadow enclosed by a quickset hedge for strolling, and an orchard. The dining room has a triple view of these various gardens through sliding windows and is adjoined by a library with a balcony overlooking the garden, by a small study and a chapel. More, too, at Chelsea interestingly developed both spatial and intellectual relationships between the garden and the library, gallery and chapel. Erasmus also pays especial attention to the decorations and iconology: the open gate of the flower garden is guarded by a painted image of St. Peter. A small chapel to the right contains a figure of Christ (but not, apparently, Christ as Gardener). Biblical inscriptions in Latin, Greek, and Hebrew accompany each of these figures. The fountain of the flower garden—a traditional feature of medieval gardens—is said by Eusebius to signify the heavenly stream for which the human soul pants.

The symbolism of all flower gardens is discussed extensively in Erasmus's chapter 3. But it is the herb garden which is fashioned most elaborately—as a kind of multidimensional lesson in divine and human artistry. This herb garden is enclosed on three sides by galleries with painted marble pillars: on the wall of one gallery is painted a fresco of trees, in whose branches are shown representatives of rare or renowned species of bird, while on the ground beneath are depicted such animals as a piping monkey, a dancing camel, and a chameleon. The fresco of the second gallery is dedicated to famous plants, especially poisonous ones, every kind of serpent, the scorpion, basilisk, and armies of ants. The third gallery shows lakes, rivers, and seas, with their fishes, amphibians, and wildlife of their shores. Eusebius frequently draws his visitors' attention to the accuracy of the frescoes: every variety of hellebore is distinguished; the poisonous plants are so realistic one fears to touch them; an attempt, however crude, is made to place every species in its natural environment.

This garden which Erasmus describes is contemporary with the rise of botanical studies in Europe, and its inclusiveness of reference recalls some of the early cabinets of curiosity, especially those in the Holy Roman Empire.[4] But the main impulse behind the garden is not scientific: it is an exercise in art, nature, and illusion for devotional ends. The herbs in their separate beds are reflected in the channels of water that flow from the central fountain. The paving stones of the galleries are painted green with representations of small flowers, while the green hedges of the garden are also painted. The "marble" of the pillars, fountains, and channels is imitated in paintwork. One of his guests is deceived, then delighted, by the deception, and Eusebius comments:

> We are twice pleased when we see a painted flower competing with a real one. In one we admire the cleverness of Nature, in the other the inventiveness of the painter; in each the goodness of God, who gives all these things for our use and is equally wonderful and kind in everything.

Nature and art cooperate to celebrate God's universe; it is the metaphysical as much as the physical world which Eusebius tends. The herb beds have scientific labels giving name and special virtue, but also banners with mottoes on them. That of the marjoram says, "Keep off, sow; I don't smell for you," and Eusebius points up the old and popular proverb by explaining that swine hate what for men is a pleasant scent.

I have spent so much time rehearsing details of this fascinating description because it epitomizes much of what I would call the utopian dimension of gardens. It draws upon literary and rhetorical traditions of garden description, with all their emphasis upon ideal and perfect places. Yet it is also in touch with—or imaginatively anticipates—actual Renaissance gardens where those ideals were realized in some shape and form: whether or not we can include More's as one of his models, Erasmus certainly knew Johann Froben's at Basel and from his correspondence it is clear that Erasmus studied, exercised, and conversed in Froben's garden as he makes Eusebius do in *The Godly Feast*. But not only is Eusebius garden a mingling of traditional and actual possibilities, it is instinct with some of the tensions which are endemic to all postlapsarian garden art. The fiction of the colloquy expects us to believe the garden is real, that it has realized in its architectural space and botanical fullness the ideals which classical and Christian literary traditions have identified with gardens. But Erasmus was perfectly aware that any garden is always and essentially a compromise between ideals located in the past and the practical exigencies and possibilities of the present. More's garden, according to Heywood, achieved only "almost perpetual verdure." Eusebius depicts the serpent and poisonous plants to remind us of the evils and inconveniences of a fallen world. Even the play between illusion and reality must recall us to a world where human art (Τεχνή) must intervene to create the fulness of the natural creation dispersed since our banishment from Eden. (This is a theme taken up prominently by botanical gardenists of the seventeenth century, and I shall be returning to it later.)

Erasmus, not surprisingly, presses his description close to irony or satire when we arrive at such an item as the labeled marjoram: for the swine and the marjoram, which also appear on the frontispiece of Sidney's *Arcadia* and of two editions (1611 and 1617) of *The Faerie Queene,* signal the animosities in nature that never existed in Eden, Arcadia, the Golden Age or any such mythical *locus amoenus*. Gardens in our world, lovesome things maybe, are always a sharp reminder of the needs that have urged man to create and cultivate them, needs that are not necessarily satisfied even then. And finally Erasmus's garden is substantially architectural: walled, with galleries and pillars, it may be seen as much as a city as a garden; indeed it takes its place (as I shall explain) at some strategic point along the human route from the Garden of Eden to the City of God.

It is here perhaps that it is worth taking up the one item of garden description which More allows himself of that Antwerp garden in the *Utopia* (fig. 11.3). We are told that the discussants take their place "on a bench covered with turfs of grass" and More repeats this feature—

11.3. Ambrosius Holbein, garden scene placed at the start of Book One of the 1518 edition of More's Utopia; *a turf seat held by wooden boards can be glimpsed especially beneath the figure of Hythlodaeus.*

the only one, as I say, singled out—at the beginning of the second part. Should we assume any particular significance in this isolated feature? Some extensive researches by Martine Paul[5] suggest that More may have wished to emphasize two features of this garden seat: first, it appears to be associated with patrician establishments and to be used by the most courtly figures therein; but at the same time (and this is the second feature) it is the most natural of a garden's artificial creation, for the seat, which we associate with indoors, is constructed of grass sods laid upon earth which is retained inside a woven wattle fencing (sometimes, brick walling was used). Does More perhaps wish to underline unobtrusively the simple, nonarchitectural elements of the garden where the utopian talks take place? Certainly the gardens in the cityscapes of the second part are firmly vegetal—no mention, for instance, of pergola or arbor. He may also have wished to suggest that those who seek to recover, if only in discourse, the ideal perfections of the world must remain (literally) close to nature.

The paradox of courtly or patrician behavior in firm alliance with true simplicity (what Spenser urges too in the sixth book of *The Faerie Queene*) is not without point for gardens and for gardens in utopias. Both gardens and utopias combine what man recall imaginatively of perfect worlds now lost with an essential element of the impossible (a point Erasmus also seems to be making). Paradoxical, too, in both gardens and utopias is their timelessness within time, as well as their naturalness that is the work of human art and craft. More's coinage of "utopia" significantly derives its etymology from a combination of the Greek for "good place" (εὐτόπος) and for "no place" (ὀυτόπος). The man who sits on that turf seat in Antwerp and discourses of utopias is called both Raphael (which signifies, "God has healed") and Hythlodaeus (dispenser of nonsense). Ideal gardens—with their illusion at least of perpetual spring—and perfect societies can only be located nowhere, in no place; to linger in both is to partake of refreshment, even perhaps some healing quality; but about both is also the tincture of nonsense. It is as much for the absurdity of his claim as for his verbal bathos that we smile at the poet's "A garden is a lovesome thing, God wot."

If we discount Erasmus's explicitly Christian lessons, his garden in *The Godly Feast* anticipates the physical disposition of many Renaissance gardens in the next hundred years. These princely gardens, like More's and Eusebius's, were realized from a combination of received garden forms and ideas in both literary and rhetorical traditions, classical largely, but subsuming the Christian. To start with, the ideal Renaissance villa (a term used to include house and garden) was likely to recall the younger Pliny's description of his villas in Tuscany and at Laurentinum (the most extensive of such descriptions from antiquity) and attempted to recreate Pliny's account of a series of spaces for different purposes and times of day; this clearly had links also with the Pindarian (*Fragments* 129–130) and Virgilian (*Aeneid,* VI, 637ff.) visions of the Elysian Fields[6] where were incorporated grounds for a whole range of activities, athletic, musical, amorous, and contemplative: "green pleasaunces and happy seats" is a version of Virgil's phrase, suggestive of a succession of garden spaces. Christian emphases could well translate such enclosures, either individually or as an ensemble, especially when they were associated with a religious house, into the closed garden of the Song of Solomon.

One Renaissance garden above all others in Italy determined the shape and spirit of the art: that was the complex begun by Bramante when he was asked to turn the Belvedere into a garden for the Papal collection of antique sculpture and at the same time to link it with the Vatican Palace by a series of ramps copied from a pagan temple-theater and by a courtyard to be used for ceremonial and entertainment purposes (fig. 11.4). Equally Utopian, too, is the determination to bring hortulan space into creative relationship with the church of St. Peter, with political ceremony, and with the Vatican libraries. In the more private gardens beyond the courtyard Pirro Ligorio later designed the casino for Pius IV, finding the prototypes for it in a whole range of antique buildings and decorating it with elaborate stucco work on the outside and frescoes (by Zuccaro) inside. The decorations unite pagan and Christian worlds; classical mythology and church fathers are drawn upon to make this elaborately wrought garden house what Burckhardt (quite rightly) called "the most beautiful resting place for the afternoon hours which modern architecture has created."[7]

Since most sixteenth- and seventeenth-century guide books to the Eternal City began their modern sections with these Vatican Gardens, their richness and emblematic fullness and their union of pagan and Christian worlds encouraged visitors to look elsewhere for such an ideal garden. Since the Belvedere courtyard provided physical, architectural models for later Italian gardens, it was in fact easy enough to find examples of its metaphysics elsewhere.

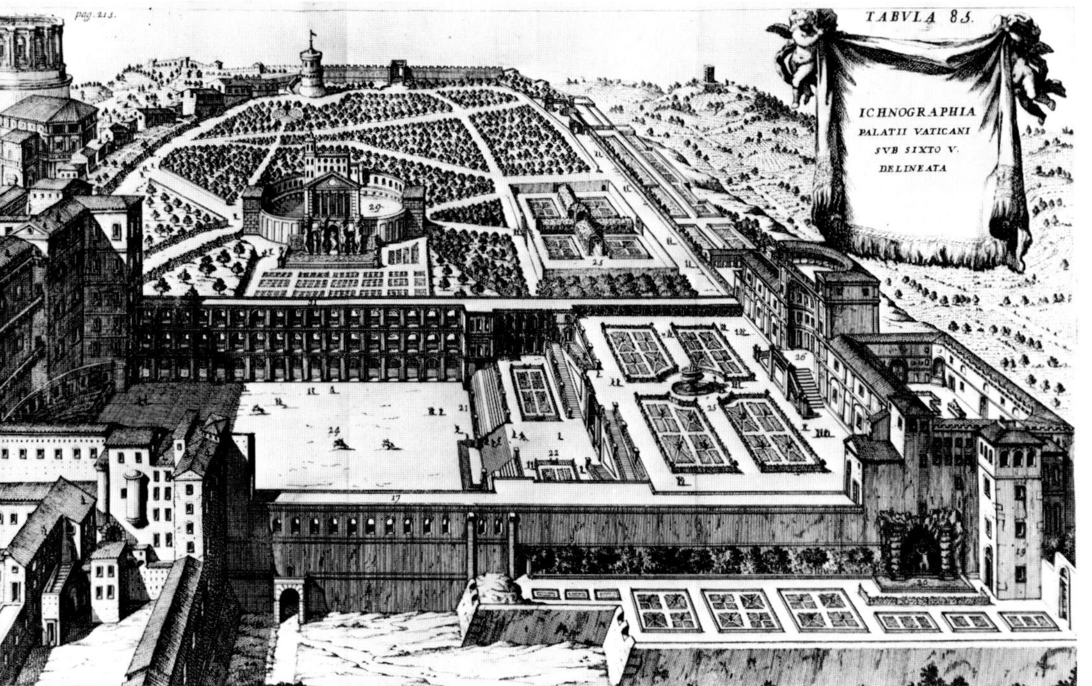

11.4. Engraving of the Vatican Gardens, Rome, from Bonanni's Templi Vaticani Fabricam *(Rome, 1696). The Belvedere Villa and descending terraces are to the right and middle; Ligorio's casino in the rear center. Hertziana Library, Rome.*

The conceit that earlier and legendary places of perfection could be realized in modern gardens was a dominant theme of designers and users alike. The Medici villa at Pratolino had its Parnassus, with a small arena for visitors to use while they listened to its concert. The d'Este gardens at Tivoli were elaborately designed to reconstitute the Gardens of the Hesperides, for Hercules (the patron alike of the Estes and the town of Tivoli) had simply brought the dragon to guard an even more perfect spot. The sight of oranges everywhere in Italy encouraged northern visitors to read into their garden settings a whole series of Hesperidean relocations. Just as Eusebius's garden had offered moral and religious lessons, so Renaissance gardens were provided with the iconography to promote virtue: Roman emperors and imitation bas-reliefs that form the perfect circle of the little garden at Villa Brenzone on Garda were installed to induce recollections of imperial values, while the gardens of the Villa d'Este with their series of forking paths realized the Choice of Hercules (one series of routes leading the visitor to representations of vice, another to ones of civic and moral probity).[8]

Sometimes, it is true, the iconography was both less precise and less uplifting. But its appeal to visions of legendary worlds, realized in modern villa complexes, was still potent. At Genoa, often the first opportunity visitors from the north had to encounter modern Italian architecture, its villas and palaces recalled the hanging gardens of Babylon, its garden enclaves such fabled places as the paradise of the Old Man of the Mountain, the Hesperides, or the Elysian Fields.[9] Garden statuary in the Doria gardens (still surviving amid the incursions of modern urbanism) took a traveler like John Evelyn into a familiar but hitherto largely literary world of ancient heroes which now seem realized before his very eyes. These Genoese palaces cast such a spell that it was perfectly apt for an earlier visitor, Jan Massys, to use the Doria gardens as background for his *Venus Cytherea* (fig. 11.5).

Gardens were thus constituted as places of hitherto lost perfections. Not perhaps surprisingly, most Renaissance iconographical programs were classicizing; but the pagan virtues had been absorbed into a Christian ethic (as at the Villa d'Este). And some gardens did, like Eusebius's, focus unequivocally upon Christian matters. Near Siena the Villa Cetinale garden is still decorated with classical figures; but its striking feature is a complete circle of stations of the cross encircling the garden. Yet if one leaves this earthly though Christian paradise and climbs the hill behind to the hermitage (palatial enough, it must be admitted, in terms of living accommodation) and from *that* vantage point (nearer

11.5. Jan Massys, Venus Cytherea, *1651. National Museum, Stockholm.*

11.6. View toward the temple from the "monster garden," Bomarzo (photograph: author).

Heaven, perhaps) looks down toward the garden, it appears diminished and minute in the Tuscan landscape. At Bomarzo (fig. 11.6), the so-called monster garden near Viterbo, a dystopia of classical legend is explicitly established in opposition to the utopian vision of God's temple at the end of the garden journey: wrestling colossi, mythical beasts, leaning houses, marine monsters, a hell-mouth, and siren-like illusions of easy virtue have all to be safely negotiated (i.e. passed in the full consciousness of their negative values) before the visitor ascends a staircase guarded by the three-headed Cerberus to take sanctuary in Vignola's magnificent and austere temple, dedicated to the true and only God and erected in memory of the deceased wife of the garden's creator, Vicino Orsini.

But as Eusebius shrewdly noted, these hortulan lessons and realizations of lost perfection depend upon the specific garden skills of bringing art and nature into creative association. This has, of course, always been a garden's particular distinction; one essential point underlying the end of Marvell's "The Garden" is that what appeared ineluctably natural ("green thoughts in a green shade") has by the end to be recognized as the gardener's art. Notions of art and of art's involvement or interference in a garden's nature have fluctuated through the ages. Eusebius's naturalistic frescoes might well strike us as naive: after all, piping monkeys and dancing camels sound as quaint as Milton meant his prelapsarian animals to appear in the Garden of Eden or as Roelandt Savery makes his in analogous visual exercises. But the theme of art and nature—whether cooperating or vying in *paragone*—is certainly crucial to gardens and, arguably, to utopias.

At least one garden, that of the Villa Lante at Bagnaia near Viterbo, established its whole iconographical program around the necessarily different roles of art and nature in the Golden Age and its dystopic successors.[10] But sixteenth- and seventeenth-century gardens everywhere elicited from visitors an appreciation of exactly this same theme; the literary traditions which sustained garden design endorsed it. In Achilles Tatius's romance of *Clitophon and Leucippe* the actual garden that adjoins a character's house is described in exactly the same detail as he had used to describe the painting of a meadow at the start of the story—crystal fountains, cloistered walls, foliage that filters sunlight to the grass beneath.[11] Similar confusions occur in Renaissance gardens and indeed it is sometimes as hard to distinguish in verbal accounts between what is actual and what is imagined or painted, as it was difficult to make such discriminations on the ground.

11.7. Jan Brueghel the Younger, The Garden of Earthly Delights, *c. 1626. The Prado Museum, Madrid.*

English visitors reported their delighted confusions: when trellis work with vines and birds turns out to be painted; when what should be a sculptured stone group of animals turns out so realistically colored and equipped with real horns and tusks that one expects them to move. Grottoes make stones into flower shapes that deceive the eye in the gloom of the cavern, which is itself artificial, resonant with many literary, especially Ovidian, references to *natural* springs in the rock. Indeed, the metamorphic world of Renaissance gardens is arguably their distinguishing feature, and Ovid's poem is drawn upon more frequently than any other source for iconographical detail and for decorative subject matter.[12] It is precisely this Ovidian coloring of garden design—water forced into a tunnel of arches, balustrades of running water which you cannot grasp, artificial birds singing, and so on—that made the Renaissance garden a fabulous place. Even giants seemed to be represented realistically—either bending down to pick up a rock to hurl at one or in the very process of metamorphosis (from rock to living being or from living being to rock is the ambiguity that makes the colossus at Pratolino so intriguing).

But the point at which the rivalries or cooperations of art and nature become most intense was in the flower garden, and this will therefore serve me conveniently as the stepping stone into that most utopian of Renaissance garden worlds: the botanical garden. The art/nature dialogue was focused in the very layout of botanical (and by inference of all) gardens. At Mantua, for example, the beds of the Duke's botanical garden were clearly the work of ingenious man, forming what Agostino del Riccio called "beautiful patterns in the forms, variously, of pyramids, maps, dragons, stars, and other *fantasie*." But other botanists attacked this artful complexity of presentation: Giovan Battista Ferrari argued that elaborately shaped beds were scientifically inappropriate—"quite unsuitable both for sowing seeds and for growing them."[13] Such pragmatic considerations obviously obtained at Leiden, where the rectangular beds were as readily accessible to the mind's categorizing and understanding as to the gardener's hands and care (fig. 11.8).

There are of course more aspects of this topic than I have space for: Keith Thomas has shown in *Man and the Natural World* that the energies which went into botanical gardens were an escape from older anthropomorphic perspectives (assessments of a plant's moral status, for example) and part of a search for the intrinsic qualities of each item in the natural world; yet this search and its physical embodiment in the precise

11.8. Seventeenth-century engraved view of the Hortus Botanicus at Leiden, with the repository of some of the nonbotanical specimens at the far end and some examples imaged below.

beds of a botanical garden also declared man's pride in his control over the world of fallen nature. A botanical garden was a possible, a feasible utopia rather than one of those that Milton derided in his *Areopagitica*: "To sequester out of the world into Atlantick and Eutopian polities, which never can be drawn into use, will not mend our condition."[14]

There was much that seemed useful to man's condition in the scientific study of the natural world. Nor did that study confine itself within botanical limits. Most botanical gardens of the sixteenth and early seventeenth centuries were linked (often physically) to cabinets of curiosity. The engraving of the Leiden Hortus displays examples from its natural history museum which was housed after 1599 in the specially built *Ambulacrum*. At Pisa, where the botanical garden was founded thirty-four years before Leiden's, adjoining the plants beds was a gallery which in 1641 Evelyn found "furnish'd with natural rarities, stones, minerals, shells, dryed Animals, etc." The inventories of the gallery and garden (which survive) show that by the time of his visit the collection included not only natural objects—what the famous Bolognese botanist, Aldrovandi, called "le cose sotterranee e le altre sopraterranee"—but landscapes, portraits of European botanists including Clusius, beautiful albums of flower paintings, birds and animals, and even religious pictures. Its gallery recalls those of Eusebius's garden, though all of his "collection" was only in painted representations.

The combination of botanical gardens and their associated cabinets of natural and artificial rarities seemed to present a utopian opportunity to reconstitute the whole natural world in its Edenic perfection. No longer did it seem necessary to speculate upon the exact situation of Eden when the fullness of Eden was beginning to be made available in many botanical gardens in Europe. The discovery of the New World as well as extensive travels into the Near and Far East brought a huge influx of new plants and other specimens (shells, native art and dress) into Europe. It seemed suddenly possible that man was in a position to design a garden which would (in John Evelyn's words) "comprehend the principall and most useful plants, and . . . be as rich and noble [a] compendium of what the whole Globe of Earth has flourishing upon her bosome."[15] The new world, with its variety of plants and trees, struck many of its first European visitors with the appearance of a garden. Thus Hakluyt reports in "A Briefe Relation of Newfoundland" of about 1582 (Everyman ed., VI, 17):

> The next morning being Sunday and the 4 of August, the Generall and his company were brought on land by English marchants, who shewed unto us their accustomed walks unto a place they call the Garden. But nothing appeared more then Nature it selfe without art: who confusedly hath brought foorth roses abundantly, wilde but odoriferous, and to sense very comfortable.[16]

When the profusion of the Americas was put together with the riches of Asia, Africa, and Europe, the potential for man's new gardens was utopian. The title page of John Parkinson's *Theatrum Botanicum* of 1640 shows the four continents contributing to this plentitude, while the first gardener, Adam, faces Solomon, representing the modern man who has the intelligence to recover Adam's knowledge, in a garden that was indeed a theater—a complete collection *and* a stage for its display (fig. 11.9).

This determination to collect together in many single places the variety of the world's natural and artistic creation is widely attested in visual evidence—luckily, since the *Kunstundwunderkammern* have been almost all completely dispersed and can only be theoretically reconstructed.[17] There is the famous engraving issued in Leiden of the Worms cabinet; a later anonymous Dutch painting at Norwich displays part of the Yarmouth collection (fig. 11.10). Or there are those paintings by Rubens and Brueghel in Madrid which bring together all of the material subject to each of man's senses. The suggestion of the profusion of the cabinet, its extension into neighboring rooms and even out into a garden beyond, is ample visual evidence of the utopian enterprise which I have been sketching. Jan van Kessel's *Europe* (Munich) repeats this popular motif; no doubt popular, too, for its demands upon painterly skills—but of course painterly virtuosity exactly answers the efforts of the virtuoso who makes such collections in the first place. We have evidence that these virtuosos' collections were recognized at once for their utopian ambitions: Christopher Arnold, afterwards Professor of History at Nuremberg, noted in 1651 his impressions of what remained of Lord Arundel's gardens and gallery beside the Thames: "certain gardens on the Thames where there are rare Greek and Roman inscriptions, stones, marbles: the reading of which is actually like viewing Greece and Italy at once within the bounds of Great Britain."[18]

11.9. Title page of John Parkinson's Theatrum Botanicum, *1640. Dumbarton Oaks, Trustees for Harvard University.*

11.10. Unknown artist, The Yarmouth Collection, *seventeenth century. Norfolk Museums Service.*

11.11. Matthaeus Merian, engraving of the Hortus Palatinus at Heidelberg, 1620: the building at the far right is thought to have contained a cabinet and laboratory.

These gardens and cabinets attest to the scientific dimension of the utopian impulse in seventeenth-century Europe (though inevitably in widely different dimensions). Many of these garden-cum-cabinets also included some form of laboratory. At the end of the famous garden created at Heidelberg by Salomon de Caus for the Elector Palatine in the 1610s was a building that (it has been convincingly argued) was a combined cabinet/museum *and* a laboratory (fig. 11.11).[19] Leiden, too, had established a chemistry laboratory alongside the botanical garden by the mid-seventeenth century. In England virtuosi likewise experimented in their gardens: Evelyn's, for example, contained a transparent beehive given him by Dr. Wilkins of Wadham, another scientist/virtuoso, whose garden in Oxford was the site of both botanical and hydraulic experiments. Evelyn's diary records many such alliances of garden and science in the houses of people he visited: Henry Winstanley, builder of the Eddystone Lighthouse, had a villa at Littlebury "with abundance of fine Curiosities all performed by clockwork"—these included both whimsical devices such as a chair that ran backward into the garden on rails, taking an unsuspecting visitor with it, and more "practical" machines which served tea and coffee in cups to the company. At Sir Thomas Browne's in Norwich Evelyn found "the whole house and garden" was "a paradise and cabinet of rarities, and that of the best collection, especially medals, books, plants, and natural things." The role of the garden in these utopian endeavors is captured well by Abraham Cowley in the first book of his *Davideis*: with an eye perhaps on Eusebius, maybe More, but certainly on Salomon's House in Bacon's *New Atlantis,* Cowley describes library, hall, and synagogue (the utopian return of the Jews to England) grouped around choice gardens, with the walls of all units adorned with maps, stories, texts, and Egyptian hieroglyphs.

But there inevitably came a time when the profusion of the world's riches seemed too large for any one cabinet.[20] Peter Mundy visiting the Tradescants' Ark in London—a botanical garden and a museum which eventually became part of the Ashmolean Museum—found a "little garden with divers outlandish herbes and flowers"; and he was "*almost* persuaded a Man might in one day behold and collecte into one place more Curiosities than hee should see if he spent all his life in Travell." That was in 1634. Gardens and cabinets bulged more and more, as collectors increased their holdings: verses prefixed to the catalogue of the Tradescants' Museum claimed

Nor court, nor shop-crafts were THINE *arts, but those*
Which Adam studied ere he did transgresse,
The wonders of the Creatures, and to dress
The worlds great Garden.

But while the Tradescant catalogue of 1634 listed some 750 species and varieties, by that of 1656 these holdings had doubled. We are again indebted to Keith Thomas for drawing attention to the "dozens of now forgotten amateur helpers and correspondents" who from Tudor times onward helped more prominent collectors by bringing items to their notice and therefore into the many botanical gardens up and down the country where local and foreign plants were grown and studied. Their efforts and the efforts of explorers meant that in the end the botanical garden of however generous dimensions could not hope to include all of the world's great garden let alone its prelapsarian profusion.

The true and full utopian dimension of the Renaissance garden probably died with the idea that one botanical garden could recover Paradise. Specialization, for one thing, intervened: when the Tradescants' collections were transferred to what would become the Ashmolean Museum, their garden was not included; since 1621 a separate botanical garden had existed at Oxford where the proper care due to plants could be given. Both Evelyn and Aubrey voiced their opinion that different materials needed different curatorial attention and expertise.

At the same time princely gardens also came under suspicion. Not the least reason for this was the frequent identification of Stuart absolutism with the garden—had not Inigo Jones often imaged the ideal world of kingly creation and power in terms of fine gardens? Indeed, all over sixteenth- and seventeenth-century Europe royal entertainments—ballets, *intermezzi,* masques, entries, progresses—used the garden as the apt metaphor for the ruler's beneficial and creative regime. The political claims implicitly made for such gardens inevitably lost them their utopian attraction when the political ideology with which they were associated came into question: Louis XIV's exercise of garden imagery at Versailles or Marly did not help the universal claims for a garden as utopia, at least in England.

The garden necessarily retained something of the ideal: if only as the perfect alliance of art and nature it could preserve its paradisical reputation. Yet the history of English gardens after the Civil Wars and the Interregnum suggest that they became personal retreats from far more than attacks upon a fallen and postlapsarian world. Utopiary rather than utopia was the order of the day.[21] For this new and reduced vision of gardens Evelyn speaks well:

> they are a place of all terrestriall enjoyments the most resembling Heaven and the best representation of our lost felicity. It is the common term and the pit from whence we were dug; we all came out of the parsley-bed—at least according to the creed of a poet [Lucretius, V, 807–810]. As no man can be very miserable that is master of a garden here; so will no man ever be happy who is not sure of a garden hereafter. From thence we came, and thither we tend; where the first Adam fell, the second arose. Kings, philosophers, and wise men spent their choicest hours in them; and when they would frame a type of Heaven, because there is nothing in nature more worthy and illustrious, they describe a garden, and call it Elysium.[22]

What that declares is that each man has the opportunity to make his garden as perfect a model of his own felicity as he can, but that the garden no longer stands for any universal ambition to bring the whole world into shape and form before one's eyes.

Yet the rhetoric of admiration for gardens continues to be used throughout the first half of the eighteenth century. It is often inert cliché; but it can also be capable of sustaining a vision of garden art as a *feasible* utopian world, subject however to more constraints, to more "natural" eventualities, than would have been admitted before. Beneath continuing claims for the garden as utopia, arcady, or the *locus amoenus* were clear recognitions of other, competing energies, disruptive and sceptical. One example will have to serve: the Elysian Fields at Stowe in Buckinghamshire (see figs. 3.1–3.4).

Here a carefully contrived cluster of temples, facing each other over the waters of what came to be called the "River Styx," suggests that the present cannot achieve the perfections of the past. A perfect and classical circular Temple of Ancient Virtue confronts a somewhat dumpy, even Gothick Temple of British Worthies across the river of death. The pagan temple contains full-length statues of a poet, a philosopher, a general, and a lawgiver (Lycurgus, this last, a creator supposedly of institutions to make Spartans austere, morally upright, simple, self-sacrificing, brave, hardy, and happy); British Worthies only has busts in niches and a larger selection must now stand for the diversity of national achievement. Behind the Temple of Ancient Virtue is a specially created heap of rubble, the Temple of Modern Virtue. Behind the Temple of British Worthies is a monument to a dog, eulogized with such solemn celebration that it calls into question the notable figures on its other side. It has the air, his ensemble, of a three-dimensional satire in the mode of Pope's *Dunciad,* and its irony finally defeats any hope that the garden can fully achieve any ideal status.

There is much in the history of the English landscape garden that suggests a prevalent skepticism toward any garden's claim to be utopian. The elegiac quality of the very idea of a garden or arcadia or Elysian Fields or world of the Golden Age is never far from the surface. We are often invited to remember that *a* garden is no substitute for *the* Garden and that each garden since the first must fade (even though, as Pope said of Stowe, "time shall make it grow"). Pope made his own garden at Twickenham a coherent antidote to Grub Street and the City; it became, as Maynard Mack has shown, a base for his career as satirist.[23] But he was forever aware that it was only his until he died (having no immediate heirs and, being a Catholic, unable to *own* property). And from 1735 its termination point was a memorial to his dead mother. This elegiac emphasis found itself echoed in many other gardens far from Twickenham, among them Shenstone's The Leasowes, created as a veritable *memento mori* to friends and poetic predecessors. Doubtless with some support from Poussin's *Et in Arcadia Ego*, the landscape garden readily adopted the tomb in the landscape as a characteristic feature until, with the establishment of the cemetery of Père Lachaise in Paris after the Revolution, the cemetery itself became a garden.[24]

I want to end this garden excursion with a few remarks on the relationships of cemetery, garden, city, and utopia. It seems perfectly apt that the new cemetery movement of the nineteenth century took its inspiration from English landscape parks and removed burial grounds from crowded and unhealthy inner cities. But these new cemeteries became in their turn as densely packed as the urban centers from which they had been removed: gardens of death became cities of the dead. All this is apt, because man's progress has also been plotted along a route that leads from the Garden of Eden at one end of time to the City of God at the other. (There are exceptions, such as the Apocalypse of Peter to whom the Lord revealed "a very great country outside of this world . . . blooming with unfading flowers and incorruptible and bearing blessed fruit." But it is essentially St. Augustine's imagery of the City of God that has prospered.)

What are the implications of man's choosing his utopian imagery from either of these termini? If he takes it from the original garden it will or should be unbounded, all nature, without the need of protection. But as William McClung has recently argued in a fascinating book on *The Architecture of Paradise,*[25] man has consistently opted for the urban imagery of a ring of walls and other protective buildings. The *hortus conclusus* already compromises the Edenic Garden with architectural components. Many representations of paradise equally hedge their bets. In Fra Angelico's *Last Judgment* the blessed celebrate in a celestial garden beneath the ramparts of a city: as McClung says, "the bastioned city satisfies as a representation of triumph, power and security, the garden as a representation of innocent delights." So too in the Utrecht codex of St. Augustine the imagery of divine urbanization exists alongside that of a fine garden (fig. 11.12).

What may explain the ascendency of an architecture over a horticulture of Paradise is the essential vulnerability of the unenclosed garden. As Bunyan put it in *The Holy City*:

> *Adam* you know, was once so rich and wealthy, that he had the Garden of *Eden,* the Paradise of pleasure, yea, and also the whole World to boot, for his inheritance; but mark, in all his Glory he was without a Wall: wherefore presently, even at the very first assault of the Adversary, he was not onely worsted as touching his Person and standing, but even stripped of all his Treasure, his Paradise taken from him.[26]

It was not only for protection that Bunyan recommended a city for his utopia; he also considered that the diversity and multitude of the blessed urged their being housed in a city. A celestial highrise. To protect a garden with a wall, then, or to provide it with buildings is to acknowledge that Eden in its pure form is irrecoverable; St. Augustine denied that the garden would be restored on earth. Furthermore the walled or claustral garden, the garden of architectural forms, satisfies because instead of reminding us elegiacally or ironically of a lost Eden it anticipates and celebrates our eventual arrival at the City of God. It secures us, too, from our fear of the unpathed wood and the unstructured wilderness, which are for Gaston Bachelard the primal dystopia.[27] Maybe—it is something about which I have long puzzled—these configurations of conscious and unconscious attitudes toward the architectural garden explain the outcry when Capability Brown tried to

11.12. St. Augustine preaches of the City of God. Utrecht Codex [MS 42], c. 1465–1474 (Utrecht University Library).

eliminate all buildings, all fences, all urban traces from his landscapes; certainly, the reaction to his work was a speedy reversion to the architectural garden by Humphry Repton, J. C. Loudon, and others.

But as the names of nineteenth-century garden history must remind us, there were reactions also to the architectural garden. Gertrude Jekyll and William Robinson promoted the horticultural paradise, whose walls—though they were necessary for social and legal reasons—were not insisted upon, not considered to be confining. A nineteenth-century fear and horror of urban crowding, of architecture used often to cramp and constrain the population, led to utopian visions of green worlds and wondrous gardens. No romance of William Morris is without its hortulan paradise; and other utopians like Carlyle and Ruskin also invoke the world of flowers and cultivation as an antidote to the dystopia of the city. Interestingly, the place in Orwell's *1984* where Winston and Julia can recover the satisfactions of love making is outside the regimented city in a pastoral landscape of bluebells and the "droning of ring-doves."[28]

There are, then, two rival imageries of gardens as utopias. One is controlled by the ultimate satisfactions of the City of God. The other recalls the pristine openness of Eden. One is architectural, the other natural, even wild (Robinson's famous book is *The Wild Garden*). Between them there is historically and ideologically a basic conflict. But in practice they have learned to compromise with each other. The paradigm of that collaboration is the garden city; but before its invention there were the gardens in the cities of More's Utopia, the nineteenth-century establishment of city parks, all of which are somehow summarized in Frank Lloyd Wright's dreams of a cityscape with intermingled gardens, or in the utopian cities projects of Henry Dreyfuss's *Democracity* at the 1939 New York World's Fair.[29]

The city is under threat once again, of course—the prime target of thermonuclear attacks: in those conditions gardens, walled or unwalled, will yield no protection. A few years ago Robert Morris envisaged his sculpture *Tomb Garden Outside the City*[30] as the mechanized burial ground after atomic disaster. Those who see either hope or the paramount need for there to be space for hope are today identified with the garden's primordial color: green. They are the Green Party or Greenpeace. Their imagery is gardenesque and they perpetuate the strong instinct of mankind to project utopias in traditional forms. We may hang representations of gardens on the walls (the marvelous Stoke Edith tapestries); we may wear fantastical headdresses in the shape of gardens to the fleshpots of Vauxhall or Ranelagh, the green retreats of eighteenth- and early nineteenth-century Londoners; we are seduced by colored ads which promise us immaculate lawns if we use their special fertilizer. These—and others—are the continuing expression of our wish for an impossible, nonsensical, healing, perfect, nowhere world.

NOTES

INTRODUCTION: READING AND WRITING THE SITE

1. *De natura deorum,* II, 60, 151–152. For an extensive exposition and discussion of these three natures see my forthcoming book, *Gardens: Theory, Practice, History,* to be published by Thames & Hudson (London, 1993).

2. J. Bonfadio, *Le lettere e una scrittura burlesca,* ed. A Greco (Rome, 1978), 96.

3. The two main writers on picturesque were William Gilpin, famous for his tour guides to various parts of Britain (see below in note 5 for his work on the Lake District), and the more theoretical Uvedale Price, *Essays on the Picturesque,* 3 vols. (London, 1810). For two modern commentaries on the picturesque cult see Christopher Hussey, *The Picturesque: Studies in a Point of View* (London and New York, 1927) and Malcolm Andrews, *In Search of the Picturesque* (Aldershot, Hants., 1989). For the bearing of the picturesque upon garden design see the relevant sections of the anthology *The Genius of the Place: The English Landscape Garden 1620–1820,* ed. John Dixon Hunt and Peter Willis (Cambridge, Mass., 1989); further citations of this will refer to its main title only.

4. *The Palm at the End of the Mind* (New York, 1972), 46. That the American poet's jar is less artful than, say, Keats's Grecian urn does not interfere with the argument offered here.

5. Gilpin, *Observations relative chiefly to the picturesque beauty . . . of Cumberland, and Westmoreland . . . ,* 3rd ed. (London, 1792), II, section xxxi.

6. Quoted in Hussey, *The Picturesque,* 119.

7. Thanks to Peter and Linda Parshall for sending me a postcard of the Larson cartoon in the first place.

8. Few question the durability of the picturesque as a source for landscape design today, but see Catharine Howett, "Systems, Signs, Sensibilities: Sources for a New Landscape Aesthetic," *Landscape Journal,* 6 (1987), especially p. 11.

9. See Augustin Berque, *Médiance de milieux en paysages* (Montpellier, 1990).

10. Two recent books have taken that particular enquiry somewhat further than previous writers: Charles W. Moore, William J. Mitchell, and William Turnbull, Jr., *The Poetics of Gardens* (Cambridge, Mass., 1989), and *The Meaning of Gardens,* ed. Mark Francis and Randolph T. Hester, Jr., (Cambridge, Mass., 1990).

11. See below, fig. 4.5 and chap. 3, note 8.

12. See below, chap. 1, notes 19 and 20.

13. The contemporary spelling *Gothick* is used throughout these essays to indicate eighteenth-century versions of this architectural style.

14. For this information I have drawn upon the *Royal Commission on Historical Manuscripts,* second report, II (1874), 82–84.

15. I have discussed these matters fully in a recent essay, "Verbal versus Visual Meanings in Garden History: The Case of Rousham," in *Garden History: Issues, Approaches, Methods,* ed. John Dixon Hunt, Dumbarton Oaks Colloquium on the History of Landscape Architecture, XIII (Washington, D.C., 1991).

16. The best introduction to this is Jean Hagstrum, *The Sister Arts* (Chicago, 1968).

17. R. Blome, *Gentleman's Recreation* (London, 1686) links both architecture and heraldry under "Ethicks" as forms which display and therefore need proper understanding or reading.

18. See my suggestions for how this partnership may be viewed in "Pope, Kent and 'Palladian' Gardening," *The Enduring Legacy: Alexander Pope Tercentenary Essays,* ed. G. S. Rousseau and Pat Rogers (Cambridge, 1988), 121–131.

1 CASTLE HOWARD REVISITED

1. Exceptions to the lack of scholarly interest in Castle Howard since Hussey's essay are Wolfgang Kaiser, *Castle Howard. Ein englischer Landsitz des frühen 18. Jahrhunderts* (Freiburg im Breisgau, 1984), and more recently Charles Saumarez-Smith, *The Building of Castle Howard* (London, 1990), which nevertheless only devotes one rather brisk chapter to the landscaping.

2. Particularly chapters 3 and 4. What I am, I suppose, also expressing is my own surprise that I did not recognize much earlier how apt was the example of Castle Howard for some of my first forays into landscape architecture history; the more surprising, too, in that I spent thirteen very enjoyable years at the University of York and for some of those lived not far from Castle Howard, which I got to know and love well.

3. Saumarez-Smith's similar task in his book is, in the absence of explicit statements, to extrapolate meanings and intentions from the architecture of the mansion itself

in order to answer the question, "who built Castle Howard and for what?" (p. xviii). I am indebted throughout my essay here to the materials gathered in this recent book, of which I was, through the kindness of its author, allowed to see a typescript at an early stage of my work.

4. I am grateful to Chris Ridgway for this suggestion and for sending me to the *Oxford English Dictionary,* which authorizes this implication.

5. Jay Appleton, "Some Thoughts on the Geology of the Picturesque," *Journal of Garden History,* 6 (1986), 274 and fig. 2.

6. Walpole to Richard Bentley, September 1753, in *The Correspondence,* ed. W. S. Lewis and R. S. Brown (New Haven, 1937), xxxv, 148.

7. For a diagram of its evolving ground plan see Kerry Downes, *Vanbrugh* (London, 1977), 28.

8. See Wolfgang Lotz, "La Rotunda: edificio civile con cupola," *Bollettino . . . Andrea Palladio,* 4 (1962), 69–73. I am grateful to Donna Salzer for this reference.

9. See *The Complete Works of Sir John Vanbrugh,* IV: *The Letters,* ed. Geoffrey Webb (London, 1928), 27–30.

10. Ibid., 159.

11. See Downes, *Vanbrugh,* 84 and note.

12. On bastion gardens, see Downes, *Vanbrugh,* 107, and note 26 below. Vanbrugh uses "bastions" in his *Letters,* 171. For Vanbrugh's love of Gothick see Downes, passim, and the letter from Tim Mowl in *Country Life* (8 February 1990), 97.

13. *The Letters,* 13–16.

14. The difficult matter of Hawksmoor's role in the work at Castle Howard has been much debated by the principal authority on them both: see Kerry Downes, *Hawksmoor* (London, 1959), *Hawksmoor* (London, 1969), *Vanbrugh* (1977), and *Sir John Vanbrugh: A Biography* (London, 1987).

15. Chris Ridgway tells me that what is now known as the Temple of the Four Winds was originally and until at least 1857 called a Temple of Diana; the present name was probably acquired during the twentieth century.

16. Cited by Kerry Downes, *Hawksmoor* (London, 1959), 243.

17. Webb, *The Letters,* 156.

18. Lord Morpeth, the son, is so reported in Vanbrugh's letter to Carlisle of 11 February 1724: *The Letters,* 156.

19. See Richard Foster Jones, *Ancients and Moderns: A Study of the Background of the Battle of the Books* (St. Louis, Mo., 1936).

20. This theme is set out economically in Thomas Gray's poem *The Progress of Poetry,* first published in 1757.

21. It is not clear whether the drawing is for the site of the present Temple of the Four Winds or of the now lost Temple of Venus, the platform alone of which survives. For the purposes of this particular discussion it is not material.

22. Kaiser, *Castle Howard,* p. 107. But it is to Robert Williams that I am indebted for the point about the ruins and for the idea that Palladio's reconstruction of the Praeneste (Palestrina) temple lay behind both his Villa Rotunda and the Temple of the Four Winds at Castle Howard.

23. The plan illustrated here as fig. 1.13 is labeled "Plan of Hinderskelfe Castle [but referring to the *new* mansion] and Wray Wood" (Victoria and Albert Museum, E 432-1951).

24. See [James Caulfield], *Memoirs . . . of the Kit-Cat Club* (London, 1821).

25. This southern garden was totally remodeled in the Victorian period when W. A. Nesfield introduced what *he* thought would represent an apt European garden style.

26. Vanbrugh calls them "bastions": Webb, *The Letters,* 171.

27. On this idea of a neo-antique garden on the south front of Castle Howard see John Harris, "Diverting Labyrinths," *Country Life* (11 January 1990), 62–65, especially p. 63. There are also precedents in the writings of the third Earl of Shaftesbury, himself such an influential figure in cultural patriotics: see his wish to have a portrait painted "in a wooded scene with ancient temple . . . in the background," in David Leatherbarrow, "Character, Geometry and Perspective: The Third Earl of Shaftesbury's Principles of Garden Design," *Journal of Garden History,* 4 (1984), 339 and fig. 10.

However, there may also be elements of Dutch garden design here (notably the green rooms, and perhaps even the bastion motif—on this see my "Anglo-Dutch Garden Art: Style and Idea," *The World of William and Mary: Politics, Commerce, Ideas and Culture,* ed. Dale Hoak and Mordecai Feingold, forthcoming, Berkeley and Los Angeles, 1992)—which would signal Charles Howard's well-known and strong identification with King William III; nor should we forget that Vanbrugh's arrest in Calais and subsequent imprisonment were caused by a public speech he made in favor of William's invasion of England in 1688.

28. Leland writes of the park having "much fair young wood in it," *Itinerary,* ed. L. Toulmin Smith (London, 1964), I, 65. That Wray Wood continued to be a crucial element of the landscape may be gauged from a 1738 woodcut, where it features prominently (see Saumarez-Smith, pl. 44). On "a political iconography of woodland" later in the eighteenth century, see Stephen Daniels, "The Political Iconography of Woodland in Later Georgian England," *The Iconography of Landscape,* ed. Denis Cosgrove and Stephen Daniels (Cambridge, 1988), 43–82.

29. Canals and pools may well be another gesture toward William III, though their handling is rather more French than Dutch.

30. See Lawrence Whistler, *The Imagination of Vanbrugh and His Fellow Artists* (London, 1954), 28–33.

31. Switzer, *Ichnographia Rustica: Or, the Nobleman, Gentleman, and Gardener's Recreation,* 3 vols. (1718), I, 87.

32. Ibid., II, 198.

33. For various descriptions of the decorations and representations of Wray Wood, see passages cited by Saumarez-Smith, 124ff.

34. These are marked as already built on the plan reproduced as fig. 1.13.

35. Cited by Saumarez-Smith, 117, from B. L. Portland Loan 29/233, folio 89.

36. Downes, *Hawksmoor* (1959), 129, 243.

37. See *Walpole Society,* 19 (1931), 117.

38. Downes, *Hawksmoor* (London, 1979), 221.

39. Ronald Paulson, *Emblem and Expression* (London, 1975), 19.

40. Cited Saumarez-Smith, 127, from John Tracy Atkyns, *Iter Boreale,* manuscript in the Yale Center for British Art, folios 23–25.

41. "[A]mphitheatrum aliquod immensum, et quale sola rerum natura possit effingere." The reference can best be appreciated in the context of Robert Castell, *The Villas of the Ancients Illustrated* (London, 1728), 80. On amphitheaters, it is worth recalling that in *I Quattro Libri* Palladio wrote of his only executed domestic building with a dome—and one much in the minds of the owner and his architects at Castle Howard—that "e circondato da altri amenissimi colli che rendono l'aspetto di un molto grande Teatro" (in Giacomo Leoni, *The Architecture of Palladio* [1721], 64).

42. William Chambers, *A Dissertation on Oriental Gardening* (1772), preface, v.

43. See Hussey, *English Gardens and Landscapes,* 126. Vanbrugh himself had doubts as to the usefulness of the word *belvedere,* preferring the more anglicized *temple* (see *The Letters,* 160). It seems to have been of some concern to him: see also "The word Corridor Madam is foreign, and signifys in plain English, no more than a Passage, it is now however generally us'd as an English Word" (*The Letters,* 71).

44. Webb, *The Letters,* 148.

45. See Saumarez-Smith, 147.

46. For this insight I take from Paul Munden's verses on the Carrmire Gate:

Rough-hewn blocks speak
out in the blurred dialect
of their local quarry;
a vernacular art which vies
with influences ancient and
foreign.

Henderskelfe, photographs of the Castle Howard Estate by Peter Heaton, poems by Paul Munden (Bulmer, York, 1989), 14.

47. The final part of this remark (from "open to all View . . .") first appeared in Switzer's *The Nobleman, Gentleman, and Gardener's Recreation* (London, 1715), xxvi. Three years later, when in 1718 Switzer published this expanded work as the three-volume *Ichnographia Rustica,* the introduction to volume III was entitled "Rural and Extensive Gardening"; the remainder of the phrase quoted here comes from his expanded remarks (III, xv) on this "Natural and Rural way of Gardening" (III, xiv).

48. Walpole, *Correspondence,* XXX, p. 257. On this see my *The Figure in the Landscape: Poetry, Painting and Gardening during the Eighteenth Century* (Baltimore, 1976), chapter 4, which discussed the landscapes associated with ancient bards and Druids. See also Stuart Piggott, *The Druids* (London, 1975), and, for a survey of their discovery and "invention," his more recent *Ancient Britons and the Antiquarian Imagination* (London, 1990).

2 THEATERS, GARDENS, AND GARDEN THEATERS

1. Georgina Masson, writing in *Queen Christina of Sweden: Documents and Studies,* ed. Magnus von Platen (*Analecta Reginensia,* I, Stockholm, 1966), 254. See below, in works cited in notes 7 and 28, for other attention to this relationship. I developed some of the Italian Renaissance materials touched upon here in my *Garden and Grove* (London, 1986), chap. 5.

2. See Warwick Wroth, *The London Pleasure Gardens of the Eighteenth Century* (London, 1896), and E. Beresford Chancellor, *The Pleasure Haunts of London* (London, Boston, and New York, 1925). For a collection of 50 color slides of views in these London garden theaters in the eighteenth and nineteenth centuries, for slides of selected playbills and theatrical events in them, and for a commentary upon their interest to theatrical history, see my *Vauxhall and London's Garden Theatres,* Theatre in Focus series (Cambridge: Chadwyck-Healey in association with the Consortium for Drama and Media in Higher Education, 1985).

3. See esp. James Granville Southworth, *Vauxhall Gardens: A Chapter in the Social History of England* (New York, 1941); Mollie Sands, *Invitation to Ranelagh 1742–1803* (London, 1946); W. S. Scott, *Green Retreats: The Story of Vauxhall Gardens 1661–1859* (London, 1955); Richard D. Altick, *The Shows of London* (Cambridge, Mass., 1978).

4. See Altick, *The Shows of London,* 250, 344, 360, and 373.

5. *The Diary,* ed. E. S. de Beer (Oxford, 1955), II, 393. Mondragone is illustrated in C. L. Franck, *The Villas of Frascati* (Levittown, N.Y., 1966). For some attempt to define "theater" in the context of a nearby Frascati villa, see Klaus Schwager, "Kardinal Pietro Aldobrandinis Villa Di Belvedere in Frascati," *Römisches Jahrbuch für Kunstgeschichte,* 9–10 (1961–1962), 379–382.

6. For the Belvedere see J. S. Ackerman, "The Belvedere as a Classical Villa," *Journal of the Warburg and Courtauld Institutes,* XIV (1951), 70–91, and Hans Henrik Brummer, *The Statue Court in the Vatican Belvedere* (Stockholm, 1970); for Palestrina, the ancient Praeneste, see John Arthur Hanson, *Roman Theater-Temples* (Princeton, 1959), 33–36.

7. For the Belvedere, see note above; for the Pitti Palace, see Roy Strong, *Splendour at Court* (Boston, 1973). Of the volumes issued by the CNRS the most relevant here are *Le Lieu Théâtral à la Renaissance,* ed. Jean Jacquot, Elie Konigson, and Marcel Oddon (Paris, 1964), esp. the essay by André Chastel, "Cortile et Théâtre," and *Les Fêtes de la Renaissance,* ed. Jean Jacquot, 2 vols. (Paris, 1956 and 1960), though there is little attention to gardens specifically. See also A. M. Nagler, *Theatre Festivals of the Medici 1539 to 1637* (New Haven, 1964).

8. *A Description of Ranelaugh Rotunda and Gardens* (1762), 8. The rotunda at Vauxhall had a stage, boxes, gallery, and a pit which could be used as an arena.

9. *Epistulae ad Familiares,* VII, 23.

10. See Lawrence Gowing, "Hogarth, Hayman,and the Vauxhall Decorations," *Burlington Magazine,* 95 (1953), 4–19.

11. An English example is recorded in the Stoke Edith hangings: see Thomasina Beck, *Embroidered Gardens* (London, 1979), 75.

12. *Elements of Architecture* (1624), 109–110.

13. Copies of Panofsky's correspondence with Weisinger are at the Institute for Advanced Study and I am grateful to Mrs. Gerda Panofsky for drawing them to my attention. Some quotations are given in Herbert Weisinger, *The Agony and the Triumph* (East Lansing, Michigan, 1964), in the course of his essay "*Theatrum Mundi*: Illusion as Reality," 58–70.

14. Besides Weisinger's essay, see also Richard Bernheimer, "*Theatrum Mundi,*" *Art Bulletin,* 38 (1956), 225–247; Jean Jacquot, "Le Théâtre du Monde de Shakespeare à Calderón," *Revue de littérature comparée,* 31 (1957), 341–372, and Anne Righter (Barton), *Shakespeare and the Idea of the Play* (Harmondsworth, Middlesex, 1962).

15. *The Citizen of the World,* letter 71; *Evelina* (Oxford English Novels edition, 1968), 193ff.

16. For Evelyn at Pratolino, see *Diary,* II, 418–419. An interesting confusion of cave (or grotto) and *cavea* (or auditorium in a theater) seems to have been made at least once during the Renaissance in documents on the Villa Lante: see Claudia Lazzaro-Bruno, "The Villa Lante at Bagnaia," *Art Bulletin,* 59 (1977), 559 and note 36.

17. Handel was presented in "the stress and strain of composition" (Scott, *Green Retreats,* 26). See also Terence Hodgkinson, *Handel at Vauxhall,* a booklet reprinted in 1969 from the *Victoria and Albert Museum Bulletin,* I (1965).

18. Quotations are from *The Vauxhall Papers* (1841), 51–53, which use contemporary descriptions.

19. "In the descent into the first garden shews itself the Colossus of Pegasus . . ." or "riseth an Island cut in the shape of a ship," in Edmund Warcupp, *Italy in Its Originall Glory, Ruine and Revivall* (London, 1660), 309–311. For the following remarks on Arundel's sculpture fragments in Cupid's Gardens see D. E. L. Haynes, *The Arundel Marbles* (Oxford, 1975), 4, my italics.

20. John Aubrey, *Natural History and Antiquities of Surrey* (1719), 282 (the remark is by Aubrey's editor). Engravings of twenty-seven of Cuper's pieces were published in this *History.* On Arundel's garden, see Roy Strong, *The Renaissance Garden in England* (London, 1979) and my *Garden and Grove.*

21. The Bodleian Library, MS Rawl. D. 1162. Many drawings of these inventions at Pratolino were made by Giovanni Guerra in the sixteenth century and are now in the Albertina, Vienna; some are illustrated in two articles on Pratolino by Detlief Heikamp, *L'Oeil,* 171 (March 1969), 16–27, and *L'Antiquità viva,* 8 (1969), 14–34.

22. For further discussion of these two Evelyn designs, see my *Garden and Grove.*

23. See Cinzia M. Sicca, "Burlington and Garden Design," in *Lord Burlington and His Circle* (London, 1982).

24. See Peter Willis, *Charles Bridgeman and the English Landscape Garden* (London, 1978), for some illustrations; but Willis does not discuss the theaters.

25. *The Works of Henry St. John, Viscount Bolingbroke* (1754), III, 318, my italics.

26. Walpole on Twickenham, I. W. U. Chase, *Horace Walpole: Gardenist* (Princeton, 1943), 28–29; on Stowe, *Horace Walpole's Correspondence,* ed. W. S. Lewis and others (New Haven, 1937), X, 314.

27. The paintings belong to the Buckingham County Museum and are illustrated and briefly discussed in John Harris, *Country Life* (15 March 1979), 707–709, and *The Anglo-Dutch Garden in the Age of William and Mary* (being the *Journal of Garden History,* 8, nos. 2 and 3 [1988]), 229–230. See also, for a discussion of the garden represented, Terry Friedman, *James Gibbs* (New Haven, 1984), 182–189.

28. The Villa Garzoni, at Collodi near Lucca, both has a small theater on the grounds and as a whole seems constructed like a steeply sloping auditorium; there were many other examples, illustrated in such books as G. B. Falda, *Li Giardini di Roma* (issued from 1670 onward). For some examples of gardens as stage settings, see Per Bjurström, *Giacomo Torelli and Baroque Stage Design* (Stockholm, 1961).

29. Per Bjurström, *Feast and Theatre in Queen Christina's Rome* (Stockholm, 1966), 23 and pl. 22. Aaron Hill's production of Handel's *Rinaldo* in 1711 showed a cascade with real water: *The Eighteenth-Century English Stage,* ed. Kenneth Richards and Peter Thomson (London, 1972), 171–172.

30. More details are given in my "Marvell, Nun Appleton and the Buen Retiro," *Philological Quarterly,* 59 (1980), 374–378.

31. There is a charming watercolor of this in John Fillinham's scrapbook, *The Public Gardens of London,* in the Guildhall Library.

32. Peter Holland, *The Ornament of Action: Text and Performance in Restoration Comedy* (Cambridge, 1979), 36. This study contains valuable discussions of the semiotics of scenery, to which I am indebted.

33. All references in the following discussion are to Stephen Orgel and Roy Strong, *Inigo Jones: The Theatre of the Stuart Court,* 2 vols. (Berkeley and Los Angeles, 1973).

34. Such garden debts (and see also the quotation from *Lord Hay's Masque* below) give some support to the theory that Jones was in Italy before his visit there with Arundel in 1613–1614; see Orgel and Strong, *Inigo Jones,* I, 20 and note 24.

35. Orgel and Strong reject Simpson and Bell's identification of this design (Orgel and Strong, *Inigo Jones,* pl. 252) for the reason that it contains only one fountain, whereas their suggestion (pl. 281) honors the text's call for fountains and grottoes in the plural. However, it seems clear that a knowledgeable gardenist would register opportunities for fountains and grottoes in the rear pavilion of pl. 252.

36. Holland, *The Ornament,* 53.

37. Ibid., 29 and 52.

38. Richards and Thomson, eds., *The Eighteenth-Century English Stage,* 187. The Thornhill sets are also discussed by Richard Southern, *Changeable Scenery* (London, 1952), 177–178.

39. See further in chaps. 4, 5, and 6 of this volume.

40. Discussed in part by Sands and Altick (see note 2, p. 96). Vauxhall's famous "Ridotto al fresco" takes its name from a word meaning resort, haunt, shelter, and so foyer of a theater.

41. Aileen Ribeiro, "The Exotic Diversion: The Dress Worn at Masquerades in Eighteenth-Century London," *Connoisseur,* 197 (1978), 7.

42. Quoted, ibid., 7.

43. On conversation pictures see the excellent discussion by Ronald Paulson, *Emblem and Expression* (London, 1975), 121–136. That the diversions of the pleasure gardens were compared with *fêtes champêtres* is clear from an engraving entitled "The Citizens fête champêtre" in a grangerized copy of *A Sunday Ramble,* which chronicles visits to some gardens, in the Bromhead Library, Senate House, University of London. On this theme generally, see Elizabeth Burns, *Theatricality* (London, 1972).

44. On Carlisle House see Ribeiro, "The Exotic Diversion," 4.

45. *Dunciad,* I, line 108; *Winter,* lines 650–651 (*The Seasons,* ed. James Sambrook, Oxford, 1972), Max Byrd, *London Transformed: Images of the City in the Eighteenth Century* (New Haven, 1978), 63.

46. He cites "Parts answ'ing Parts, shall slide into a whole" and comments "As if his Ldsps fine Gardens were to be just such another Scene of Lewdness as Cupids Gardens or Faux-Hall" (the Twickenham edition of Pope's poetry, III.ii.183).

47. See Ribeiro, "The Exotic Diversion," 11.

48. Relevant passages in the Penguin text of the novel are pp. 120–121 for Mat's reactions, 123–125 for Lydia's, and 388 for the *Theatrum mundi* reference.

49. Fielding's verses are quoted by Ribeiro, "The Exotic Diversion," 3, and the others are taken from an engraving of Ranelagh in the Guildhall Library.

50. *A Tour . . . of Great Britain* (7th ed., 1769), II, 172.

51. *Life of Johnson* (Oxford Standard Authors edition, 1961), 959. Max Byrd has a brief but illuminating discussion of Boswell's playing with new identities (*London Transformed,* 65).

3 EMBLEM AND EXPRESSION IN THE EIGHTEENTH-CENTURY LANDSCAPE GARDEN

1. MS annotation to William Mason's *Satirical Poems,* published in an edition of the relevant poems by Paget Toynbee (Oxford, 1926), 43.

2. *Observations on Modern Gardening* (London, 1770), 150–151.

3. An interesting exception is the figure of Melancholy, which is discussed later in this essay. For a more extended and somewhat different discussion of the growing lack of familiarity with emblematic imagery and learned allusions during the eighteenth century, see the following essay.

4. The engravings commissioned in 1739 by Sarah, the widow of Charles Bridgeman, one of the landscape architects who had worked at Stowe, were published in

1746 and have been reprinted as *Stowe Gardens in Buckinghamshire laid out by Mr Bridgeman . . .* (London, 1987), with descriptive notes by George Clarke.

5. I. W. U. Chase, *Horace Walpole: Gardenist* (Princeton, 1943), 14.

6. See Maynard Mack, *The Garden and the City: Retirement and Politics in the Later Poetry of Pope 1731–1743* (Toronto, 1969), 70–72. For some of the many images of this legendary spot (it was extensively celebrated), see my *Garden and Grove: The Italian Renaissance Garden in the English Imagination* (Princeton, 1986), pl. 103, or Raymond Keaveney, *Views of Rome from the Ashby Collection in the Vatican Library* (London, 1988), plate on p. 211.

7. Laurence Whistler, Michael Gibbon, and George Clarke, *Stowe: A Guide to the Gardens* (rev. ed., Stowe, 1968), 18. I am especially grateful to George Clarke for sharing with me his extensive and expert knowledge of the Stowe gardens. Mr. Clarke is at present completing a history of the gardens.

8. For Trumbull's advice to Pope on Homer, see the *Correspondence of Alexander Pope,* ed. George Sherburn, 5 vols. (Oxford, 1956), I, 45; on Horace, see *Imitations of Horace,* Twickenham edition, IV, xxxvi–xxvii. All further references to Pope's poetry will be to volume and page of this edition. For further commentary upon cultural translation and adaptation, see the first two essays in this collection.

9. First edition, 1748, 19–20. Later editions of Gilpin's *Dialogue* in the British Museum (see, for example, 578 d. 4) are bound with forty engravings of the temples in the gardens, some of which are discussed here. For an introduction to Gilpin's text, see Augustan Reprint Society, no. 176 (Los Angeles, 1976).

10. M. J. Gibbon, "Gilbert West's Walk through the Gardens in 1731," *The Stoic,* 24 (March 1970), 62. Mr. Gibbon writes of the busts in their original home, Gibbs's Building.

11. The lines, with the one omitted in brackets, run:

> *Hic manus, ob patriam pugnando vulnera passi;*
> *[quique sacerdotes casti, dum vita manebit]*
> *quique pii vates, et phoebo digna locuti;*
> *inventas aut vitam excoluere per artis;*
> *quique sui memores aliquos fecere merendo. (11.660–664)*

12. The full inscription is quoted in Gilpin's *Dialogue,* 3d ed. (1751), 15–16. This edition contains all the inscriptions from the garden temples that I discuss. On Milton's role here, see my "Milton and the Making of the English Garden," *Milton Studies,* 15 (1981), 81–105.

13. See Whistler, Gibbon, and Clarke, *Stowe: A Guide to the Gardens,* 22. An added complexity is that the parish church of Stowe was kept standing in the Elysian Fields, adding its emblematic voice to this cluster of architectural meanings. A

collection of visitors' responses to the Stowe gardens has been edited by George Clarke, *Descriptions of Lord Cobham's Gardens at Stowe (1700–1750),* Buckinghamshire Record Society, no. 26 (1990).

14. This Georgic preserve may be seen in several of Sarah Bridgeman's views (Clarke, ed., *Stowe Gardens*), notably to the right of the view of the Rotunda. Recently Maynard Mack has offered further testimony of the presence to "even the most ordinary sensibility" of Virgil's poem: see *The Garden and the City,* 19–20.

15. See Robert Castell, *The Villas of the Ancients Illustrated* (1728), 76.

16. The Temple of Venus and the Hermitage at Stowe appear in the illustrations to "The Idle Lake" and "Archimago's Cell," which are reproduced in my *William Kent,* cat. nos. 77 and 73. For a discussion of Rousham see my forthcoming essay, "Verbal versus Visual Meanings in Garden History," in *Garden History: Issues, Approaches, Methods,* ed. John Dixon Hunt (Dumbarton Oaks Colloquium on the History of Landscape Architecture, XIII).

17. See Gilbert West, *Stowe, the Gardens, . . .* (1732), II, 28–32 and note.

18. In Maynard Mack's book *The Garden and the City,* especially the first three chapters, and in Frederick Bracher, "Pope's Grotto: The Maze of Fancy," *Essential Articles for the Study of Alexander Pope,* ed. Maynard Mack (Hamden, Conn., 1968). See also note 26 below.

19. Joseph Spence, *Observations, Anecdotes and Characters of Books and Men,* ed. James M. Osborn (Oxford, 1966), I, 257; Mack's discussion of the passage occurs in *The Garden and the City,* 37–40.

20. Switzer, *Ichnograhica Rustica* (1718), II, 197.

21. See, for a similar mixture, the view of Miserden in Johannes Kip, *Théâtre de la Grande Bretagne* (1716).

22. Bolingbroke's letter is cited by Mack, *The Garden and the City,* p. 27. Walpole, later, also testified to the "multiplied scenes" of Pope's garden: see Chase, *Horace Walpole: Gardenist,* 28–29.

23. A similar equation occurs in James Thomson's "Spring"; see *The Seasons,* ed. James Sambrook (Oxford, 1981), 26ff.

24. See my *William Kent,* cat. nos. 10–11, and the figures in the Twickenham edition of *Essay on Man.*

25. John Serle, *A Plan of Mr. Pope's Garden . . .* (1745), 5–7. There are in the Huntington Library some sketches of the interior of the Grotto that bear out the sense of variety that I am stressing here.

26. Always a contentious problem, this still remains so: see the largely proleptic account of Pope's gardening in Morris Brownell, *Alexander Pope and the Arts of*

Georgian England (Oxford, 1978), as opposed to the more historically grounded account by Peter Martin, *"Pursuing Innocent Pleasures": The Gardening World of Alexander Pope* (Hamden, Conn., 1984).

27. *Correspondence,* IV, 228.

28. Mack, *The Garden and the City,* 73.

29. Ibid., pl. 22.

30. *Correspondence,* IV, 267 and II, 296.

31. Written by an anonymous contributor to *The Newcastle General Magazine, or Monthly Intelligencer* for 1748. The piece is now conveniently reprinted by Mack, *The Garden and the City,* pp. 237ff.

32. *Correspondence,* II, 296, my italics.

33. *Correspondence,* II, 264. These considerations of Pope were subsequently developed first into an article for *The Art Quarterly* (Spring 1974) and finally into the second chapter of my *The Figure in the Landscape: Poetry, Painting and Gardening during the Eighteenth Century* (Baltimore, 1976; pbk. ed., 1989). These final pages are retained here to complete the argument of the essay.

34. "Contemplative life is not only my scene, but it is my habit too" (*Correspondence,* I, 454); elsewhere he tells of the "imaginary entertainments" he enjoys in his grotto (ibid., I, 163).

35. See G. K. Hunter, "The 'Romanticism' of Pope's Horace," in *Essential Articles for the Study of Alexander Pope,* ed. Maynard Mack (London, 1964).

36. Spence, *Anecdotes,* I, 252.

37. Ibid., I, 255. See also Pope's various responses to the differing scenes at Netley Abbey: "A New Pope Letter," *Philological Quarterly,* 65 (1966), 409–418. For a more thorough discussion of pictures and the garden, see the following essay.

38. Passages quoted are *Night Thoughts,* ed. G. Gilfillan (Edinburgh, 1853), 255–256, 258, and 326–327 respectively.

39. The phrase is from one of the poems by William Butler Yeats on the country estate of Lady Gregory, "Coole Park and Ballylee, 1931," where he self-consciously registers his own responses to the wintry landscape of the park.

40. Joseph Warton, *Essay on the Genius and Writings of Pope* (1782), II, 411.

41. *Correspondence,* ed. P. Toynbee and L. Whibley, 3 vols. (1935), II, 899.

42. *The Spectator,* no. 414 (25 June 1712): see *The Genius of the Place,* ed. Hunt and Willis, 141.

4 *UT PICTURA POESIS, UT PICTURA HORTUS*, AND THE PICTURESQUE

1. *Letters from England,* ed. Jack Simmons (London, 1951), 165.

2. See especially chap. 14. *Northanger Abbey* was in draft by 1799, probably revised in 1809. Recently Malcolm Andrews, *The Search for the Picturesque* (Aldershot, Hants., 1989) has studied the tourism and the landscape aesthetics of this "science" between 1760 and 1800.

3. Martin Price, "The Picturesque Moment," in *From Sensibility to Romanticism: Essays Presented to Frederick A. Pottle,* edited by F. W. Hilles and Harold Bloom (New York, 1965). Neither Christopher Hussey, *The Picturesque: Studies in a Point of View* (London, 1927), nor David Watkin, *The English Vision: The Picturesque in Architecture, Landscape and Garden Design* (London, 1982), consider the timing of the picturesque vogue. The only reference, and then only in passing, to some connection between the picturesque and *ut pictura poesis* seems to be by John Garham, "Ut pictura poesis," *Dictionary of the History of Ideas* (New York, 1973), IV, 473.

4. *The Works,* edited by E. T. Cook and A. Wedderburn (London, 1903–1912), VIII, 235–237. For some skepticism concerning the usefulness of the term *picturesque,* see Kenneth Woodbridge, "Irregular, Rococo or Picturesque," *Apollo,* 108 (1978), 356–358.

5. Addison, *The Works* (London, 1720), III, 497. *Landskip* was a word of Dutch origin, signifying "painted landscape."

6. Pope, recorded by Joseph Spence in *Observations, Anecdotes and Characters of Books and Men,* ed. James M. Osborn (Oxford, 1966), I, 252 and 253 respectively.

7. It should be obvious, but Morris Brownell frequently uses Pope's invocations of *picturesque,* especially from the Homer translations, to argue teleologically; see his *Alexander Pope and the Arts of Georgian England* (Oxford, 1978), and my assessment in *Review,* 3 (1981), 155–164.

8. *The Twickenham Edition of the Poetry of Pope,* ed. M. Mack (New Haven, 1967), VIII, 233–234.

9. For a typical example of the expected connections between visual image and literature, see Jonathan Richardson's "Argument in Behalf of the Science of a Connoisseur" and its consideration of paintings by Michelangelo in terms of literary texts by Dante and Villani, in *Two Discourses* (London, 1719), 26ff.

10. Dryden, *Of Dramatic Poesy and Other Critical Essays,* ed. George Watson (London, 1962); the remark on *decorum* quoted later in this paragraph is from II, 195. On Dryden's essay see Dean Tolle Mace, "Dryden, Poussin and the Parallel of Poetry and Painting in the Seventeenth Century," in *Encounters,* ed. J. D. Hunt (London, 1971).

11. Quoted by Peter J. Connelly, "Pope's *Iliad: Ut Pictura Translatio,*" *Studies in English Literature,* 21 (1981), 445. On pictorialism in Pope's Homer, see also David Ridgley Clark, "Landscape Painting Effects in Pope's Homer," *Journal of Aesthetics & Art Criticism,* 22 (1963), and Jean Hagstrum, *The Sister Arts* (Chicago, 1958), 210–222 and 229–233.

12. *Twickenham Edition,* VIII, 32, a note to Book X, line 677.

13. *The Correspondence,* edited by George Sherburn (Oxford, 1956), I, 167–168. It is hard to imagine this scene as Philips presents it in any way like the picturesque of Gilpin or Price. Similarly, when Pope remarked that "All gardening is landscape-painting" (see note 6 above) he was reputedly speaking while looking through the gateway at the Oxford Botanical Garden—hardly a vista to appeal to the later picturesque experts.

14. *Twickenham Edition,* X, 390–391.

15. Ibid., VII, 3. Spence connects Pope's "ideas afterwards for gardening" with his literary taste and judgment in the 1700s: *Observations,* I, 251.

16. David Jacques half-heartedly suggests that Pope's bowling green might have been considered "in the Great Light of a History Painting": *Garden History: The Journal of the Garden History Society,* 4 (1976), 42.

17. I have discussed this fully in "Pope's Twickenham Revisited," in *British and American Gardens in the Eighteenth Century,* ed. Peter Martin (Williamsburg, Va., 1984).

18. See Kenneth Woodbridge, *The Stourhead Landscape,* rev. ed. (London: The National Trust, 1982), 47–49, and Elisabeth MacDougall, "*Ars Hortulorum*: Sixteenth-Century Garden Iconography and Literary Theory in Italy," in *The Italian Garden,* ed. David R. Coffin (Washington, D.C., 1972), 53–58.

19. See Spence, *Observations,* I, 257, and Maynard Mack's commentary on this in *The Garden and the City* (Toronto, 1969), 37ff.

20. Félibien's words about Poussin: see André Félibien, *Entretiens* (Trévoux, 1725), 139.

21. These matters are more fully set out in my forthcoming essay on Rousham: "Verbal versus Visual Meanings in Garden History," in *Garden History: Issues, Approaches, Methods,* ed. John Dixon Hunt (Dumbarton Oaks Colloquium on the History of Landscape Architecture, XIII).

22. Spence, *Observations,* I, 423.

23. [Gilpin], *A Dialogue upon the Gardens . . . at Stow* (Buckingham, 1748), 19–21.

24. For the "scenes" of Pope's garden noticed by Henry St. John, Viscount Bolingbroke, see *The Works of Henry St. John, Viscount Bolingbroke* (1754), III, 318; for

Pope on Hotwells, see *Correspondence,* IV, 201; for poetic scenes see *Windsor Forest,* lines 17, 261, and 426 inter alia; cf. "A pretty kind of savage Scene" from Pope's "Imitation of the Sixth Satire of the Second Book of Horace," line 177. The difficulty of taking the parallels between garden and theater scenery further is the absence of enough surviving examples of the latter.

25. David Solkin, *Richard Wilson: The Landscape of Reaction* (London, 1982), 115.

26. See, for example, Betsy Rosasco, "The Sculptural Decorations of the Garden of Marly: 1679–1699," *Journal of Garden History,* 4 (1984), 95ff.

27. Félibien, *Entretiens,* 150. Poussin evidently used a model theater to compose some of his paintings; see Anthony Blunt, *Nicolas Poussin* (Washington, D.C., 1967), 242–245; see also Oskar Bätschmann, *Nicolas Poussin: Dialectics of Painting* (London, 1990), 27–29. William Gilpin, interestingly, continued to invoke the stage as a model for picturesque scenes: see *Three Essays* (2d ed., 1794), 140.

28. *Conference . . . (London, 1701),* folio a[1] recto. For a discussion of the "legible body" see Norman Bryson, *Word and Image: French Painting of the Ancient Régime* (Cambridge, 1981), chap. 2.

29. John Macky, *A Journey through England . . .* (London, 1724), I, 61. On Rigaud's drawings see Jacques Carré, "Through French Eyes; Rigaud's drawings of Chiswick," *Journal of Garden History,* 2 (1982), 133–142, where further examples of gesturing spectators can be found.

30. The portrait by Richardson is in the Yale Center for British Art. Unfortunately, the obelisk—though visible enough in the left background of the painting—does not show sufficiently in reproduction.

31. See Frank Simpson, "Dutch Paintings in England before 1760," *Burlington Magazine,* 95 (1953), 39–42, and Frank Herrmann, *The English as Collectors* (London, 1972).

32. "Philanactophil" [E. Bolton], *Nero Caesar . . .* (1624), 181.

33. See *A Philosophical Enquiry . . .,* ed. J. T. Boulton (Notre Dame, Ind., 1968), lxxvii–lxxviii, 164–165, 167–172, and passim.

34. A useful commentary on these psychological developments as they affect the imagination is Ernest Tuveson, *The Imagination as a Means of Grace: Locke and the Aesthetics of Romanticism* (Berkeley and Los Angeles, 1960).

35. See *The Renaissance Imagination,* edited by Stephen Orgel (Berkeley and Los Angeles, 1975), 51–74; the examples cited in my paragraph are those invoked by Gordon. That Addison should choose to be skeptical of traditional alliances between the arts in an essay on medals is perhaps significant: it was the study of ancient texts and images on medals in the closing years of the seventeenth century (the *Histoire Métallique*) that established a high point in the French elaboration of *ut*

pictura poesis. I have looked at some further revisions of these French theories in my inaugural lecture at Leiden University: *A Handle on "Tristram Shandy": or, Uncle Toby's Wound and Other Words and Images* (Leiden, 1984).

36. Joseph Spence, *Polymetis* (1747), 2–3.

37. Spence, *Observations,* I, 408.

38. Ibid., 414.

39. Respectively: ibid., II, 647; I, 415–416; I, 426; I, 419.

40. Joseph Spence, *An Essay on Pope's Odyssey,* pt. II (1727), 2ff. Brownell, *Alexander Pope,* 125ff. has suggested, not altogether plausibly, that this is in fact Spence's description of Pope's own garden at Twickenham.

41. Spence, *Polymetis,* 292.

42. Ibid., 83–88.

43. Ibid., 290.

44. Warton's *The Enthusiast* (1744), in *The Genius of the Place,* ed. Hunt and Willis, 241. On Spence's role in garden history see the series of articles in *Garden History: The Journal of the Garden History Society,* 6, no. 3 (1978), 7, no. 3 (1979), and 8, nos. 2–3 (1980).

45. Thomas Whately, *Observations on Modern Gardening* (1770), 151 and 146–150. See also the previous essay.

46. See note 43 above. On Brown's "languages" see Robert Williams, "Making Places: Garden-Mastery and English Brown," *Journal of Garden History,* 3 (1983), 382–385.

47. For Addison, see *The Works,* I, 43ff. (for *Letter*) and II, preface (for *Remarks*); for Pope, see *Twickenham Edition,* VI, 157.

48. See Solkin, *Richard Wilson,* 37–55. I am indebted to Solkin for much of my emphasis on Wilson.

49. Quoted by Solkin, ibid., 16.

50. *The Idler,* 79 (20 October 1759).

51. Solkin, *Richard Wilson,* especially 19, 26, 31, and passim.

52. *The Walpole Society,* 36 (1956–1958), 45.

53. William Whitehead, *Elegies, with an Ode to the Tiber* (London, 1757), 21.

54. Quoted by John Butt, *The Augustan Age* (London, 1950), 136–137; Shenstone was writing to Bishop Percy in November 1760. An example of Shenstone's

"Language of Reflexion" might be Pope's lines from *Windsor Forest,* "Here Order in Variety we See/Where all things differ, yet where all agree," which allude to the idea of *concordia discors;* presumably it was to this same theme that Gilpin wished to allude when he placed the lines on the title page of his Stowe *Dialogue* (see note 23 above). It is difficult to see them—except teleologically—as "the epigraph of the picturesque school of landscape" (Brownell, *Alexander Pope,* 100), and then it is their prescription for formal effect alone rather than the collaboration of notional and formal that was relished.

55. *Analytical Review,* 20 (1794), 259. The reviewer's initials are given as "R.R."

56. See Uvedale Price, *Essay on the Picturesque* (1794), I, 23–25, 105–107, and 155.

57. "A Journal to Italy by Doctor Cuninghame," Pierpont Morgan Library MS, MA 3159, ff. 49 and 119–120.

58. *Remarks on Rural Society; with Twenty etchings of Cottages, from Nature; and some observations and precepts relative to the picturesque* (1797), 9. What perhaps marks this later picturesque so strongly is its lack of moral emphasis: neglected cottages in the older picturesque would have signaled some message about human action or its lack (see, for instance, Pope's *Epistle to Bathurst,* lines 179–198).

59. *Essay upon Prints* (3d ed., 1781), 3. For Gilpin's dislike of Dutch painters, see his letter quoted by C. P. Barbier, *William Gilpin: His Drawings, Teaching and Theory of the Picturesque* (Oxford, 1963), 114.

60. *The Letters of Thomas Gainsborough* (Greenwich, 1963), 99. See also Price, *Essay on the Picturesque,* I, 16–17, satirizing gardens pruned of such visual "business."

61. *The Diary of Joseph Farington,* ed. K. Cave, VIII (New Haven, 1982), 3033.

62. J. H. Pott, *An Essay on Landscape Painting* (1782), 13–14; Robert Morris, *An Essay upon Harmony* (1739), 15. This associationism became, of course, a fundamental part of Richard Payne Knight's picturesque.

63. On Gilpin, see W. D. Templeman, *The Life and Works of William Gilpin* (Urbana, Ill., 1939), 228; for Wordsworth's (unexecuted) plan, see *The Letters of William and Dorothy Wordsworth, The Later Years,* ed. E. de Selincourt (Oxford, 1937–1939), I, 185.

5 SENSE AND SENSIBILITY IN THE LANDSCAPE DESIGNS OF HUMPHRY REPTON

1. Since this essay was first published in 1978, Repton studies have been boosted by the exhibition at the Sainsbury Centre for Visual Arts, the University of East Anglia (and later at the Victoria and Albert Museum, London), and its catalogue by George Carter, Patrick Goode, and Kedrun Laurie, *Humphry Repton, Landscape Gardener, 1752–1818* (1982), as well as by a series of articles notably by Stephen Daniels including "Humphry Repton at Sustead," *Garden History,* 11 (1983), 57–

64, and (with S. Seymour) "Landscape Design and the Idea of Improvement 1730–1900" in *An Historical Geography of England and Wales,* ed. R. A. Dogshon and R. A. Butlin (London, 1990), 487–520; and see also note 63 below. The standard work on Repton is Dorothy Stroud, *Humphry Repton* (London, 1962), but see also Edward Hyams, *Capability Brown and Humphry Repton* (London, 1971).

2. *Headlong Hall and Nightmare Abbey* (Everyman Library, London, 1965), 29.

3. Ibid., 34 and 58.

4. Watkin, *Thomas Hope, 1769–1831, and the Neo-classical Idea* (London, 1968), 136. Watkin still sees Repton as a creature of "picturesque eclecticism" in his later book, *The English Vision: The Picturesque in Architecture, Landscape and Garden Design* (London, 1982), 84.

5. Duckworth, *The Improvement of the Estate* (Baltimore, 1972), 47, 42. Still more recently, Charles W. Moore, William J. Mitchell, and William Turnbull, Jr., *The Poetics of Gardens* (Cambridge, Mass., 1989), 44, register Repton as a "prolific exponent of picturesque composition." The exhibition catalogue (note 1) also contains an essay on "The Picturesque Controversy" by Patrick Goode.

6. See, for instance, (though admittedly an extreme example), Stephen Daniels, "Landscaping for a Manufacturer: Humphry Repton's Commission for Benjamin Gott at Armley in 1809–10," *Journal of Historical Geography,* 7 (1981), 379–386. See also Daniel's essay on "The Political Landscape" in the exhibition catalogue (note 1).

7. *Architectural Review,* 95 (1944), 125.

8. J. C. Loudon, *The Landscape Gardening and Landscape Architecture of the Late Humphry Repton, Esq.* (London, 1840; reprinted 1969), 132.

9. Cited by Stroud, *Repton,* 27–28. See also Repton's constantly adumbrated sense of garden history and his awareness of Continental styles to rival the English (e.g., ibid., 132).

10. See especially his preface to *Fragments on the Theory and Practice of Landscape Gardening,* in Loudon, *Landscape Gardening,* 409–410.

11. Ibid., 259. For Whately, see *Observations on Modern Gardening,* 5th ed. (London, 1793), 154ff.

12. A drawing of the Stowe scene by Jacques Rigaud, upon which the 1739 engraving, published by Sarah Bridgeman, was based, is reproduced in *The Genius of the Place,* ed. Hunt and Willis, pl. 61. The Babworth scenes are illustrated in Stroud, *Repton,* 33.

13. The poem was published in 1732 and a footnote to the lines quoted explains that the reference is to "Statues of Apollo, the Nine Muses, and the Liberal Arts and Sciences placed round the Parterre."

14. Alexander Pope, *Correspondence,* ed. George Sherburn, 5 vols. (Oxford, 1956), II, 309.

15. See George Clarke, "Grecian Taste and Gothic Virtue," *Apollo,* 97 (1973), 566–571.

16. Nikolaus Pevsner, *Studies in Art, Architecture and Design,* 2 vols. (New York, 1968), I, 140.

17. Loudon, *Landscape Gardening,* 56–58.

18. Ibid., 262.

19. Ibid., p. 58 note.

20. Cited in the Repton catalogue (see note 1), 21.

21. Loudon, *Landscape Gardening,* 413–414.

22. Ibid., 441 (my italics) and 412.

23. Ibid., 119.

24. See *The Three Wartons: A Choice of Their Verse,* ed. Eric Partridge (London, 1927), 72ff. Warton's imagery for "natural" scenes seems to be derived from pictures.

25. *A Dialogue upon the Gardens . . . at Stowe* (1748; rpt. Los Angeles, 1976), 23ff.

26. *Correspondence,* ed. P. Toynbee and L. Whibley, 3 vols. (Oxford, 1935), II, 899.

27. Loudon, *Landscape Gardening,* 327.

28. E. H. Gombrich, *Art and Illusion* (Princeton, 1961), vii and passim.

29. Pevsner, *Studies,* I, 142.

30. Loudon, *Landscape Gardening,* 101, and with reference to fig. 5.4 here.

31. Ibid., 228 note.

32. Ibid., 365.

33. For a brief discussion of the French tradition of pictures of garden use, see chap. 9 below.

34. Ibid., 101.

35. Ibid., 235 note.

36. Ibid., 102–103.

37. Ibid., 111. On Foxley see Denis Lambin, "Foxley: The Prices' Estate in Herefordshire," *Journal of Garden History,* 7 (1987), 244–270.

38. Loudon, *Landscape Gardening,* 103.

39. The Red Book for Brandsbury is in the Dumbarton Oaks Garden Library.

40. Quoted in Stroud, *Repton,* 108.

41. Loudon, *Landscape Gardening,* 111.

42. Ibid., 592. Lord Sidmouth's house, "before and after," is illustrated in ibid., 481–482, and in *The Genius of the Place,* pl. 101.

43. Loudon, *Landscape Gardening,* 78.

44. Ibid., 100.

45. The Red Book records that Repton was "on the spot" in August and in October 1795 and worked out his designs at home the following February. The Red Book survives at Blaise Castle, which is now in the hands of the Bristol City Museum. Extracts are included in *The Genius of the Place,* 359–365.

46. Jane Austen, *Novels,* ed. R. W. Chapman, 6 vols. (Oxford, 1966), V, 85.

47. Loudon, *Landscape Gardening,* 96. Blaise Castle, and Repton's treatment of its "castleness," may usefully be compared to Castle Howard: see chap. 1 above.

48. See, for example, the designs for Wingerworth House (Loudon, *Landscape Gardening,* 462). Pevsner (*Studies,* 1, 152) reminds us that among Repton's contemporaries was a flourishing school of British watercolorists, with whom he has some obvious affinities.

49. Loudon, *Landscape Gardening,* 105n and 81.

50. For instance, ibid., 413–414.

51. Austen, *Novels,* III, 57. Austen's rejection of Repton (perhaps through ignorance of his work) is puzzling, especially since, as I attempted to argue in the film, *Mansfield Park: Improvement,* made by the BBC for the Open University nineteenth-century novel course, Reptonian ideas and values seem to lie at the center of the novel and provide it with a sustaining metaphor. Mavis Batey connects *Mansfield Park* and Repton's work that Jane Austen might have known at Adlestrop and Stoneleigh in "Jane Austen and Stoneleigh," *Country Life* (30 December 1976), 1974–1975.

52. Samuel Kliger, "Jane Austen's *Pride and Prejudice* in the Eighteenth-Century Mode," *University of Toronto Quarterly,* 16 (1947), 365.

53. Austen, *Novels,* II, 154.

54. Ibid., II, 245.

55. Ibid., II, 246.

56. Ibid., IV, 358. For Repton on avenues, see Loudon, *Landscape Gardening,* 62ff. and 504.

57. Ibid., 572. See also: "I wish to make my appeal less to the eye than to the understanding" (p. 120).

58. Ibid., 410.

59. Austen, *Novels,* I, 56.

60. Ibid. (*Northanger Abbey*), V, 197.

61. Ibid., V, 111. The similar observation by Price is cited by Duckworth, *Improvement of the Estate,* 96n.

62. See Loudon, *Landscape Gardening,* 342, and Stroud, *Repton,* 136ff.

63. *Novels* (*Persuasion*), V, 40. On the relation of landscape taste to moral and social status, especially as it is to be tracked in Repton's works, see Stephen Daniels, "Humphry Repton and the Morality of Landscape," *Valued Environments,* ed. John R. Gold and Jacquelin Burgess (London, 1982), 124–144.

64. Loudon, *Landscape Gardening,* 124.

65. Ibid., 36–37.

66. Ibid., 47.

67. Ibid., 509.

68. Yet he can retain such a fence at Barningham Hall and accompanies the recommendation with intricate calculations to determine at what distance from a terrace and of what height the fence should be (ibid., 416).

69. Ibid., 541.

70. Ibid., 52.

71. Ibid., 540.

72. Ibid., 421.

6 PICTURESQUE MIRRORS AND THE RUINS OF THE PAST

1. The phrase is Tennyson's, "Locksley Hall," line 182.

2. In *Proceedings of the American Philosophical Society,* 107 (1963), 273–288.

3. For Bridgeman, see Peter Willis, *Charles Bridgeman and the English Landscape Garden* (London, 1978); on Brown see Dorothy Stroud, *Capability Brown* (3d ed.,

London, 1975), Robert Williams, "Making Places: Garden-mastery and English Brown," *Journal of Garden History,* 3 (1983), 382–385, and my own *The Figure in the Landscape,* 218ff.

4. These matters were taken up and developed in my *Garden and Grove* and later, in more detail, in *William Kent.*

5. See Quentin Skinner, "Meaning and Understanding in the History of Ideas," *History and Theory,* 8 (1969), 24. Skinner's whole argument is also of general relevance to the problems of historical analysis which I treat here.

6. Martin Price, "The Picturesque Moment," in *From Sensibility to Romanticism,* ed. F. W. Hilles and Harold Bloom (New York, 1965), 286.

7. Respectively, H. M. McLuhan, "Tennyson and Picturesque Poetry" (originally published in *Essays in Criticism* of 1956), in *Critical Essays on the Poetry of Tennyson,* ed. John Kilham (London, 1960), 74, and Price, "The Picturesque Moment," 270–275.

8. See Northrope Frye, "Towards Defining an Age of Sensibility," *ELH,* 23 (1956), 144–152.

9. *The Picturesque: Studies in a Point of View* (London, 1927), 4.

10. See Malcolm Andrews's study of picturesque tourism, *The Search for the Picturesque* (Aldershot, Hants., 1989).

11. This is the topic of chap. 4 above.

12. This conventional but nonetheless interesting remark is cited by W. D. Templeman, *The Life and Works of William Gilpin* (Urbana, Ill., 1939), 228.

13. Marcel Röthlisberger, *Claude Lorrain: the Paintings,* 2 vols. (New Haven, 1961), I, 41.

14. Thomas Gray, *Works,* ed. Edmund Gosse (London, 1884), I, 250 and 260.

15. Thomas Gray, *The Works, with Memoirs by William Mason* (London, 1827), 287n.

16. See illustrations and further details of all these optical items in the short article by Deborah Jean Warner, "The Landscape Mirror and Glass," *Antiques,* 105 (1974), 158–159. However, Peter Bicknell, *The Picturesque Scenery of the Lake District* (Winchester and Detroit, 1990), 194, argues that a "claude glass" was a set of transparent tinted filters, and the mirror used by the artist in the Gainsborough drawing reproduced here was referred to as "Gray's glass" after the poet who made its use famous.

17. Gray, *Works,* ed. Gosse, 281.

18. See, for example, Dora Panofsky, "Narcissus and Echo," *Art Bulletin,* 31 (1949), 112–120.

19. *The Seasons,* ed. James Sambrook (Oxford, 1972), "Summer," lines 1247–48.

20. *The Genius of the Place,* ed. Hunt and Willis, 273.

21. Quoted by W. W. Manwaring, *Italian Landscape in Eighteenth-Century England* (New York, 1925), 186.

22. Price, "The Picturesque Moment," 271.

23. The traditional emphases upon idealized landscape may be represented by Reynolds in his *Discourses;* for the rival concern with specificity see a most interesting article by Barbara M. Stafford, "Toward Romantic Landscape Perception: Illustrated Travels and the Rise of Singularity as an Aesthetic Category," *Art Quarterly,* new series I (1977), 89ff.

24. J. Aikin, *Letters from a Father to a Son,* 2d ed. (London, 1794), 266.

25. *The Genius of the Place,* 119–121; but also see above, chap. 1, for another explanation of Vanbrugh's suggestion.

26. William Gilpin, *A Dialogue Upon the Gardens . . . at Stow* (1748), Augustan Reprint Society, 176 (1976), 5.

27. Aikin, *Letters from a Father,* 266 and 269. For more recent reflections on the mind's response to ruins see Georg Simmel, "Die Ruine," in *Philosophische Kultur* (Potsdam, 1923), 135–143, and Robert Ginsberg, "The Aesthetics of Ruins," *Bucknell Review,* 18 (1970), 89–102.

28. Gilpin, *Dialogue,* 19–21; see above in chap. 3 for Stowe; for Turner and Byron, see my "Wondrous Dark and Deep: Turner and the Sublime," *The Georgia Review,* 30 (1976), 139–164.

29. *The Genius of the Place,* 210.

30. Ibid., 180.

31. "A New Pope Letter," *Philological Quarterly,* 45 (1966), 409–418.

32. *The Genius of the Place,* 210.

33. Ibid., 291–292.

34. Compare *The Genius of the Place,* 284 (the 1757 work) and 321 (that of 1772). Chambers published his Kew designs in 1763.

35. This is discussed in more detail in chap. 3.

36. Marvell's "Upon Appleton House," stanzas xi ff.; Walpole, in *The Genius of the Place,* 313. For commentary upon Marvell's detailed reading of the Nun Appleton ruins and its provenance in Italianate gardens, see my *Andrew Marvell, His Life and Writings* (London, 1978), 96ff.

37. See Roland Mortier, *La Poétique des ruines en France* (Geneva, 1974), especially chap. 7.

38. Aubrey wrote that "as Pythagoras did guess at the vastness of Hercules' statue by the length of his foot, so amongst these ruins are remains enough left for a man to guess what noble buildings were made by the piety, charity and magnanimity of our forefathers . . . [ruins] breed in general minds a kind of pity and set the thoughts a-work to make out their magnificence as they were when in perfection," quoted by Ian Dunlop, *Palaces and Progresses of Elizabeth I* (London, 1962), 197. See also Margaret Aston, "English Ruins and English History," *Journal of the Warburg and Courtauld Institutes,* 36 (1973), 231–255.

39. H. V. S. and M. S. Ogden, *English Taste in Landscape in the Seventeenth Century* (Ann Arbor, Mich., 1955), especially 43–44, 138–139, and 160–161.

40. See Hunt, *The Figure in the Landscape,* pl. 42 and p. 82.

41. Yorke's account of Fountains Abbey is in *The Genius of the Place,* 237–239; the poem, also quoted there, is taken from Thomas Gent, *The . . . History . . . of Rippon* (1733); Gilpin's visit is recorded in his *Northern Tour* (1786), II, 180–181.

42. Joseph Spence, *Polymetis* (1747), 290.

43. William Gilpin, *Three Essays* (London, 1792), 7 and 28.

44. See Hunt, *The Figure in the Landscape,* 36–48.

45. *Anti-Jacobin Review,* 5 (January 1800), 28–37.

46. See Kenneth Woodbridge, *Landscape and Antiquity: Aspects of English Culture at Stourhead 1718 to 1838* (Oxford, 1970), 33ff.

47. Vanbrugh's remark is discussed above in chap. 1. For Addison, see *Spectator,* no. 414; Robert Castell, *The Villas of the Ancients Illustrated* (London, 1728), even invoked the authority of the younger Pliny whom he translates as saying that round his Tuscan villa "it would not appear as real Land, but as an exquisite Painting: there is that Variety of Landskip wheresoever you cast your Eye" (p. 58 [i.e., 82])—*landskip* being a Dutch word signifying a painted landscape.

48. Walpole, *Correspondence,* XXXV, 149.

49. See above in chap. 5.

50. See Gillian Cohen, "Visual Imagery in Thought," *New Literary History,* 7 (1976), 513–523.

51. *The Genius of the Place,* 348.

52. Gray, *Works,* ed. Gosse, 254. For an excellent discussion of the Lake District as a tourist site see Malcolm Andrews, *The Search for the Picturesque* (Aldershot, Hants., 1989), chap. 7.

53. An early picturesque paradigm perhaps is recorded by St. Jerome: when returning one night from visiting the catacombs, he was overcome with the sight and with their early Christian associations and strove to capture the experience by quoting an apt passage from the *Aeneid*: see *Hieronymi . . . Operum* (Paris, 1704), III, cols. 979–980.

54. Quoted in *Elizabeth Montagu, Queen of the Blue-Stockings,* ed. E. J. Climenson, 2 vols. (London, 1906), I, 53–54. The same phrase of Pope's ("a browner horror on the woods") is quite deliberately—because italicized—invoked at Roche Abbey by Arthur Young in his *Eastern Tour* (1771). Perhaps the idea appealed because of its similarity to the tonal coloring cast by a Claude glass over a scene.

55. See Donald D. Eddy, "John Brown: 'The Columbus of Keswick,' " *Modern Philology,* 73 (1976), 80. Eddy reconstructs Brown's famous letter in this article.

56. For Lodore Falls, see Manwaring, *Italian Landscape,* 192–193. Mrs. Carter's remarks are quoted by Manwaring on p. 174.

57. Quoted in ibid., 177.

58. Quoted in ibid., 195. The remark was made in 1792.

59. See Eddy, "John Brown," 80.

60. Walpole, *Correspondence,* XIII, 181.

61. Quoted by Manwaring, *Italian Landscape,* 174.

62. Jane Austen, *Novels,* ed. R.W. Chapman, 6 vols. (Oxford, 1966), II, 154, and V, 111.

63. Louis Marin, interview in *Diacritics* (Summer 1977), 48.

64. For further discussion of some of these matters see the following two essays. See also Stephen J. Spector, "Wordsworth's Mirror Imagery and the Picturesque Tradition," *ELH,* 44 (1977), 85–107, as well as many more discussions cited by Spector.

7 JOHN RUSKIN AND THE PICTURESQUE

1. All quotations are taken from *The Works of John Ruskin* (Library Edition), ed. E. T. Cook and A. Wedderburn, 39 vols. (London, 1903–1912), with references to volume and page number—here, VII, 9. Ruskin's major works are available in many other editions, readily available in second-hand book stores, but it is by convention as well as for scholarly convenience that references are given to the Library Edition of his many writings.

2. Letter to *The Daily Telegraph,* 8 October 1878. Ruskin is not the most consistent or systematic of writers—as he himself said: "I do not intend, however, now to pursue the inquiry in a method so laboriously systematic . . ." (V, 18). That remark

seems to me more representative of Ruskin's actual practice than the attempt to shape him into a systematic thinker made by G. P. Landow, *The Aesthetic and Critical Theories of John Ruskin* (Princeton, 1971). However, Landow's book and Robert Hewison's *John Ruskin, the Argument of the Eye* (London, 1977) are two works that address themselves to the subject of Ruskin and the picturesque.

3. William Gilpin, *Three Essays* (London, 1792), 41. On Gilpin generally, see Carl Paul Barbier, *William Gilpin, His Drawings, Teaching and Theory of the Picturesque* (Oxford, 1963).

4. On this topic see Helen Gill Viljoen, *Ruskin's Scottish Heritage* (Urbana, Ill., 1956), 107 and 227 note 23.

5. *The Ruskin Family Letters,* ed. Van Akin Burd, 2 vols, (Ithaca, N.Y., 1973), 117–118. The father's letters are full of his picturesque discoveries: "You must see Bury St Edmond fine picturesque Bridge & Churches . . ." (p. 557).

6. See the discussion of Turnerian landscape painting in chap. 8.

7. This was one of the subjects in his "first sketchbook," according to *Praeterita* (XXXV, 77); the drawing, at Vassar College Art Gallery, dates from 1835, his sixteenth year. Another early drawing of what his editors at least call a "ruin" near Ambleside is reproduced by them in II, facing p. 201.

8. *The Diaries,* ed. Joan Evans and J. H. Whitehouse (Oxford, 1956), I, 32. And for a similar section of the valley of Chamounix, see *Diaries,* I, 14–16.

9. The American insight is echoed by Cadwallader D. Colden, a New York canal builder: "Did we live amidst ruins and . . . scenes indicating present decay . . . we might be as little inclined as others, to look forward"; quoted by David Lowenthal, "The Place of the Past in the American Landscape," *Geographies of the Mind,* ed. David Lowenthal and Martyn J. Bowden (Oxford, 1975), 93.

10. See also the "inventions of such incidents and thoughts as can be expressed in words as well as on canvas" (III, 112).

11. Cf. "[On the Proper Shapes of Pictures and Engravings]" in Ruskin, *Works,* I, 235–245, with Loudon, *The Landscape Gardening and Landscape Architecture of the late Humphry Repton. . .* (London, 1840), 32n.–38n.

12. Loudon, *Landscape Gardening,* 592.

13. An interesting discussion of the languages of scenery—whether endemic or derived from some exercise of what Ruskin would come to distrust as the "pathetic fallacy"—and an enquiry into the significance of *The Poetry of Architecture* in Ruskin's career which complements my considerations here is Harold L. Shapiro, "*The Poetry of Architecture*: Ruskin's Preparation for *Modern Painters,*" *Renaissance and Modern Studies,* 15 (1971), 70–84.

14. *Diaries,* I, 63.

15. Gilpin, *Three Essays,* 20.

16. See his early verses on Skiddaw and Derwent Water (II, 265–266), where the "ruins" of the first, a mountain, are also celebrated. For other uses of the picturesque cliché of the mirror of lake waters see *Iteriad,* ed. J. S. Dearden (Newcastle upon Tyne, 1969), 33–34.

17. See also John James Ruskin in February 1840, perhaps taught to look at reflections carefully by his son's essays on *The Poetry of Architecture,* "In winter if quite still the absence of strong light gives such a complete mirror like steel with every object so clearly reflected that it is a wonder altogether" (*Ruskin Family Letters,* 674). E. T. Cook's *Life of Ruskin* (London, 1911), I, 143, notes that Ruskin's various accounts of reflection were invoked approvingly in Sir Montagu Pollock's *Light and Water* (1903).

18. *Collected Poems of Shelley,* ed. Neville Rogers (Boston, 1968), 485.

19. On Ruskin's use of typological strategies see the discussion by G. P. Landow in *The Aesthetic and Critical Theories* and his most recent account of the same topic in the very useful volume *Literary Uses of Typology,* ed. Earl Miner (Princeton, 1977).

8 RUSKIN, "TURNERIAN TOPOGRAPHY," AND *GENIUS LOCI*

1. John Russell, *Turner in Switzerland,* with survey and notes by Andrew Wilton (Zurich, 1976), 122.

2. David Hill, *Turner in Yorkshire* (York, 1980), 93.

3. In Russell and Wilton, *Turner in Switzerland,* 20. See also Henri Zerner, "About Landscape," in *The Rudolf L. Baumfeld Collection of Landscape Drawings and Prints* (Los Angeles, 1989), 29–32.

4. All Ruskin references will be given in the text to the standard edition, *The Works of John Ruskin* (Library Edition), ed. E. T. Cook and A. Wedderburn, 39 vols. (London, 1903–1912), though *Modern Painters* is readily available in many other editions.

5. *Ruskin in Italy,* ed. Harold I. Shapiro (Oxford, 1972), 172–176.

6. In *Portrait of an Artist as a Young Man* Joyce's hero, Stephen Daedalus, invokes Thomas Aquinas in his formulation of an aesthetic that must address the thingness of things (*quidditas*); while Duns Scotus's interest in this-ness (*haecceitas*) sustains many of Hopkins's perceptions of identity and meaning in things and persons.

7. Russell and Wilton, *Turner in Switzerland,* 110.

8. See Geoffrey H. Hartman, "Romantic Poetry and the Genius Loci," in *Beyond Formalism: Literary Essays 1958–1970* (New Haven, 1970), and C. S. Lewis, "Genius and Genius," *Studies on Mediaeval and Renaissance Literature,* ed. Walter Hooper (Cambridge, 1966).

9. See Martin Butlin and Evelyn Joll, *The Paintings of J. M. W. Turner,* rev. ed., (New Haven, 1984), 55 and pl. 81.

10. Blake, *The Marriage of Heaven and Hell,* pl. 11.

11. Coleridge, *Collected Letters,* ed. E. L. Griggs, 6 vols. (London, 1956–1971), II, 865–866.

12. Ironically, after his "unconversion" in 1858 Ruskin began to manipulate, albeit rather idiosyncratically, the language and symbols of *genius loci* which he had earlier considered moribund. We may see the beginnings of his recovery of a mythological syntax of place in the magnificently inventive deconstruction, at the very end of *Modern Painters,* of Turner's *Apollo and Python* and *The Goddess of Discord Choosing the Apple of Contention in the Garden of the Hesperides.* The serpents on their rocks, the maidens guarding the golden apples, are all read as revealing Turner's sense of the meaning of the places depicted. And later, in books such as *The Queen of the Air* and *Deucalion,* Ruskin pursues a brilliant interrogation of spirit of place via its classical languages.

13. See the important essay on "Wordsworth, Inscriptions and Romantic Nature Poetry" in Hartman's *Beyond Formalism;* a quotation from this essay follows in the paragraph.

14. Turner uses inscriptions for instance on the canvases of *Apullia in Search of Apullus vide Ovid* (1814), where a name is inscribed on a tree, and *The Bay of Baiae* (1823), in which some verses of Horace are carved on a rock.

15. This creative encounter of subject and object becomes a key issue in romanticism: one famous narrative of such an event is Coleridge's "The Rime of the Ancient Mariner," and Coleridge also tackles it theoretically in his discussion of the imagination in *Biographia Literaria,* chap. 13.

16. A recent discussion of these two paintings is concerned primarily with Turner's debts to literature and little with questions of *genius loci* and landscape architecture: Andrew Wilton, *Painting and Poetry: Turner's "Verse Book" and His Work of 1804–1811* (London, 1990), 47–60 and catalogue nos. 35, 44, and 56.

17. See Morris Brownell, *Alexander Pope's Villa: Views of Pope's Villa,* catalogue of exhibition at Marble Hill House (London, 1980). On the "genius" of Pope's villa and its Thames site see Maynard Mack, *The Garden and the City: Retirement and Politics in the Later Poetry of Pope 1731–1743* (Toronto, 1969), 11ff., but especially 23–24.

18. *The Sunset Ship: The Poems of J. M. W. Turner,* ed. Jack Lindsay (London, 1966), 117.

19. Thomas Love Peacock, *The Genius of the Thames: A Lyrical Poem in Two Parts* (London, 1810), has some notes by the author (pp. 115–125) which offer a most useful contemporary commentary upon *genius loci.*

20. The point is made by Julius Bryant, *Finest Prospects: Three Historic Houses: A Study in London Topography* (London, 1986), 87.

21. James Thomson, *The Seasons and The Castle of Indolence,* ed. James Sambrook (Oxford, 1987), 76.

22. On Turner and aeolian harps see Wilton, *Painting and Poetry,* 69ff.

23. See above, chap. 3.

24. John Gage, *Colour in Turner: Poetry and Truth* (London, 1969), 143ff.

25. I am aware that this modifies the more categorical position of my earlier essay (chap. 3 above). I am indebted to Stephen Bending for suggestions on how expressive landscape features were still needed to invoke the preciser syntax of the older emblematic traditions. But it should be noted in connection with Turner that Hugh Blair's *Lectures on Rhetoric and Belles-Lettres* (London, 1783), which Turner consulted while preparing his Royal Academy lectures, warned against "supernatural machinery" and "incredible fictions" (II, 424–425).

26. Whately, *Observations on Modern Gardening* (London, 1770), 150; also see 119–120.

27. Turner's responses to patrons' estates are surely parallel to some of the considerations which led Humphry Repton to propose highlighting certain features in many of his commissions: see Stephen Daniels, "Humphry Repton at Sustead," *Garden History,* 11 (1983), 57–64; Stephen Daniels and S. Seymour, "Landscape Design and the Idea of Improvement 1730–1900," in *An Historical Geography of England and Wales,* ed. R. A. Dogshon and R. A. Butlin (London, 1990), 487–520; Stephen Daniels, "Landscaping for a Manufacturer: Humphry Repton's Commission for Benjamin Gott at Armley in 1809–10," *Journal of Historical Geography,* 7 (1981), 379–386; and Daniels's forthcoming essay "Landscaping and Estate Management in Later Georgian England," *Garden History: Issues, Approaches, Methods,* ed. John Dixon Hunt (Washington, D.C., 1991).

28. See Hill, *Turner in Yorkshire,* pp. 35–52.

29. See *The Figure in the Landscape: Poetry, Painting and Gardening during the Eighteenth Century* (Baltimore, 1976), chap. 5.

30. See above, chaps. 3 and 4.

31. Wordsworth, "Lines composed a few miles above Tintern Abbey" (1798), lines 106–107.

32. See above, note 15.

33. Thomas Warton, *The Poetical Works* (Oxford, 1802), 99–103.

34. For example, two views of St. Agatha's Abbey, Yorkshire, painted at different times and with very different intentions and effects; they are reproduced in Hill, *Turner in Yorkshire,* nos. 129 and 130.

9 FRENCH IMPRESSIONIST GARDENS AND THE ECOLOGICAL PICTURESQUE

1. The most useful attention to garden subject matter is contained in the exhibition catalogue *A Day in the Country: Impressionism and the French Landscape* (New York: Los Angeles County Museum of Art, Chicago Art Institute, and Réunion des Musées Nationaux, 1984) which devotes one section (part III, section 6) to "Private and Public Gardens." Also, Robert L. Herbert, *Impressionism: Art, Leisure and Parisian Society* (New Haven, 1988) has a section devoted to gardens, pp. 254–263. For another discussion of garden motifs to which I am indebted but which I find inattentive to specifically gardenist perspectives, see Paul Hayes Tucker, *Monet at Argenteuil* (New Haven, 1982). However, a major work like John House's *Monet: Nature into Art* (New Haven, 1986), while it does not omit to refer to gardens among the painter's subjects, never sees them as having any special significance.

2. It is a huge subject, and begins to burst its seams here; but I intend to develop this essay into a full-length book study, with some comparative glances at the social-gardenist worlds of American impressionism. At that stage greater attention will be given to the many garden paintings of Gustave Caillebotte, on whom see two recent books cited in note 26 below. Meanwhile, I take much for granted in the art historical scholarship of French impressionism, upon which I have depended considerably in order to make my own points relevant to garden history.

3. "Mon Salon: IV. Les Actualistes," *L'Évenèment Illustré* (24 May 1868).

4. T. J. Clark, *The Painting of Modern Life: Paris in the Art of Manet and His Followers* (Princeton, 1984) has been of great stimulation to me in this work, even if in the end I want to quarrel with the small role Clark gives to gardens in impressionism.

5. See S. Giedion, *Space, Time and Architecture,* 4th ed. enlarged (Cambridge, Mass., 1963), 648–664. On gardens and green space in Paris see Denise Le Dantec and Jean-Pierre Le Dantec, *Splendeurs des Jardins de Paris* (Paris, 1991), a typescript of which the authors let me read during the final stages of my revisions of this essay.

6. See William Robinson, *The Parks, Promenades, and Gardens of Paris* (London, 1869), 551, quoting Edouard André, on how "the chief gardeners and the city architects were often called upon to extemporize shady avenues in a few days."

7. Ibid., 657–659.

8. Ibid., 82 and 85.

9. Ibid., xxi–xxii.

10. The Goncourts noted how public life had taken over the private (cited in *The Painting of Modern Life,* Clark, 34); so too with gardens in the city.

11. In *The English Flower Garden* (1883) his plan of a "nongeometrical town garden" actually utilized ideas he had discussed in the Parc Monceau chapter in *Parks.* On Robinson's contradictions see David Ottewill, *The Edwardian Garden* (New Haven, 1989), 53 and 67.

12. Victor Fournel, *Paris Nouveau et Paris Futur* (Paris, 1865), 124 and (for following quotation) 125, in his sixth chapter, attacking developments in "Les parcs et jardins." By contrast, see Robinson's enthusiasm for the Parc Monceau, *Parks,* 48–58.

13. "L'administration actuelle aime beaucoup les grilles neuves: peut-être en abuse-t-elle un peu" (Fournel, *Paris Nouveau,* 103).

14. Clark (*The Painting of Modern Life,* 27–28) tellingly quotes a passage from Zola's *L'Assommoir,* chapter 8, where Gervaise and Goujet climb toward Montmartre: they exclaim, "you'd believe you were in the countryside." Herbert (*Impressionism,* 188) narrates Renoir's delight in discovering an abandoned garden outside a studio he rented in Montmartre (see fig. 9.1).

15. *Le Bal Public,* sold at Christie's, New York, 1990.

16. See for instance Vincent van Gogh's *The Guinguette at Montmartre* (1886) in the Musée d'Orsay, Paris.

17. The point is made in François Loyer, *Paris Nineteenth Century: Architecture and Urbanism* (New York, 1988), 314.

18. Clark discusses and cites this considerable literature extensively, and I am indebted to his work for this aspect of my argument.

19. Quoted in Tucker, *Monet at Argenteuil,* 126: the date was 1845.

20. See Clark, *Painting of Modern Life,* 9 and 33, the latter extrapolating from Victor Hugo's lament for the old Paris.

21. Clark, *Painting of Modern Life,* 194–195 and, for the painting not reproduced here (Museum of Fine Arts, Boston), his color pl. XX. On Argenteuil as a town caught between picturesque beauty and new commercial exploitation, see Tucker, *Monet at Argenteuil,* 15–20 and passim.

22. Just as Clark finds writers were "in a cleft stick about the countryside" (*Painting of Modern Life,* 148), so in his turn he seems to be with the garden, perhaps because his argument cannot allow any haven from the uneasy worlds of city and suburb which he probes so convincingly.

23. This is another essay in itself, for some elements of which see the following essay here.

24. Clark, *Painting of Modern Life,* 157. Cf. "And landscape, for Monet as for many other painters . . . was the one genre left" (ibid., 182)—but did the genre of landscape not come to include gardens?

25. "The suburbs and the near countryside were also gardens in the quieter sense of the term" (Herbert, *Impressionism,* 255), whatever that means.

26. Cited by Clark, *Painting of Modern Life,* 191–192 and fig. 89, perhaps forgetting that Caillebotte lived and painted his garden at Petit Gennevilliers: see Kirk Varnedoe, *Gustave Caillebotte* (New Haven, 1987) and Pierre Wittmer, *Caillebotte en Jardin* (Saint-Just-en-Chausée, 1990, with an American edition announced from Abrams in 1991).

27. Robert Caze, quoted in *Painting of Modern Life,* 149–150, where the next remark by Blanche is also quoted. Pissarro, who rather despised the garden subjects of his fellow impressionists (see Herbert, *Impressionism,* 260), actually represents one of these globes of silvered glass (fig. 9.8).

28. Quoted in Tucker, *Monet at Argenteuil,* 38 and 39.

29. See Fréderic Bazille's painting of the terrace at Méric (Cincinnati Art Museum, and *A Day in the Country,* no. 79) and Manet's *The Bench,* painted in a rented garden at Versailles during the summer of 1881 (Herbert, *Impressionism,* pl. 260).

30. Quoted in Tucker, *Monet at Argenteuil,* 125, first from Jules Janin, *La Normandie* (1862) and then from Eugène Chapus, "La vie à Paris: le charactère de la société parisienne actuelle; les maisons de la campagne," *Le Sport* (5 September 1860).

31. Tucker, *Monet at Argenteuil,* 41, notes that one hundred meters to the right of this painting was a tannery, so that these gardens are given no protection from that industrial view.

32. The appearance of modern park benches in private gardens has been noted (above, note 29); Herbert remarks how Caillebotte's metal chairs, boxed trees, and paths "would suit a corner of a Parisian park" of the new mode (*Impressionism,* 258).

33. I invoke Ezra Pound's clarion call to modernist poets: "Make it New."

34. I am thinking of specific literary examples: novels are full of them; but Andrew Marvell's poem "The Garden" is a sharp exploration of what it means to think a garden is wholly natural until abruptly brought up against its inherent artifice.

35. Not, as in some British conversation paintings, the mercantile classes aping the status and behavior of country gentry, but bourgeois happy being bourgeois.

36. Clark's figures 117 and 118 suggest the kind of public leisure against which that of the impressionist garden defined itself. Clark invokes Veblen's *The Theory of the Leisure Class* on how the new social classes "consume" or "perform" the leisure suddenly available to them (*Painting of Modern Life,* 204).

37. Hence, I suppose modern commentators' rather odd invocation of the biblical "hortus conclusus": see House, *Monet,* 18; Tucker, *Monet at Argenteuil,* 134; and Clark, *Painting of Modern Life,* 194–195.

38. Quoted in Clark, ibid., 178.

39. And in the Exposition Universelle this display of power in landscape architecture was extended, in modern fashion, to the industrial and commercial sector.

40. Thus House (*Monet,* 18), though without specific reference to garden subjects: "The paintings themselves were intended to be seen in Paris, and thus to contribute to metropolitan debates about city, suburb and country, and about modernity in landscape painting."

41. For example, Tucker, *Monet at Argenteuil,* 135ff., and Clark *Painting of Modern Life,* 207.

42. On conversation pictures see especially Mario Praz, *Conversation Pieces* (University Park, Penn., 1971). The *Oxford English Dictionary* defines "conversation" as "the action of consorting or having dealings with others; living together. . . ."

43. See Charles F. Stuckey, *Berthe Morisot, Impressionist* (New York, 1987), 45.

44. We even know that some of Morisot's subjects would not pose for her in a garden: see Stuckey, ibid., 31.

45. Walter Annenberg Collection, reproduced in Herbert, *Impressionism,* fig. 182; see also the similar situation painted by Manet inside a greenhouse, ibid., fig. 183 or *A Day in the Country,* fig. 52.

46. There is a classical bust in the Melun riverside garden painted by Stanislaus-Henri Rouart (Louvre), but this is a rare appearance of statuary in private gardens.

47. D. Wildenstein, *Claude Monet; Biographie et catalogue raisonné,* 4 vols. (Lausanne and Paris, 1974–1985), I, letter 203.

48. This point is also made in passing by Herbert about Renoir (*Impressionism,* 254).

49. See also Stephen Gwynn, *Claude Monet and His Garden* (New York, 1934), especially 58, and Claire Joyes, *Claude Monet: Life at Giverny* (New York and Paris, 1985), 24.

50. See Eugène Deny, *Jardins et Parcs Publics* (Paris, 1893), 88–99, for the responsibilities of Alphand and Barillet-Deschamps for this landscape style. But its genealogy and credit were a source of some typical French argumentation: see Denise Le Dantec and Jean-Pierre Le Dantec, *Reading the French Garden* (Cambridge, Mass., 1990), 189–211. Stuckey fails to take into account how the changes made to the Bois under Haussmann might be viewed (see *Berthe Morisot Impressionist,* 16).

51. Except, it should be noted, that the Baron considered Louis XIV's great landscape designer André Le Nôtre "undemocratic": *Memoires du Baron Haussmann,* 2 vols. (Paris, 1890ff.), I, 183.

52. Fournel, *Paris Nouveau,* 115. Paul Valéry tells us that Mallarmé thought the Bois de Boulogne "a meager affair": see his essay on Berthe Morisot, in *Degas, Manet, Morisot,* trans. David Paul (Princeton, 1960), 117.

53. Fournel, *Paris Nouveau,* 111–112.

54. César Daly writing (with approval) in 1862; quoted in Clark, *Painting of Modern Life,* 43.

55. See the survey of journalism, popular literature, and horticultural publications, including plant catalogues, in *A Day in the Country,* especially pp. 207–209. Monet built greenhouses at Giverny in 1892.

56. See Mac Griswold, *Pleasures of the Garden* (New York, 1987), 115, and the previous note.

57. A painting by Manet of "Monet working in his garden" is in the Metropolitan Museum. Compare the National Trust in England, in whose many glossy publications there is never any hint of the gardeners who necessarily maintain these "natural" arcadias!

58. I owe this useful point to Herbert, *Impressionism,* 303.

59. Work had featured prominently in eighteenth-century English garden paintings: see the images of Hartwell House, for example, reproduced in John Harris, *The Artist and the Country House* (London, 1979), 188–189. Caillebotte's paintings are more attentive to the role of the gardener: see my "Caillebotte and the gardens of French Impressionism," *Apollo,* 124, 354 n.s. (August 1991), 138–139.

60. Compare in this respect the so-called cottage garden.

61. H. Ciolkowski, quoted by Rewald in his introduction to Stephen Shore, *The Gardens of Giverny: A View of Monet's World* (New York, 1983), 70 (emphasis added); Lamartine is quoted in ibid., 13.

62. This commonplace was announced in antiquity by Aristotle, Longinus, and Quintilian, and rehearsed in terms of horticulture in Shakespeare's *The Winter's Tale,* Act IV.

63. Robinson, *Parks,* 93. However, Robinson did later hedge his bets on carpet bedding with a chapter on "Summer Bedding" in *The English Flower Garden,* first published in 1883.

64. This "school" also came to include—as an extreme manifestation—Ian L. McHaig, though his focus was little upon gardens: for which see his "Nature Is More Than a Garden," in *The Meaning of Gardens,* ed. Mark Francis and Randolph T. Hester, Jr. (Cambridge, Mass., 1990), 34–37.

65. Rewald, in Shore, *Gardens of Giverny,* 9.

66. Clark, *Painting of Modern Life,* 21.

67. For example, the painting by Monet of his first rented house at Argenteuil (2 rue Pierre Guienne), recently given to the National Gallery of Art, Washington, D.C., is largely a construction, at the very least a creative manipulation of the

actual site: see Charles S. Moffett's entry on the painting in *Art for the National: Gifts in Honor of the 50th Anniversary of the National Gallery of Art* (Washington, D.C., 1991), 166.

68. Meyer Schapiro, *Modern Art* (New York, 1978), 192.

69. See the "Preface" and "Foreword to the New Edition" in *The Wild Garden,* 4th ed. (London, 1894), xxii ff.

70. See for example Michel Serres's recent *Le contrat naturel* (Paris, 1990), and, for some commentary on it, Augustin Berque, *Médiance de milieux en paysages* (Montpellier, 1990), 63 and 72.

71. Joris Karl Huysmans, *Against the Grain* [*A Rebours*], chap. 8 (New York, 1931), 187.

10 THE PICTURESQUE LEGACY TO MODERNIST LANDSCAPE ARCHITECTURE

1. Yve-Alain Bois, "A Picturesque Stroll around Clara-Clara," *October,* 29 (1984), 61.

2. Steven R. Krog, "The Language of Modern," *Landscape Architecture,* 75, no. 2 (1985), 56.

3. Elizabeth B. Kassler, *Modern Gardens and the Landscape* (New York, 1964). For instance, her biased and overgeneralized notion of Renaissance and Baroque aesthetics—"man's triumph over nature" (p. 5)—or her characterization of the nature/art dialectic in the English landscape garden (pp. 9ff.). That this latter is still a subject which contemporary landscape architects seem unwilling to register as complex and philosophically demanding may be seen from the historical aspects of Diana Balmori, "Architecture, Landscape, and the Intermediate Structure: Eighteenth-Century Experiments in Mediation," *Journal of the Society of Architectural Historians,* 50 (1991), 38–56.

4. James C. Rose, "Freedom in the Garden: A Contemporary Approach in Landscape Design," *Pencil Points* (October 1938), 643. Even the far more cogent essays of Eckbo, Kiley, and Rose in the *Architectural Record* of 1939 and 1940 are flawed by their showing little depth of history—what is "new" to them is often "déjà vu" to a longer historical perspective. A selection of these writings which I examine here is to be reprinted in the volume of the Berkeley conference to which a version of this essay was first read: *Modern Landscape Architecture: A Critical Review,* edited by Marc Treib (forthcoming from the MIT Press).

5. John Barrell, *The Political Theory of Painting from Reynolds to Hazlitt* (New Haven, 1986).

6. See, for excellent accounts of this, Ernest Tuveson, *The Imagination as a Means of Grace: Locke and the Aesthetics of Romanticism* (Berkeley and Los Angeles, 1960), and Christopher Fox, *Locke and the Scriblerians: Identity and Consciousness in Early Eighteenth-Century Britain* (Berkeley and Los Angeles, 1988).

7. This has been discussed above in chaps 1, 3, and 4.

8. The availability of different models was a staple argument among the picturesque theorists: see the selection from Richard Payne Knight's poem *The Landscape* reproduced in Hunt and Willis, *The Genius of the Place,* 342–344.

9. Shaftesbury's use of these descending orders of control in a garden is discussed by David Leatherbarrow, "Character, Geometry and Perspective: The Third Earl of Shaftesbury's Principles of Garden Design," *Journal of Garden History,* 4 (1984), 332–358. For the even larger context of three natures within which a garden's control of nature may be cited, see my forthcoming book *Gardens: Theory, Practice, History,* to be published by Thames & Hudson in 1993.

10. See, for example, George Cumberland visiting Hafod in picturesque Wales after his travels abroad, though interestingly his patriotism lets him adjust his scale to allow Welsh scenery still to be sublime: *An Attempt to Describe Hafod* (London, 1796), vi–vii.

11. See the introduction to this volume.

12. See above in chap. 4.

13. A glance at any selection of books on present-day garden design will quickly enforce this point about the grip of the picturesque upon modern design.

14. See, for example, Lawrence Halperin, *Freeways* (New York, 1966) and Christian Zapatka, "The American Freeways," *Lotus International,* 56 (1989).

15. This point was made by Richard Schermerhorn, "Landscape Architecture—Its Future," *Landscape Architecture,* 23, no. 4 (1932), 286. I am also indebted to Marina Adams, "Designing along the Right Lines," unpublished paper on British Rail and its missed opportunities in landscape architecture.

16. *Landscape Architecture,* 32, no. 1 (January 1942), 65: "but when Mr. Tunnard has been longer among us, when he has had time to acquaint himself with the people and the pattern of life in our villages and on our rich farms . . ."

17. André Vera, *Le Nouveau jardin* (Paris, 1912), iii.

18. See for example Hazel Conway, "The Manchester/Salford Parks: Their Design and Development," *Journal of Garden History,* 5 (1985), 231–260.

19. See Fletcher Steele eyeing the other modernist arts in *Landscape Architecture,* 20, no. 3 (1930), 161.

20. For example Guevrekian's *Garden of Light and Water* of 1925 yields a fascinating cubist vision on paper that one cannot believe would have survived in so interesting a cubist environment upon the ground; it is illustrated in J. Marrast, *MCMXXV Jardins* (Paris, 1926), pl. 14 and 15.

21. *Landscape Architecture,* 22, no. 4 (1932), 301.

22. Ralph H. Griswold in ibid., 298. The absurdity of this remark—the idea that "cottage gardens" were somehow a Renaissance style and not in fact invented by the romantic period—still went unappreciated by the audience at Berkeley where this lecture was originally delivered: they wouldn't laugh at this quotation even when incited to do so!

23. Deborah Nevins, "An Interview with Mary Miss," *The Princeton Journal,* 2, 96–97.

24. Any casual survey of illustrations in books on Victorian gardening will quickly show that the order of the day was unadventurous uniformity, from which a few gloriously improbably examples stand out. See also Michael Waters, *The Garden in Victorian Literature* (Aldershot, Hants., 1988).

25. Laurie Olin seems to make the same plea indirectly when he criticizes the current "anti-cultural stance that eschews aesthetic concerns," *Landscape Journal,* 7, no. 2 (1988), 150.

26. The career of Tunnard is in this sense typical, as Lance Neckar has argued in "Strident Modernism/Ambivalent Reconsiderations: Christopher Tunnard's *Gardens in the Modern Landscape,*" *Journal of Garden History,* 10 (1990), 237–250. I am indebted to this essay for various other perspectives upon Tunnard.

27. "Private Delight and the Communal Ideal," *Landscape Architecture,* 31 (January 1941), 70. To which one might respond, with E. M. Forster, that we are also born alone and die alone. See also Steele in the same journal, 22, no. 4 (1932), 299.

28. See *The Economist* (12 August 1989), "Eastern Europe Survey," 15.

29. See Peter Willmott, *Community Initiatives: Patterns and Prospects* (London, 1989) for such a skeptical view. There also seems some confusion between designing space for use by a group and the designing of space by a user group.

30. Compare the research that has been done into how people want their office spaces designed, which is by no means the same as getting users to do the designing. However, see the excellent results of Mark Francis's research, an interim report of which makes heartening reading: *Gardens in the Mind and in the Heart: Some Meanings of the Norwegian Garden* (Davis, Cal., 1989).

31. For Byrd and Harkness, see Michael van Valkenburgh, *Transforming the American Garden: 12 New Landscape Designs* (Cambridge, Mass., 1986); for Las Colinas see *Landscape Architecture,* 75, no. 5 (1985), 64–67.

32. See Robin Karson, *Fletcher Steele, Landscape Architect: An Account of the Gardenmaker's Life, 1885–1971* (New York, 1989).

33. Christopher Tunnard, "Modern Gardens for Modern Houses: Reflections on Current Trends in Landscape Design," *Landscape Architecture,* 32 (January 1942), 58.

34. For Frances Butler, see her "Mappus Mundi: The Portuguese Immigrant Garden in California," *Places,* 4, no. 3 (1987), 33–43. Both Wesmacott and Lassus discuss their work in *The Vernacular Garden,* ed. John Dixon Hunt and Joachim Wolschke-Bulmahn, Dumbarton Oaks Colloquium on the History of Landscape Architecture, XIV (Washington, D.C., forthcoming).

35. See "The Landscape Approach of Bernard Lassus. Translated and Introduced by Stephen Bann," *Journal of Garden History,* 3 (1983), 79–107; also Sutherland Lyall, *Designing the New Landscape* (New York, 1991), 76–83, for the main example of an executed project at Rochefort-sur-Mer.

36. See Stephen Bann, "A Description of Stonypath [old name for Little Sparta]," *Journal of Garden History,* I (1981), 113–144; and Yves Abrioux, *Ian Hamilton Finlay: A Visual Primer* (Edinburgh, 1985).

37. Kassler, *Modern Gardens,* 14.

38. See also above, chap. 8, note 6.

39. See *Landscape Architecture,* 20, no. 3 (1930), 162.

40. See, for instance, James C. Rose, "Freedom in the Garden," *Pencil Points* (October 1938), 639ff.

41. Yet he claims that "style evolves naturally from the subjective" without pausing to ask what informs style: "Freedom in the Garden," 642.

42. Eliot addressed these matters in his 1921 essay on "The Metaphysical Poets." See also the entry on "dissociation of sensibility" in *Princeton Encyclopedia of Poetry and Poetics,* enlarged ed., (Princeton, 1974), 195–196.

43. See the fuzzy thinking on this theme in his "Fine Art in Landscape Architecture," *Landscape Architecture,* 24, no. 4 (1934), mainly 177–178. It is perhaps the very brevity of his essay (was this supposed to be in a functional, modernist spirit?) that disables his thinking. It is a fault, incidentally, that continues to disturb much current writing on landscape design. Even the more historically and culturally experienced authors of the recent *Poetics of Gardens* completely misunderstand the seventeenth-century mind when they say of the Oxford Botanical Garden that it was "made for the intellect rather than for the senses." See Charles W. Moore, William J. Mitchell, and William Turnbull, Jr., *The Poetics of Gardens* (Cambridge, Mass., 1988), 113.

44. A whole article could and should be written about the modernist obsession with axes: Fletcher Steele is muddled and ambiguous in his attitudes—see *Landscape Architecture,* 20, no. 3 (1930), 177—while Ralph H. Griswold is sentimentally hostile to straight lines laid on a rolling landscape (what else is Vaux-le-Vicomte?)—see ibid., 22, no. 4 (1932), 294, and so on.

45. This is a point well made by Barbara Sarudy in her discussion of eighteenth-century gardens of the Chesapeake: see *Journal of Garden History,* 9, no. 3 (1989).

46. Moore, Mitchell, and Turnbull, *Poetics of Gardens,* 81, 217, and 188, among other places.

47. Laurie Olin calls this "translation" (*Landscape Journal,* 7, no. 2 [1988], 149).

48. Ibid., 150.

49. See William Howard Adams, *Robert Burle Marx: The Unnatural Art of the Garden* (New York, 1991), and Sima Eliovson, *The Gardens of Roberto Burle Marx* (Portland, Or., 1991).

50. See Lyall, *Designing the New Landscape,* 114–121.

51. See Claudia Lazzaro, *The Italian Renaissance Garden* (New Haven, 1990), in index under "Third Nature."

52. There are several signs that this revivification of landscape architecture theory is taking place: see, for example, the special issue of *Landscape Journal,* 7, no. 2 (1988), guest-edited by Anne Whiston Spirn, entitled "Nature, Form and Meaning."

53. See this theme discussed above in relation to the Castle Howard landscape (chap. 1).

54. See the issue of *Places* devoted to "The Future of Urban Open Space," 6, no. 1 (1989).

55. For brief glimpses of these perspectives see J. C. N. Forestier, *Gardens* (New York, 1924), 8 and 11; Eckbo, *Landscape for Living* ([New York,] 1950), foreword; and Ian McHarg's account of his childhood as a preamble to *Design with Nature* (Garden City, N.Y., 1969).

POSTSCRIPT: GARDENS IN *UTOPIA*: UTOPIA IN THE GARDEN

1. My quotations are taken from the Penguin edition of More's *Utopia* (Harmondsworth, 1965). There is a considerable literature on this famous book, some of which is footnoted in a recent article by Athanasios Moulakis, "Pride and the Meaning of *Utopia,*" *History of Political Thought,* 11 (1990), 241–256. Moulakis makes the point that More's work is dramatic, not discursive (p. 256), an emphasis which it is also crucial to make about many gardens.

Our contemporary renewal of interest in community urban garden projects shares some of these older utopian concerns: see the relevant articles in *The Meaning of Gardens,* ed. Mark Francis and Randolph T. Hester (Cambridge, Mass., 1990).

2. [Ellis] Heywood, *Il Moro* [Florence, 1556], ed., trans., and with introduction by Roger Lee Deakins (Cambridge, Mass., 1972), pt. I, 4–5.

3. *The Colloquies of Erasmus,* ed. Craig R. Thompson (Chicago, 1965), 46. The passages concerning the garden cited below are to be found on 50–55 and 76–78.

4. The point is made by Marilene Allen, "Literary and Historical Gardens in Selected Renaissance Poetry," Ph.D. dissertation, University of Edinburgh, 1980, to which I was much indebted in writing this piece originally.

5. See her "Turf Seats in French Gardens of the Middle Ages," *Journal of Garden History,* 5 (1985), 3–14.

6. Pindarian fragments 129 and 130, in *Pindar* (Loeb Classics), ed. John Sandys, 588–591; Virgil, *Aeneid,* VI, 637ff.

7. On the belvedere see the discussion and bibliography in David R. Coffin, *The Villa in the Life of Renaissance Rome* (Princeton, 1979), 69–87 and 109–110; on the casino see Graham Smith, *The Casino of Pius IV* (Princeton, 1977).

8. On the Villa d'Este's program see David R. Coffin, *The Villa d'Este at Tivoli* (Princeton, 1960), chap. 5.

9. See my *Garden and Grove: The Italian Renaissance Garden in the English Imagination* (London, 1986), index under "Genoa."

10. See Claudia Lazzaro-Bruno, "The Villa Lante at Bagnaia," *Art Bulletin,* 59 (1977), 553–560.

11. Achilles Tatius, *Clitophon and Leucippe* (Loeb Classics), ed. S. Gaselee, 5–9.

12. See my *Garden and Grove* for further details.

13. See Lucia Tongiorgi Tomasi, "Projects for Botanical and Other Gardens: A Sixteenth-Century Manual," *Journal of Garden History,* 3 (1983), 1–34. Claudia Lazzaro, *The Italian Renaissance Garden* (New Haven, 1990), also discusses the planting of these gardens, though without much attention to the notion of the *paragone*.

14. Milton, *Complete Prose Works* (New Haven, 1959), II, 526.

15. Evelyn, cited by John Prest, *The Garden of Eden: The Botanical Garden and the Re-creation of Paradise* (New Haven, 1981), 47, from Evelyn's manuscript "Elysium Britannicum" (Christ Church College Library, Oxford), pt. II, chap. xvii.

16. *Hakluyt's Voyages,* selected and edited by Richard David (Boston, 1981), 314.

17. See generally on this theme the various essays collected in *The Origins of Museums: The Cabinets of Curiosities in Sixteenth and Seventeenth-Century Europe,* ed. O. R. Impey and A. G. MacGregor (Oxford, 1985).

18. Quoted by David Masson, *Life of Milton* (London, 1881), IV, 350.

19. See Richard Patterson, "The *Hortus Palatinus* at Heidelberg and the Reformation of the World," *Journal of Garden History,* 1 (1981), 97.

20. See the discussion of this topic by John Prest in *The Garden of Eden.*

21. The pun, alas, is not mine, but Glenn Lewis's: see *Paradise/Le Paradis* (Ottawa, 1981), 31.

22. From Evelyn's manuscript "Elysium Britannicum," pt. I, chap. i.

23. Mack, *The Garden and the City: Retirement and Politics in the Later Poetry of Pope, 1731–1743* (Toronto, 1969).

24. See Richard A. Etlin, *The Architecture of Death: The Transformation of the Cemetery in Eighteenth-Century Paris* (Cambridge, Mass., 1984), and the special issue ("Cemetery and Garden") of *Journal of Garden History,* 4 (1984).

25. McClung, *The Architecture of Paradise: Survivals of Eden and Jerusalem* (Berkeley and Los Angeles, 1983), to which I am much indebted for this final section of my postscript.

26. Bunyan, *Christian Behaviour, The Holy City,* etc., ed. J. Sears McGee (Oxford, 1987), 99.

27. Gaston Bachelard, *The Poetics of Space* (Boston, Mass., 1964), especially chap. 8.

28. George Orwell, *1984* (New York, 1949), 125–127.

29. These and other examples are illustrated in *Dreams and Nightmares: Utopian Visions in Modern Art,* a catalogue by Valerie J. Fletcher (Washington, D.C., 1963).

30. Illustrated in ibid.

INDEX

Italicized page numbers indicate illustrations.

6-92